THE LAST DAYS IN ISRAEL

CANADA-ISRAEL COMMITTEE
2221 YONGE STREET, SUITE 502
TORONTO, ONTARIO M4S 2B4

Canada-Israel Committee
1075 Bay Street, Suite 525
Toronto, Ontario M5S 2B1

CASS SERIES: ISRAELI HISTORY, POLITICS AND SOCIETY
Series Editor: Efraim Karsh
ISSN: 1368-4795

This series provides a multidisciplinary examination of all aspects of Israeli history, politics and society, and serves as a means of communication between the various communities interested in Israel: academics, policy-makers, practitioners, journalists and the informed public.

1. *Peace in the Middle East: The Challenge for Israel*, edited by Efraim Karsh.
2. *The Shaping of Israeli Identity: Myth, Memory and Trauma*, edited by Robert Wistrich and David Ohana.
3. *Between War and Peace: Dilemmas of Israeli Security*, edited by Efraim Karsh.
4. *US–Israeli Relations at the Crossroads*, edited by Gabriel Sheffer.
5. *Revisiting the Yom Kippur War*, edited by P. R. Kumaraswamy.
6. *Israel: The Dynamics of Change and Continuity*, edited by David Levi-Faur, Gabriel Sheffer and David Vogel.
7. *In Search of Identity: Jewish Aspects in Israeli Culture*, edited by Dan Urian and Efraim Karsh.
8. *Israel at the Polls, 1996*, edited by Daniel J. Elazar and Shmuel Sandler.
9. *From Rabin to Netanyahu: Israel's Troubled Agenda*, edited by Efraim Karsh.
10. *Fabricating Israeli History: The 'New Historians'*, second revised edition, by Efraim Karsh.
11. *Divided Against Zion: Anti-Zionist Opposition in Britain to a Jewish State in Palestine, 1945–1948*, by Rory Miller.
12. *Peacemaking in a Divided Society: Israel After Rabin*, edited by Sasson Sofer.
13. *Israeli–Egyptian Relations: 1980–2000*, by Ephraim Dowek.
14. *Global Politics: Essays in Honour of David Vital*, edited by Abraham Ben-Zvi and Aharon Klieman.
15. *Parties, Elections and Cleavages; Israel in Comparative and Theoretical Perspective*, edited by Reuven Y. Hazan and Moshe Maor.
16. *Israel and the Polls 1999*, edited by Daniel J. Elazar and M. Ben Mollov.
17. *Public Policy in Israel*, edited by David Nachmias and Gila Menahem.

Israel: The First Hundred Years (Mini Series), edited by Efraim Karsh.
1. *Israel's Transition from Community to State*, edited by Efraim Karsh.
2. *From War to Peace?* edited by Efraim Karsh.
3. *Politics and Society Since 1948*, edited by Efraim Karsh.
4. *Israel in the International Arena*, edited by Efraim Karsh.
5. *Israel in the Next Century*, edited by Efraim Karsh.

The Last Days in Israel

ABRAHAM DISKIN

FRANK CASS
LONDON • PORTLAND, OR

First published in 2003 in Great Britain by
FRANK CASS PUBLISHERS
Crown House, 47 Chase Side, Southgate
London N14 5BP

and in the United States of America by
FRANK CASS PUBLISHERS
c/o ISBS, 5824 N.E. Hassalo Street
Portland, Oregon, 97213-3644

Website: www.frankcass.com

Copyright © 2003 Abraham Diskin

British Library Cataloguing in Publication Data

ISBN 0-7146-5421-3 (cloth)
ISBN 0-7146-8383-3 (paper)
ISSN 1368-4795

Library of Congress Cataloging-in-Publication Data

A catalog record for this book is available
from the Library of Congress

All rights reserved. No part of this publication may be reproduced, stored in or introduced into a retrieval system or transmitted in any form or by any means, electronic, mechanical, photocopying, recording or otherwise, without the prior written permission of the publisher of this book.

Typeset in Palatino 10.5/13pt by Cambridge Photosetting Services
Printed in Great Britain by MPG Books Ltd, Victoria Square, Bodmin,
Cornwall

… Let not your prophets and your diviners,
that be in the midst of you, deceive you,
neither hearken to your dreams
which you cause to be dreamed.
For they prophesy falsely unto you …
Jeremiah 29: 8–9

Contents

List of Tables	ix
Introduction	1
1. Basic Problems and Basic Objectives	5
The Basic Social Dilemma and Israeli Democracy	5
The Jewish State: Demography and the Legal Norm	8
The Security Equation: Motivation and Means	15
Social and Political Polarization: Democracy, Jewishness, Security, and Peace	22
2. The Constitutional Revolution and the Breakdown of Balances between the Branches of Government	33
The Judiciary: 'Make Us a King to Judge Us'	33
The Legislative and the Executive: The Courage to Repent before the Fall	41
3. The Party Map	55
Roots and Development, 1949–92	55
The New Party Map, 1996–99	66
The Power of the Political Center	69
4. Days of Storm and Stress	79
From Rabin to Peres: 'Yes to Peace—No to Violence'	79
From Peres to Netanyahu: The Shifting Sands of Parity	87
The Netanyahu Government: In the Absence of Checks and Balances	95
The 1999 Elections	101
The Barak Government: From Dilemma to Dilemma	113
The Sharon Government	125
5. Conclusion: Solutions in the Absence of a Solution	131
Notes	136

Appendices 141
i. The Declaration of the Establishment of the State of Israel 143
ii. Basic Law: Human Dignity and Freedom 146
iii. Basic Law: Freedom of Occupation 148
iv. The Palestinian National Charter 150
v. Declaration of Principles on Interim Self-Government Arrangements 156
vi. Report of the Sharm el-Sheikh Fact-Finding Committee 163
vii. Palestinian-Israeli Security Implementation Work Plan 166
viii. Basic Profiles of Israel, Gaza Strip, West Bank, and Selected Middle Eastern Countries 170
ix. Knesset Elections: 1949–99 171
x. The Governments of Israel: 1949–2002 173

Bibliography 177

Index 185

List of Tables

1.	Population of Israel, 1948–98	9
2.	Sources of Population Growth, 1948–98	10
3.	World Jewish Population and Israeli Jewish Population, 1939–98	10
4.	Immigration, 1919–98	11
5.	Immigration of Jews and Non-Jews, 1989–98	12
6.	1948 Refugees and their Offspring by Current Place of Residence	14
7.	Size of Armies in the Middle East in 1983 and 1994	20
8.	Number of Paragraphs Dealing with Democracy, Jewishness, Security, and Peace in the Statements of Aims Submitted by the Political Parties to the Registrar of Parties	24
9.	Public Opinion Regarding the Importance of Peace, Security, and the Jewish and Democratic Nature of the State	25
10.	Index of Polarization Regarding the Importance of Peace, Security, and the Jewish and Democratic Nature of the State	27
11.	Public Opinion Regarding Territorial Concessions and Arab Aspirations to Destroy Israel, 1999	29
12.	Index of Polarization Regarding Territorial Concessions and Arab Aspirations to Destroy Israel, 1996 and 1999	30
13.	Ideological Self-Definition of Voters on Eve of Elections to the 15th Knesset	74
14.	Reasons for Supporting Parties in the 1996 Elections	92
15.	Replies to the Question 'Should Israel Agree to a Division of Jerusalem within the Framework of a Peace Agreement with the Palestinians?' in a 1996 Election Poll	92

16. Election results from votes for Prime Minister 93
    (29 May 1996)
17. Responses to the Statement: 'It Is Easier to Vote for the 94
    Small Parties in Knesset Elections Now That the Prime
    Minister is Elected Directly'
18. Knesset Election Results (29 May 1996) 95
19. Election results from votes for Prime Minister 102
    (17 May 1999)
20. Effective Number of Parties in the Knesset Following 103
    Elections, 1949–99
21. Knesset Election Results (17 May 1999) 104
22. Reasons for Supporting Parties in the 1999 Elections 106
23. Preferences for Prime Minister among Party Supporters 107
    in the 1999 Elections
24. Election results from votes for Prime Minister 107
    17 May 1999) by Type of Community
25. Fifteenth Knesset Election Results in Selected Cities 109
26. Fifteenth Knesset Election Results in Jewish and Arab 109
    Settlements
27. Fifteenth Knesset Election Results in Old and New Towns 110
28. Fifteenth Knesset Election Results in Kibbutzim and 111
    Moshavim
29. Fifteenth Knesset Election Results in Judeah and Samaria 111
    and in the Golan Heights
30. Representation of Selected Population Groups in the 112
    Fifteenth Knesset
31. Participation in Previous Knessets among Members of 113
    the 15th Knesset
32. The Political Map after Elections to the 15th Knesset 114
33. Possible Coalitions in the 15th Knesset 116
34. The 28th Government: Ministers, Ministries, and Period 120
    of Current Service
35. Election results from votes for Prime Minister 126
    (7 February 2001)
36. The 29th Government (7.3.01) 128

Introduction

Scientific research makes it possible to base predictions on its findings and conclusions. However, the social sciences in general and political science in particular are far from being exact sciences. It is therefore reasonable to expect that an investigator in these fields whose predictions come true will be quite pleased with himself. But there is a fly in the ointment. Those investigators studying the societies in which they live and whose values they have assimilated along with attendant emotional resonance face both a danger and frustration. The danger is that to mix values and feelings with scientific method makes it hard to achieve an objective and analytical approach to findings and data. The frustration is that dire predictions that come true hardly do one's heart good.

Under the circumstances, it may be said that much of what is presented in this book was written with a heavy heart. For, to my regret, many of the findings presented in this study do not augur well for the future. This is true with regard to the threat to Israel's existence, the tangled constitutional web that Israel has spun for itself, the fragmented political system, the ruling elite, and the functioning of all three branches of government. Everything is connected. The conclusions are not encouraging and change is not always possible.

Chapter 1 of the study sets forth the main objectives and basic problems confronting Israel. Its first section presents the conceptual-theoretical framework to which the rest of the book is bound, whether explicitly or implicitly. Here I describe the basic dilemma of society, its democratic solution, and the uniqueness of Israeli society and democracy. The chapter's second section concerns itself with the demographic and legal aspects of Israel as a Jewish state. The third section examines the security threat in the light of the balance of power, the motivation of each side, and the peace process. The fourth section examines alternative views of the basic values mapped out in the previous sections—democracy, Jewishness, security and peace—through an analysis of the positions of the political parties and the public.

Chapter 2 focuses on the constitutional framework of the State of Israel. The first section discusses the revolution undergone by the judiciary in its outlook and standing, particularly in the early 1990s, which has given it potentially far-reaching powers. The second section discusses the revolution produced by the direct election of the Prime Minister (subsequently rescinded). Some of the unfortunate results of this latter innovation are also discussed in the fourth chapter of the study.

Chapter 3 deals with changes in the political party map. Political parties are the corner stone of any political system. In Israel, a well-developed and multifunctional party system existed before the establishment of the state. A short review of its evolution since elections to the First Knesset (Parliament) fills out the historical dimension necessary for an understanding of the political system as such. Aside from introductory and concluding remarks, this chapter is arranged chronologically. Its individual sections are divided according to elections that represented significant turning points in the political life of Israel. In addition, basic patterns of political conduct are examined, which dictate—among other things—the way coalition governments are formed and the built-in causes of their stability or instability. The concluding section deals with the political center, both because of its importance in the game of politics and because of the relatively poor showing of centrist parties in Israel.

Chapter 4 surveys the political history of recent years—years of instability and domestic and foreign problems that could foreshadow the collapse of the system. The sections of this chapter analyze elections, governments, and political activity of the 1992–2002 period.

In the concluding chapter, I take a new look at some concepts deriving from game theory. If the first part of this book regarded the Prisoner's Dilemma as the basic social dilemma that institutional, political, and valuational systems attempt to resolve, the concluding chapter touches upon the very important contribution, in my view, that game theory can make. It is easy to show, through the mathematical models of the theory, the theoretical and actual prevalence of 'no-solution' situations in political and social life. Furthermore, public life in Israel, under present circumstances, may entail intractable confrontations. Internalization of this truth is the key to any hope and possibility of a better future.[1]

The present study summarizes various analyses that I made of the Israeli political system in different contexts throughout the 1990s. Much of it was written before the elections to the Fifteenth Knesset. Thus only those pages dealing with the constitutional revolution, the section on the Sharon government, and some of the material on the Barak government were written more recently. For example, the analysis of the coalition options available to Ehud Barak was written before he formed his government in June 1999. Everything has of course been reviewed before handing in the final manuscript, though few changes had to be made.

The Floersheimer Institute for Policy Studies has served as a congenial environment for the work done on this book. The concerns of the Institute are not limited to the descriptive and theoretical side of research, but also extend to ways of improving both the processes of policy making and their implementation. The foundations of the State of Israel and Israeli society have been undermined in many ways in recent years. If the written word can point to basic problems, it may also be able to contribute to their solution. We can only hope that this will be the case and that many dire predictions that have not yet come true will prove to be false.

I wish to thank Frank Cass Publishers for showing an interest in this work even before it was translated from the Hebrew, and the Floersheimer Institute for Policy Studies for helping me prepare it. Many others also helped, both in gathering data and with helpful comments. Special thanks go to my translator, Fred Skolnik; to members of the Central Election Committee and especially its director, Tamar Edri; to the people at Malam Systems Ltd and in particular Claude Eluz; to the national superintendent of elections at the Ministry of the Interior, Ehud Shilat; to the director of the Knesset archives, Rivka Marcus; to Professor Efraim Karsh; to Professor Amiram Gonen; to Professor Tzvi Ophir; and to Professor Paul Abramson; and to Professor David Ricci for their tremendous help and friendship. More than anyone, I wish to thank my wife, Dr Hanna Diskin, who opened my eyes to many aspects of the subject and without whose help I would be guilty of even more errors and flights of fancy.

1
Basic Problems and Basic Objectives

THE BASIC SOCIAL DILEMMA AND ISRAELI DEMOCRACY

Every society and every political system is by definition threatened by divisions and cleavages that separate its various elements. At the same time, it is rare that those elements come into all-out conflict, for generally those participants in a sociopolitical system have common interests. However, the desire of each of the participants to advance private interests produces results calling to mind the Common Goods Dilemma (or the Prisoner's Dilemma).[2] Selfish decisions on the parts of individuals (or groups) produce results that are harmful not only to society as a whole but often to each of the participants. These negative results naturally become more pronounced when a society is threatened externally.

Solutions to this problem may be divided into three types: (1) those involving *coercion* (or at least the imposition of agreements) between different components of the society) by the governing authorities; (2) those involving the promotion of social *solidarity* by decision makers (at all levels)[3]; and (3) those involving the perception of the basic social dilemma as a *repetitive phenomenon*.[4] Such a perception may restrain selfish or sectarian short-term considerations by decision-makers out of an awareness of long-term consequences.

Representative democracy is the only form of government that guarantees, by definition, not only recourse to the first type of solution but also to the other two.[5] It should be emphasized, however, that recourse to all three types of solutions is present in every human society. It goes without saying that democracies, like all other types of governments, resort to coercion. From the moment a government is elected until such time that new elections are held, the authorities employ various forms of coercion. Furthermore, social solidarity existing under democratic regimes derives both from recognition of commonly accepted basic rights and the understanding that the rules of the game, which apply equally to all participants in the election process, are a prerequisite of fair competition. And finally, the phenomenon of repetitiveness in the democratic solution is bound up with the fact that elected bodies are limited to a defined term of office and must face the nation again at election time. In this sense, the tendency of certain new democracies to postpone elections occasionally or resort to other expedients[6] undermines the basis of the democratic experience.

There are those who will regard this description of democracy as too abstract and limited. However, any attempt to broaden or sharpen it is doomed to failure. Arrow's Impossibility Theorem[7] is only one illustration of the internal contradictions characterizing democracy.[8] The democratic process is not perfect, and it is even difficult to guarantee a consistent and 'positive association' between the will of the voter and the composition of the elected body. It goes without saying that the correlation between the will of the voter and the norms, policies, and activities of elected officials[9] is even weaker. This is particularly true given the shift of focus that occurs between election time and the subsequent period in which the elected serve their terms.

This said, elections in democracies nonetheless have three basic characteristics. These are: (1) that elections are held at regular intervals; (2) that there is at least a tendency of 'positive association' between the will of the voter and the results of the election; and (3) that elections are general and permit the replacement of the ruling élite.

Israel is one of approximately 30 countries that can be defined as a stable democracy, but it is far from being a perfect democracy. The country's original Basic Laws define it as a 'Jewish-democratic' state. A number of other important documents underscore this definition. Today, however, the number of non-Jews living under Israeli rule (including those in the areas under the administration of the Palestinian Authority) is approaching the number of Jews living under Israeli rule. Residents of Israel[10] who are not Jews do not, for the most part, enjoy full political rights, formally or otherwise, including the right to vote or run for office; although Israel has treated the new residents forced upon it in the aftermath of the Six-Day War more liberally than did older and more exalted democracies under similar circumstances. Palestinians have received broader rights under Israeli rule than they did in Arab countries, but the very size of the Palestinian population renders the definition of Israel as a Jewish and democratic state problematic. It is no wonder, then, that the status of the Palestinian population and the status of the territories where they are concentrated have stood at the center of Israel's political debate since 1967. Nonetheless, for many years, most of Israel's political leadership, both right wing and left wing, remained blind to the far-reaching significance of this situation.

In the long term, Israel's existence is threatened both by the problems entailed by its nature as a Jewish-democratic state and by major security problems.[11] In this sense, Israel differs from other democracies that are engaged in shaping their way of life but not in guaranteeing their very existence.

On the home front, Israel also faces social problems more complicated than those faced by most other democracies. Israel is split ethnically, economically, ideologically and politically. It is enough to mention in this context the cleavage between the religious and nonreligious populations, which is different in nature from similar situations in other Western countries; the divisions over the Arab–Israel conflict; the political implications of ethnic inequality; the economic inequality that has deepened in recent years; and the tensions produced by the mass immigration of the 1950s and 1990s.[12]

As a result of the functional problems of Israeli democracy and other circumstances connected in part with power struggles within and among the branches of government, the basic features of Israel's constitutional framework have changed in recent years. While Israel was far from functioning as an optimal democracy before these changes took place, this evolution has made it much more difficult for the system to operate than in the past.

The last two Knesset elections have produced a political map very different from the previous one. Sociopolitical cleavages have become deepened, the strength of the big parties has declined significantly, there are signs of still greater polarization, the strength of the sectarian parties has grown significantly, and party control over voters and the elected has weakened. These developments are partly linked to the change in the constitutional framework and the social and demographic problems mentioned above. Each of them is sufficient to produce dire results. It goes without saying that taken together they do not augur well for Israel.

8 *The Last Days in Israel*

THE JEWISH STATE: DEMOGRAPHY AND THE LEGAL NORM

The Zionist enterprise has always rested on two principal foundations. Overtly, today, more than ever before, Israel stands on two solid feet. There has never been so many Jews in Israel and Israel's military might has never been so great. Nonetheless, a closer look reveals that Israel's position in regard to these two factors is shaky indeed.

Demographic factors are what originally gave the Zionist State hope for the future. From the time of the Peel Commission's partition plan (1937) the international community supported the creation of a Jewish state within boundaries to be determined according to the concentrations of the Jewish and Arab populations in the Land of Israel.[13] As is known, the Jews were a minority in Mandatory Palestine at the time the state was founded. Notwithstanding, UNSCOP's partition plan and its adoption[14] by the General Assembly of the United Nations on 29 November 1947 was first and foremost based on the concentration of Jewish settlements[15] in Eastern Galilee, the Jezreel Valley, the Coastal Plain, and Jerusalem. In these circumstances, most Jewish leaders supported partition and opposed the creation of a binational state. This approach was founded not only on the principle of 'catch as catch can', but primarily on the understanding that the Zionist enterprise could not prevail in a demographic war for *all* the Land of Israel.

Despite its success, Zionism today faces challenges and stumbling blocks similar to those faced by the founding fathers. Today's demographic problem expresses itself in two ways: (1) in the decrease of the Jewish population relative to the non-Jewish population; and (2) in the challenge to the definition of Israel as a Jewish state.

In the territory west of Jordan—that is to say, the territory that includes Israel within the borders of the pre-Six-Day War 'Green Line' and the territories occupied by Israel in 1967 and now partially under Palestinian control—the percentage of non-Jews has been over 40 percent for a number of years. If one takes into account the hundreds of thousands of foreign workers residing in Israel today and deducts those Israelis who have emigrated but are still listed in the Population Registry, it is doubtful whether the Jews are a majority. Numerical data that would allow a precise calculation are not available. However, statistics on arrivals and departures in Israel can serve as an indicator. In 1998 the number of tourists departing from Israel exceeded the number arriving by 111,633. Some of the surplus may be attributed to those who arrived in Israel as tourists before 1998 with the aim of settling in the country. The number of temporary residents entering the country exceeded those leaving by 9,594. Part of this surplus may be attributed to the arrival of non-Jewish foreign workers.

During the first 50 years of Israel's existence, its total population increased by a factor of 6.9 (see Table 1). In this period the Jewish population increased by a factor of 6.7. In the last 40 years the proportion of non-Jews has doubled, and it now represents a fifth of Israel's population within the Green Line.

The main reason for the decline in the share of the Jewish population is related to natural increase. The fertility and birthrate among Moslem Arabs residing in Israel is much higher than among most sectors of the Jewish population.[16] It is true that over the years overall birthrates have dropped, so that differences are now somewhat smaller, but in the absence of Jewish immigration these differences are still enough to threaten the Jewish nature of the state even within the Green Line. Moreover, the fertility rate in the Gaza Strip (and to a somewhat lesser extent in Judeah and Samaria) is among the highest in the world.

A good indication of what is in store for the Jewish majority within the Green Line can be garnered from its age structure. Jewish births in 1998 represented 68.2 percent of the total. In the same year, Jewish children under the age of five represented 69.6 percent of the total for their age group and Jewish children aged 5–14 already represented 73.8 percent. The share of Jews in every age group (including children) declines almost every year.

The relative drop in the Jewish population and the increase in the Arab population, deriving from patterns of natural increase, were

Table 1: Population of Israel, 1948–98

	Total Thousands	Jews Thousands	%	Non-Jews Thousands	%
1948*	872.7	716.7	82.1	156.0	17.9
1958	2,031.7	1,810.2	89.1	221.5	10.9
1968	2,841.1	2,434.8	85.7	406.3	14.3
1978	3,737.6	3,141.2	84.0	596.4	16.0
1988	4,476.8	3,659.2	81.7	817.6	18.3
1998	6,041.4	4,785.1	79.2	1,256.3	20.8

Source: Central Bureau of Statistics (1999), pp. 2–6.
*End-of-the-year data, with the exception of 1948 for which the date is 8 November 1948.

Table 2: Sources of Population Growth, 1948–98

		Total Growth	Natural Increase	Migration Balance	Immigration	Emigration
Total Population	Thousands	5,197.2	3,018.4	2,178.8	2,737.8	559.0
	%	100.0	58.1	41.9	52.7	−10.8
Jews	Thousands	4,192.5	2,132.4	2,060.1	2,611.1	551.0
	%	100.0	50.9	49.1	62.3	−13.1
Non-Jews	Thousands	1,004.7	886.0	118.6	126.6	8.0
	%	100.0	88.2	11.8	12.6	−0.8

Source: Central Bureau of Statistics (1999), pp. 2–8.

offset to a great extent by mass immigration (see Table 2). Half the increase in the Jewish population over the first 50 years of statehood came from immigration. If we factor in Jewish emigration we find that the contribution of immigration to the increase in the Jewish population reached over 60 percent.[17]

The share of Israeli Jews in the world Jewish population has also risen steadily over the years (see Table 3). If in the period of the British White Paper, on the eve of World War II, the share of Jews living in the Land of Israel relative to the world Jewish population was just 3 percent, today their share is nearly 40 percent, according to official estimates. In actual fact, the figure is higher, since a large part of the substantial Jewish population in North America is undergoing an accelerated process of assimilation. These trends represent an impressive victory for the Zionist movement, but they also indicate that the sources of future immigration are drying up.

The rate of immigration to Israel over the years has not been steady. It was very high in the period following the War of Independence. In comparison with the size of the existing Jewish population at the time, the number of newcomers represents an

Table 3: World Jewish Population and Israeli Jewish Population, 1939–98

	World (millions)	Israel (%)
1939	16.6	3
15.5.1948	11.5	6
1970	12.6	20
1980	12.8	25
1990	12.9	30
1998	13.1	37

Source: Central Bureau of Statistics (1999), pp. 2–10.

almost unprecedented surge of immigration on any scale (see Table 4). No one will deny that problems of acclimatization during this period are still felt today in various political, social and economic processes. The average annual number of immigrants in those early years was twice as high as in the years of mass immigration in the 1990s. In addition, it should be taken into account that the existing population at the beginning of statehood was very small. Early immigration was mostly from Arab countries. It included the remnant of European Jewry as well, which also underwent the melting-pot experience under very difficult conditions.

The collapse of the Soviet Union (beginning in 1989) set in motion the second largest wave of immigration since the establishment of the state. Within two years, nearly 400,000 people arrived in Israel. Subsequently the pace slackened, but during the entire decade of the 1990s a million immigrants reached Israel from the former Soviet Union. Former residents of the Soviet Union now constitute the largest immigrant group living in the country. There can be no question that the character of this group changed Israeli society radically. Today Soviet immigration is nearing its end. This can be seen, among other things, in the number of non-Jews among the immigrants (see Table 5). According to Israel's Law of Return even the non-Jewish descendants of Jews have the right to immigrate. At the beginning of the current wave (1989–95), non-Jewish immigrants comprised fewer than 10 percent of the total; in recent years they have comprised over 30 percent.

Today, no potentially large group of Jewish immigrants can be found anywhere in the world. The only large group of Jews outside Israel resides in the United States, and there are no indications that

Table 4: Immigration, 1919–98

Period	Total Immigration Absolute Numbers	Annual Mean	USSR Absolute Numbers
1919–14.5.1948	482,857	17,017	52,350
15.5.1948 - 1951	687,624	189,689	8,163
1952–1960	297,138	33,015	13,743
1961–1964	228,793	57,198	4,646
1965–1971	199,035	28,434	24,730
1972–1979	267,580	33,448	137,134
1980–1989	153,833	15,383	29,754
1990–1997	822,823	102,853	709,094
1998	56,722	56,722	46,509

Source: Central Bureau of Statistics (1999), pp. 5–6.

Table 5: Immigration of Jews and Non-Jews, 1989–98

	Total Thousands	Jews Thousands	%	Non-Jews Thousands	%
1989	25.8	25.1	97	0.7	3
1990	201.5	195.6	97	5.9	3
1991	178.2	168.1	94	10.1	6
1992	79.9	71.9	90	8.0	10
1993	80.3	70.7	88	9.6	12
1994	83.2	78.1	94	5.1	6
1995	79.4	75.4	95	4.0	5
1996	75.0	56.4	75	18.6	25
1997	70.2	48.2	69	22.0	31
1998	59.8	39.8	67	20.0	33
Total	933.3	929.3	89	104.0	11

Source: Central Bureau of Statistics (1999), pp. 2–8.

it feels inclined to leave for Israel. The total number of North American immigrants is quite low, and in the absence of unforeseen and earth-shattering circumstances (for which one would hardly wish) it is hard to imagine large-scale immigration. At the same time, opinion polls in Israel indicate increasing perception of the option of emigration as legitimate and increasing intentions to take up this option. The conclusion to be drawn from all the above is that the proportion of the Jewish population will continue to decline significantly in the future in the 'Little Israel' of the Green Line as well.

The demographic problem is not only linked to the above data but also to the 'post-Zionist' tendency to negate the Jewish character of Israel, which is expressed by seeking to alter its definition from a 'Jewish-democratic' state to a state belonging to 'all its citizens'. Today, this tendency seems to characterize the overwhelming majority of Israel's Arab citizens and many of its Jews. It is interesting that this challenge to the Jewish nature of the state comes at a time when its 'Jewish-democratic' nature is being shored up in very important Basic Laws—namely, the Basic Law: Freedom of Occupation and the Basic Law: Human Dignity and Freedom, which we shall discuss further on.

The first important instrument to deal with the latter issue was Article 7a of the Basic Law: the Knesset. This article, whose purpose was to keep certain political parties out of the Knesset, was passed as an amendment in 1985. The immediate goal was to deal with the election of Rabbi Meir Kahane, representing Kach in the Knesset after the 1984 elections. As in Article 21 of the Basic Law[18] of the German Federal Republic (West Germany) dating from 1949, the Israeli legislator expressed his conviction that those threatening the democratic process must be kept from participating in it. The following is the language of Article 7a:

> A list of candidates shall not participate in Knesset elections if its objects or actions, expressly or by implication, include one of the following:
> 1. Negation of the existence of the State of Israel as the state of the Jewish people;
> 2. Negation of the democratic character of the state;
> 3. Incitement to racism.[19]

The legislator repeated this stricture in similar language in Article 5 of the Law of Political Parties (1992), amending the registration of parties:

> A party shall not be registered if its objects or actions, expressly or by implication, include one of the following:
> 1. Negation of the existence of the State of Israel as a Jewish and democratic state;
> 2. Incitement to racism;
> 3. Service as a front for illegal activity, when this is reasonably certain.[20]

We need not discuss how the idea of a Jewish state came to be mixed together with the idea of a democratic state. It is worth noting, though, that contradictions among normative principles are not always avoidable, i.e., under most circumstances, contradictions can be found in any normative system. In fact, the tensions that exist here are mild compared with the contradictions to be found among the normative principles characterizing Israel's constitutional framework, as is the case in the most progressive democracies. Moreover, the national character of democratic countries is not unique to Israel. It is the rule with regard to awarding and denying citizenship to foreigners on the basis of country of origin.

Furthermore, a precedent was set even before the above laws were passed, in the well-known verdict rendered in Election Appeal 1/65: *Ya'akov Yardor* vs *Central Election Committee for the Sixth Knesset*, known to the public under the name of the 'El-Ard Petition'.[21] In its decision the Supreme Court upheld by a majority vote (Chief Justice Shimon Agranat and Justice Yoel Sussman against Justice Chaim Cohen) the disqualification of the Socialist Party by the Central Election Committee. What stood out in this decision was the attention paid by the three justices to the right to protect itself even when it has no explicit authority to do so and despite the political nature of its Central Election Committee. Much weight was given to arguments like the one advanced by the chairman of the Committee in a letter to the legal representative of the list. There he said that 'the present list of candidates constitutes an illegal association, since its initiators deny the integrity of the State of Israel and its very existence.'

However, legal steps that were possible before the new legislation was enacted did not even arise in the 1999 elections to the Fifteenth Knesset. Thus there are currently a number of Knesset members who challenged, both before and after the elections, Israel's continued existence as a Jewish state.

The spirited attacks of Arab and other Knesset members on the Jewish nature of democratic Israel go hand in hand with the demand to realize the 'right of return' of the 1948 refugees (and Arabs uprooted in 1967). The declared aim of Arab–Israeli politicians and other Arabs, and first and foremost Arafat and all the official spokesmen of the PLO and the Palestinian Authority, is 'full' implementation of the decisions of the UN. In other words, their intent is to bring about recognition of the right of nearly 4 million Palestinians (refugees and their offspring) to return to Israeli territory within the bounds of the Green Line (see Table 6). Practically speaking, argue the more moderate advocates of this demand, the idea is for hundreds of

Table 6: 1948 Refugees and their Offspring by Current Place of Residence

Current Place of Residence	Absolute Numbers	In Refugee Camps (%)	In Other Locations (%)
Jordan	1,554,375	17.9	82.1
Lebanon	375,218	55.8	44.2
Syria	381,163	29.2	70.8
West Bank	579,987	27.0	73.0
Gaza Strip	818,771	54.7	45.3
Total	3,709,514	32.5 (1,203,828)	67.5 (2,505,686)

Source: Ha-Aretz, 23.7.2000, p. b3 (Based on UNRWA data for 31.3.2000. Excluding residents of other countries).

thousands to return and for the Jews who seized their property to be evicted, and for those who renounce their right to return to be compensated more than generously. Postponing discussion of such a major claim in peace talks with the Palestinians could undermine agreements reached with them and with other Arab parties.

THE SECURITY EQUATION: MOTIVATION AND MEANS

The strength of a system engaged in an actual or a potential armed conflict is a function of the material resources at its disposal and the level of motivation among its members. Any analysis of the balance of power between Israel and those who threaten its existence should take these factors into account.

The importance of motivation in the military equation appears time and again in the twentieth century. Thus among many democratic nations one finds a mix of high military capability with a low level of motivation in actual or potential conflicts with nondemocratic nations

This is particularly noticeable in the United States, some of whose citizens were isolationist at the outset of both world wars. The same held true for reactions in the public and in the media to government actions in the Vietnam War, not only toward the end, but from the beginning. The most recent example is the way the Gulf War was terminated. In some instances, of course, the lack of motivation can be justified. Nonetheless, the American example shows that even the most apparently powerful of nations becomes a paper tiger when material might is applied in the absence of motivation. Recent evidence suggests that the Bush government weighed the lessons of the past when planning its response to the attack of 11 September 2001.

The importance of the motivation factor in democratic regimes derives from the values adhered to by many segments of the population, including those that are influential in determining the national agenda, as well as from the standing of leaders and their dependence on these same segments of the population, and from the free flow of information, unlike the situation in the nondemocratic countries. Those who are to be harnessed to the war effort find themselves in a situation characteristic of the basic social dilemma, where private considerations do not always add up to deference to public interests. Democracy provides the individual and society with an optimal framework for the business of living compared with any other known system of government. But the priorities of the individual in such a society tend to embrace short-term considerations, which democracy may inspire more than any other kind of regime. Thus Israel today suffers from a clear-cut decline in motivation with regard to possible involvement in a military conflict of any kind. Earlier, an aspiration to strike at Israel's morale as a means of achieving victory (however partial) gave birth to the idea of a 'war of attrition' among the Arabs, and first and foremost among them Nasser after the 1967 war. As is known, his war of attrition ended with the attrition of the Arab side, and hostilities ended in August 1970 with the ceasefire agreements. The fact that these agreements did not protect Israel when it came to the 1973 war in no way detracts from Israel's endurance until that time. Afterwards, though, the Yom Kippur War itself was what diminished Israel's ability to stand firm in a conflict that is basically one of 'attrition'.

This turning point in the level of motivation and endurance under conditions of attrition expressed itself in all the major clashes since 1973 and characterized growing segments of Israel's population. The phenomenon was very noticeable in the Intifada, the Gulf War, and Lebanon. It should be emphasized, however, that decisions made by the Israeli leadership in recent years were not necessarily mistaken. There can be no doubt that some of these decisions were right and probably would have been made under other circumstances as well. Nevertheless, the decline in motivation and morale was not lost on the other side. In each of the cases mentioned above, not only was Israel affected but also its allies. The dangers of cooperating with Israel were made apparent to everyone. The second Intifada, which broke out at the end of September 2000, and the riots among Israeli Arabs that came on its heels, were undoubtedly influenced by a perception of Israeli weakness in the face of a strategy of attrition.

The decline in motivation has many causes. The Jewish population of Israel has paid a heavy price in the long-standing conflict with the Arab world. I have already suggested elsewhere that it is precisely weariness on both sides that can contribute to resolving difficult conflicts such as the one Israel is involved in. However, in this case Israelis currently seem more weary of the conflict than their antagonists.

Commensurately, the scale of values that has hitherto characterized broad segments of Israeli society has undergone a radical change (to a great extent as part of a global trend). The sanctification of individual and personal values as opposed to collective values, the inclination toward short-term gain, and the marked decline in national solidarity today characterize Israel more than ever before.

Moreover, we are also witnessing a change in the 'perception of the enemy'. The vulgar language that was once directed against Israel in every conceivable forum is no more. It is now generally limited to internal consumption (also in the Arab countries with which Israel has peace treaties). In addition, Israel now maintains relations across the Arab world that did not exist in earlier generations, whereby we are witnessing a tendency toward realpolitik among some Arab leaders. For all these reasons the other side is perceived as less of a threat than before.[22] Nonetheless, despite all these changes, the desire to destroy Israel has not vanished.[23]

In addition, there has also been a change in the way Israel is perceived by its own citizens. On the one hand, there is the doubtful view that Israel's security situation is better than ever. 'Israel is the "bully" of the Middle East,' as one of its dovish leaders likes to say, 'and it has no reason to be afraid of any of the other children in the nursery.' On the other hand, there is a growing feeling of guilt in the public at large as well as among leaders, academic figures, and other members of the élite over Israel's 'sins' against the Palestinians.

Israel is of course not totally blameless. For example, most of the 1948 refugees were indeed expelled from their homes in the war period; most residents of the occupied territories were born after the 1967 conquest and even the parental generation grew up under this reality; and it is difficult to convince the next of kin of Intifada victims that the occupation has been an enlightened one, even if most of these victims are the responsibility of the Palestinians. Still, though no one can deny the wretchedness of large parts of the Palestinian population, it appears that the fault lies mostly with the decisions made by the Palestinian leadership at all its varied levels and with the support of the Palestinian public for unworthy leaders and criminal and destructive notions. That is, the fault does not lie entirely with the policies or actions of Israel, which can in fact lay claim to relative, but not perfect, enlightenment in comparison with the behavior of leading democracies under similar circumstances. The one-sided view of the history of the conflict, laying all the blame at the feet of Zionism and Israel, as is the habit today among 'new historians', 'critical sociologists', and all kinds of postmodernists, has no basis in fact.[24]

Despite flagging motivation, Israeli views on the Arab–Israel conflict and other subjects are not uniform. On the one hand, almost every sector of the Jewish population indicates a clear desire for peace. On the other hand, together with this desire there is deep concern over the stated and hidden intentions of the Arabs.[25]

The Arab world too lacks uniformity. We have already mentioned above the change in style and the increasing willingness not only to enter into talks with Israel but also to achieve reconciliation. The changes derive from internal developments in various Arab communities and from a more realistic assessment of the balance of power and deterrence. Likewise, on more than one occasion, it has become apparent to the Arabs that some of their aims can be achieved politically. In the period between the Six-Day War and the Yom Kippur War the popular slogan was, 'What was taken by force will be returned by force'. For many Arabs, this battle cry seems anachronistic today. On the other hand, the utopian vision of a 'new Middle East',[26] promulgated by Israeli architects of the Oslo Accords and their supporters, has little substance.

Israel was born in sin: on this point there is almost complete consensus in the Arab world, including Arab countries that have signed peace treaties with Israel and achieved friendly relations. The doves in the Arab world are prepared to tolerate Israel for lack of choice and, out of concern for the future, to renounce their previous aspiration to restore what was 'stolen'. But no one in the Arab world, including moderate leaders, is prepared to concede the justice of the creation of the Zionist entity.

What is more, there are those in the Arab world who, by their behavior, demonstrate anti-Zionist feelings even more pronounced than in the past. Prominent among them are Moslem fundamentalist groups, Shiite and Sunni, whose followers are prepared to sacrifice their lives fighting Israel and Zionism.

It is well known that within a few years of the triumph of Islam in the seventh century the Moslems had ruled Jerusalem and built the Dome of the Rock. The Holy City stood united in the heart of the Moslem Empire. Except for the Crusader period, Moslem rule in the country was unbroken until the end of World War I. Therefore, most Arabs could not and would not reconcile themselves to the 'colonialist-imperialistic' policies of Europe, to Herzl's idea of 'transforming a religion into a nationality', or to the absorption of the persecuted Jews of Europe and other places 'at the expense of the legal inhabitants of the country' who had occupied it since time immemorial.

At the two extremes of Arab views on the existence of Israel, one finds those ready for reconciliation, in spite of their basic hostility, and those who are unwilling to give up the idea of destroying Israel and continue to proclaim their intentions publicly.[27] This division of opinion expresses itself within the Palestinian leadership. On the one hand, it spawns the PLO National Covenant, which is second to none in militancy, and on the other hand it promotes serious negotiations with Israel, agreement to the existence of two states side by side in the future, and 'abrogation of the Covenant by a special committee'. Arafat has resolved this apparent contradiction on a number of occasions by invoking the 'Big Dream'. That is, he seeks today a realistic compromise and to live alongside Israel but does not give up the dream of a Greater Palestine. Perhaps it is this dream that explains why the home page of the Internet site identified with the Palestinian Authority displays a map of the country highlighting 412 Arab villages on the 'Israeli' side of the Green Line that were wiped out by Israel in the 1948 war. Moreover, textbooks used in schools under the control of the Palestinian Authority routinely speak of the destruction of Israel as 'the only alternative'. In fact, the aim of destroying Israel is given prominence in kindergartens, grade schools, universities, mosques, the mass media, militant outbursts and official political statements. Ironically the word 'peace' is interpreted by many Arab spokesmen as corresponding to 'destruction of the Zionist entity'.

Israel has a clear interest (going back to 1967), if only demographic, in reaching an agreement whose end result is the establishment of a Palestinian state. Moreover, it is reasonable and worthwhile for Israel to increase its efforts to find a just solution for the Palestinians. But the hope for a situation that will see hostility eliminated with a sweep of the hand is unrealistic. If and when such a process indeed evolves it will continue for years and it is doubtful that it will obviate extreme positions.

Beyond motivation, the defense equation depends on material resources. To examine changes in the balance of such resources, it is worth presenting a number of scenarios that could lead to the destruction of the state. Unfortunately, a number of these indeed exist.

In the past it was customary to speak of a 'worst-case' scenario threatening Israel's existence. The reference was to a broad coalition of Arab armies cooperating in a conventional attack against Israel.

Even during periods when it was clear that Israel was capable of dealing successfully with each of the Arab armies separately, cooperation between them was seen as a serious challenge to the Israel Defense Forces. Nonetheless, whenever such a coalition confronted Israel, it was Israel that triumphed. In recent years, it would seem that this kind of 'worst-case' scenario has become less likely than it was in the past. There are a number of reasons for this: the weakening of pan-Arab and pan-Islamic ideologies; the peace treaties with Egypt and Jordan; the reconciliation of a greater number of Arab countries to the existence of the State of Israel; the demilitarization of the Sinai Peninsula; the certainty that Israel has nuclear weapons; and the processes of modernization occurring in various Arab countries.

Comparison of the conventional means of warfare at Israel's disposal with those in possession of its enemies, always showed a balance of power less favorable to Israel than it really was (see Table 7). That is, the numbers for men, planes, tanks, and other conventional means of warfare always appeared to indicate Israeli inferiority. This has remained true in recent years as well. For example, Syria has more tanks than Israel, and the armed force mobilized by Iran during its war with Iraq was double the number in the Israeli regular army and reserves.[28] Nonetheless, Israel's advantages in conventional warfare are even greater today than in the past. This is reflected in the technological level of military equipment and the quality of its fighting forces. After all, the 'average Israeli tank' is much more effective than the 'average Syrian tank'. Nonetheless, it

Table 7: Size of Armies in the Middle East in 1983 and 1994

Country	1983 Soldiers (Thousands)	1983 Total Number of Tanks	1983 High Quality Tanks	1984 Soldiers (Thousands)	1984 Total Number of Tanks	1984 High Quality Tanks
Israel	130	3,650	600	136	3,845	1,930
Egypt	320	2,400	1,000	320	2,800	1,000
Iran	1,000	1,000	–	340	1,500	200
Iraq	875	3,700	1700	350	2,100	900
Jordan	70	917	230	85	1,067	375
Libya	60	3,000	1,300	50	2,710	360
Saudi Arabia	63	450	450	102	900	600
Syria	300	3,700	2,100	306	4,800	1850

Source: Heller, 1984, pp. 260–1, Kam, 1996, p. 401. Similar tendencies, with different numbers, were published by other sources, such as *Janes* or the International Institute for Strategic Studies (London).

should be mentioned that on the eve of the Yom Kippur War the Israeli regular army was considered good enough to stop a combined Syrian–Egyptian attack.[29] In actuality, the business was more protracted than imagined.[30] As to the question of motivation, however, the situation is different today from anything known in the past. The change in the level of motivation has led to a situation where the quality of manpower in the permanent army is steadily declining in comparison with the quality in Israeli society as a whole.

The motivation factor is the main one in the second scenario concerning the destruction of Israel, namely the attrition scenario. In the past the idea of defeating Israel by wearing it down was seen as unrealistic. This was attested to by the way in which the Six-Day War commenced after a waiting period, and by the way the War of Attrition ended in 1970. Unfortunately, patterns of behavior of increasingly large segments of Israeli society in every conflict since the Yom Kippur War, together with the improvement in means of warfare and the rise in motivation among Arab forces, make the attrition scenario more likely than in the past. Attrition may occur through terrorism, conventional military means, rebellion, and limited use of weapons of mass destruction. Extensive attrition could lead first of all to a rapidly developing wave of emigration, producing a domino effect whose end is unforeseeable. On the other hand, the determined response of the Jewish public to the violent events since the end of 2000 conceivably points to a turn for the better in everything connected with motivation and the ability to withstand a war of attrition.

The third scenario, the use of weapons of mass destruction against Israel is seen by many today as distinctly possible, and the most dangerous of all possibilities. Countries that have in the past stated their desire to obliterate the Zionist entity now have at their disposal chemical and biological weapons of destruction and the means to deliver them. In addition, Israel did not use all the means at its disposal to prevent countries such as Iran from developing nuclear weapons. The upshot of this is that actors who deny Israel's right to exist are closer than ever to obtaining such weapons. Nonetheless, one can detect sparks of sanity in Iran as well as in other 'crazy' nations. Israel, of course, has not only the means but also a 'second-strike capability' operable under the most arduous conditions. However, the question is: what is the good of the insane Mutual Assured Destruction (MAD) scenario after taking the first hit? It will be remembered that for a long time the United States had an (automatic) Launch on Warning policy, meant to serve as a deterrent. Israel's policy has been almost the exact opposite. Conceivably, it will have to rethink its position when hostile nations complete their nuclear development. As was shown, for example, by the launching of missiles against Israel during the Gulf War, and in view of the difficulties in developing antimissile systems, it would appear that the other side too would have not only first-strike but also second-strike capabilities. From the above it is clear that Israel should have added to the combination of early warning, deterrence, and interception an unequivocal strategy of preventing the development of such weapons by any means available.

SOCIAL AND POLITICAL POLARIZATION: DEMOCRACY, JEWISHNESS, SECURITY, AND PEACE

The above discussion highlights four concepts that more than anything reflect the basic problems characterizing Israel's political system: democracy, Jewishness, security, and peace. Different people of course understand these concepts very differently. But the way they are used by politicians and perceived by the public can offer a key to basic positions among different groups in Israel.

Some people argue that among these four concepts there exist not only tensions but also contradictions. Thus, among those who wish to turn Israel into a country belonging to 'all its citizens', some see in the Jewish symbols of the state, in laws such as the Law of Return and in the relevant sections of the Basic Laws and the Law of Political Parties, an attack on democracy. For years, many in all the main political camps were convinced that peace would come at the price of giving up territorial defense assets along with other concessions. We have already mentioned above, in the context of the motivation factor, the tension that could arise between democracy and security needs. The demonic characterization of Judaism and Zionism by the framers of the PLO Covenant and others casts into bold relief the argument that there exist contradictions between the Jewish nature of the state and each of the other concepts.

In contrast, there are those who deny that there is any tension among these concepts and even point to their mutual dependence. A good example is the use of the slogan 'Peace and Security' by politicians from all the parties. What degree of importance the various parties attach to these concepts, and to the dependence or contradictions among them, can be learned, among other things, from the official 'statements of aims' they submit to the Registrar of Parties (see Table 8).[31] With the exception of the One Nation Party, all the parties that won seats in the Fifteenth Knesset mention at least one of these four components in their 'statement of aims'. Reference, or absence of reference, to these concepts, is not coincidental. Thus, no reference is made to the Jewish nature of the state or to the subject of security in the official 'statements of aims' of the dovish or Arab parties: Ratz, Mapam, Shinui, the Islamic Arab Party, the Arab Democratic Party, and the Israel Communist Party (Hadash). In contrast, the Jewish religious parties generally give broad scope to the idea of the Jewishness of the state. The National Religious Party, Agudat Israel, Degel ha-Torah, Shas, Moledet, and Tekumah mention it but not any of the other three concepts in their 'statements of aims'. All four concepts are mentioned in the 'statements of aims' of the Likud, the Center Party and Herut. To the last of those we can add the One Israel Party if we take into account its three founding members: the Israel Labor Party, Gesher, and Meimad.

Prior to the 1999 elections, between 19 April and 5 May, I polled a representative sample of Israeli voters. A total of 995 respondents participated in the poll, selected in 28 statistical clusters, and they were interviewed face to face. Among other things I asked the respondents to what extent they agreed or disagreed with the following four statements:

1. 'It is important that the government make every effort to achieve peace.'
2. 'It is important that the government make every effort to ensure the security of the country.'
3. 'It is important that the government make every effort to preserve the Jewish nature of the state.'
4. 'It is important that the government make every effort to preserve the democratic nature of the state.'

The replies of respondents serve only as a partial index of their views on the four basic concepts discussed in this section. The third statement is somewhat problematic, since some of the respondents undoubtedly interpreted it in religious (and not demographic) terms and perhaps even in the context of religious-party participation in the coalition. Despite the problem of interpretation, the overwhelming

Table 8: Number of Paragraphs Dealing with Democracy, Jewishness, Security, and Peace in the Statements of Aims Submitted by the Political Parties to the Registrar of Parties

Party	Total Number of Paragraphs	Democracy	Jewishness	Security	Peace
One Israel	6	–	–	2	2
Labor	8	5	–	1	2
Gesher	10	10	8	1	1, 2
Meimad	3	3	1–3	3	–
Likud	5	2	1, 2	1, 5	1
Shas	4	–	1–4	–	–
Ratz	3	3	–	–	1
Mapam	3	1	–	–	3
Yisrael ba'Aliyah	4	–	2, 3	4	–
Shinui	4	1	–	–	3
Center Party	17	1–4, 8	1–5, 9, 12	6	5, 6
Mafdal	5	–	1–3, 5	–	–
Agudat Yisrael	1	–	1	–	–
Degel ha'Torah	4	–	2, 3	–	–
Ra'am	5	4	–	–	2
Mada	3	2	–	–	3
Moledet	3	–	1, 2, 3	–	–
Herut	6	4	1, 3	2	2
Tekuma	3	–	1, 2	–	–
Yisrael Beitenu	12	(1), (7–10)	5	(11), (12)	(11), (12)
Maki (Hadash)	6	4	–	–	1
Balad	8	1	–	–	7, 8
One Nation	10	–	–	–	–

Source: Data supplied by the Registrar of Parties.

majority of respondents were inclined to 'agree' or 'agree strongly' to this statement as well (see Table 9).

The respondents were inclined to agree with a combination of the above statements. 61 percent agreed (or agreed 'strongly') that the government should make 'every effort' in all four areas. This is a very impressive result given the fact that only 69 percent agreed to the statement concerning the Jewishness of the state. Nonetheless, the tensions at play among the various concepts were apparent in the low (and even negative) correlation between each pair. The most popular combination was between security and democracy: 93 percent of the respondents agreed that the government should make an effort in both areas, but the Spearman correlation[32] between replies to the two questions was just 0.169. The strongest correlation was obtained between government efforts to ensure security and to

Table 9: Public Opinion Regarding the Importance of Peace, Security, and the Jewish and Democratic Nature of the State

'It is important that the government make every effort to ...	N	Absolutely agree (1)	Agree (2)	Maybe (3)	Disagree (4)	Absolutely disagree (5)	Mean Position
'achieve peace;	988	63.7%	27.0%	5.4%	2.6%	1.3%	1.51
'ensure the security of the country;	979	80.4%	15.2%	2.8%	0.7%	0.9%	1.27
'preserve the Jewish nature of the state;	989	39.2%	29.7%	14.2%	8.5%	8.4%	2.17
'preserve the democratic nature of the state.'	985	81.2%	15.6%	2.1%	0.4%	0.7%	1.24

Source: Public opinion survey, 1999.

preserve the Jewish nature of the state. The correlation coefficient here was 0.294, but the percentage of agreement with the two statements was only 69. Low negative correlations (–0.209 and –0.079, respectively) were obtained for the combinations 'peace–Jewish nature' (89 percent support) and 'Jewish nature–democratic nature' (67 percent support). The combination 'peace and democracy' received 89 percent support with a correlation of 0.246, while the most familiar combination, 'peace and security', received 87 percent support and a correlation of just 0.146 between the two.

The conclusion to be drawn from the above is that there is very widespread support for the values inherent in all four concepts. However, this support is given varying degrees of emphasis among different population groups, reflecting in effect the tensions at play among the different issues. At the same time, as was apparent from previous studies,[33] agreement with generally accepted basic principles tends to grow weaker, and polarization between the different camps tends to grow stronger, when the general position is broken down into specific questions and the public falls under the sway of divisive events such as elections.[34]

What is the level of polarization on various issues? Is Israeli society really so divided over basic political issues? Is the polarization in basic political positions linked to identification with a particular political camp? What is the level of polarization in positions among different social groups in comparison with the level of polarization among different political groups? Such questions have immediate electoral relevance. Thus, for example, it may be assumed that when the polarization between political groups is greater than the polarization between social groups, the positions in question will have a greater effect on how votes are cast.[35]

The extent of polarization between two given groups was examined by comparing the mean position in each. The absolute value of the difference in the mean positions of each group was divided by 4, which represents the greatest possible difference. Maximum polarization yields a polarization index of 1. This is obtained when all members of one group share the same extreme position ('strongly agree') and all members of the other group share the opposite extreme position ('strongly disagree'). The index of minimum polarization is 0. This is obtained when the mean position of both groups is identical.

The level of polarization was measured among five pairs of responding groups:

1. Jews whose fathers were of African or Asian origin (the number of respondents was 270–271 for the different questions) against Jews whose fathers were of European or American origin (264–268 respondents). The second group did not include immigrants from the former Soviet Union during the past 20 years so as not to distort the basic level of polarization under the effect of the generally right-wing positions of these immigrants.

2. Lowest income group (156–159 respondents) against highest income group (154–162).

3. Lowest education group (76–77) against highest education group (156–157).

4. Jews (899–903) against non-Jews (66–74, not including non-Jewish immigrants).

5. Netanyahu supporters (285–291) against Barak supporters (416–418) prior to the 1999 elections.

The results obtained generally indicate a fairly low level of polarization between the mean positions of the different groups with regard to all four of the concepts we examined (see Table 10). Polarization by ethnic division, level of income, and level of education stood at

0.05 or less, except on the question of the Jewish nature of the state, where it ranged from 0.10 to 0.17, which is also quite low.

The highest levels of polarization were between Jewish and Arab respondents. Understandably, the polarization was most marked on the question of the Jewish nature of the state (0.65). A high level of polarization was also found on the question of the effort to be invested in security (0.31).

The polarization between Netanyahu and Barak supporters was not marked. On the issue of peace it was 0.15. A more significant degree of polarization was found on the question of the Jewish nature of Israel. Here it was 0.27. For each of these issues the degree of polarization was far higher than in the case of the different social categories, with the exception of the Arab–Jew division.

The collapse of the sense of solidarity in Israeli society is therefore not related to any great differences in positions related to social inequality. Instead, we may assume that it is the result of the increasing legitimization of self-centered and sectarian patterns of behavior among both leaders and the led. Political identification is apparently no less strong than social identification. The cleavages characterizing Arab–Jewish relations on both the social and the valuation levels are the most marked of all. In all cases examined

Table 10: Index of Polarization Regarding the Importance of Peace, Security, and the Jewish and Democratic Nature of the State

'It is important that the government make every effort to …	Jewish Ethnicity	Income Level	Level of Education	Jews vs Non-Jews	Netanyahu Supporters vs Barak Supporters
'achieve peace;	0.01	0.02	0.03	0.12	0.15
'ensure the security of the country;	0.02	0.07	0.01	0.31	0.02
'preserve the Jewish nature of the state;	0.10	0.17	0.13	0.65	0.27
'preserve the democratic nature of the state.'	0.00	0.05	0.02	0.11	0.08

Source: Public opinion survey, 1999.
0 = minimal polarization; 1 = maximal polarization.

the question of the Jewish nature of the state produced the greatest degree of polarization.

As stated, a relatively high degree of polarization is revealed when basic positions are broken down into specific issues. Below we examine the polarization over possible concessions within the framework of peace agreements with the Palestinians and Syria, and over perception of Arab aspirations to destroy Israel.

The statements for which the extent of agreement was examined were the following:

1. 'In return for a peace agreement with the Palestinians, should the settlements in Judeah, Samaria and the Gaza Strip be evacuated?' (hereafter 'evacuation of settlements').

2. 'In the framework of a peace agreement with Syria, should Israel give back the Golan Heights?' (hereafter 'return of the Golan Heights').

3. 'In the framework of a peace agreement with the Palestinians, should Israel give up the Jordan Valley?' (hereafter 'abandonment of the Jordan Valley').

4. 'In the framework of a peace agreement with the Palestinians, should Israel agree to the division of Jerusalem?' (hereafter 'division of Jerusalem').

5. 'Would the Arab world seek to destroy the State of Israel if it could?' (hereafter 'Arab aspirations to destroy Israel').

6. 'Would Syria seek to destroy the State of Israel if it could?' (hereafter 'Syrian aspirations to destroy Israel').

7. 'Would the Palestinians seek to destroy Israel if they could?' (hereafter 'Palestinian aspirations to destroy Israel').

Generally speaking, most respondents were inclined not to give up all of the Golan Heights, the Jordan Valley or any of Jerusalem (see Table 11). Most marked was the opposition to a division of Jerusalem, with a majority 'strongly' disagreeing. In contrast, a small majority agreed to evacuate settlements, with fewer than a third against. A clear majority believes that the Arab world in general (as well as Syria and the Palestinians in particular) would seek to destroy Israel if it could. Distrust of Syria runs quite deep, which accords with findings in previous studies.

Table 11: Public Opinion Regarding Territorial Concessions and Arab Aspirations to Destroy Israel, 1999

	Absolutely agree (1)	Agree (2)	Maybe (3)	Disagree (4)	Absolutely disagree (5)	Mean positions
Evacuation of settlements	31.6%	21.2%	17.0%	16.0%	14.2%	2.60
Return of the Golan Heights	9.2%	7.8%	17.5%	28.7%	36.8%	3.76
Abandonment of the Jordan Valley	7.4%	8.2%	16.3%	36.5%	31.6%	3.77
Division of Jerusalem	9.6%	8.4%	11.0%	19.4%	51.6%	3.95
Arab aspirations to destroy Israel	31.2%	28.7%	21.8%	10.6%	7.7%	2.34
Syrian aspirations to destroys Israel	35.1%	29.2%	18.9%	11.3%	5.5%	2.23
Palestinian aspirations to destroy Israel	31.9%	29.5%	20.8%	10.8%	7.0%	2.32

Source: Public opinion survey, 1999.

Changes in the degree of the polarization of positions in recent years can be demonstrated by comparing the above poll with a similar one conducted on the eve of the 1996 elections, between 7 and 17 May (see Table 12). A total of 1,064 voters were polled then (with the same 28 statistical clusters as in the 1999 poll).

All the positions examined reveal considerable polarization between Jewish and Arab respondents and between supporters of the 'right-wing' and 'left-wing' candidates in the last two elections. Generally speaking, however, the polarization between Jews and Arabs is much greater than between right-wing and left-wing voters, reaching almost the highest level possible.

In general it can be said that the level of polarization has not changed significantly. However, we know from numerous previous studies that positions on issues such as these are not ironclad, changing according to circumstances. This is apparently the reason for the slight reduction in the polarization between Jews and Arabs on the question of Arab aspirations to destroy Israel. Between the 1996 and 1999 elections there was a slight alleviation of suspicion among some of the Jewish population concerning the intentions of various Arab entities. It should nevertheless be emphasized that, in 1999 as well, polarization over perception of the enemy remained

Table 12: Index of Polarization Regarding Territorial Concessions and Arab Aspirations to Destroy Israel, 1996 and 1999

	Jews vs. Non-Jews (1996)	Jews vs. Non-Jews (1999)	Netanyahu Supporters vs. Peres Supporters (1996)	Netanyahu Supporters vs. Barak Supporters (1999)
Evacuation of settlements	0.54	0.67	0.56	0.55
Return of the Golan Heights	0.69	0.63	0.15	0.33
Abandonment of the Jordan Valley	0.66	0.63	0.25	0.21
Division of Jerusalem	0.70	0.72	0.22	0.31
Arab aspirations to destroy Israel	0.64	0.46	0.17	0.26
Syrian aspirations to destroys Israel	0.65	0.45	0.16	0.23
Palestinian aspirations to destroy Israel	0.61	0.42	0.19	0.19

Source: Public opinion surveys, 1996, 1999
0 = minimal polarization
1 = maximal polarization

very high. The level of polarization jumped again following the events of the 'Al-Aqsa Intifada'.

'Return of the Golan Heights' and 'division of Jerusalem' were seen as more likely in 1999. Some voters, mainly those of dovish disposition, changed their positions over these issues, deepening the rift between the left and the right.

Especially worthy of note is the extent of willingness to evacuate the settlements. The disagreement between the right and the left over this issue was considerable both in 1996 and 1999, reaching the level of polarization between Jews and Arabs.

The following conclusions may be drawn from all of the above:

a) There is very broad basic support for the principles of democracy, Jewishness, security and peace.

b) The issue of the Jewishness of the state provokes greater division than the others, apparently because it is perceived in terms beyond the demographic context.

c) Political polarization over these issues, as could be seen from our examination of the aims of the parties and the positions of voters, is generally no less severe than social polarization. Consequently it may be concluded that there is a connection between these issues and the way both elected officials act and voters cast their ballots.

d) The political polarization between Jews and Arabs is the most marked of all the categories of social polarization.

e) Specific questions on the subject of the Arab–Israel conflict, that is, on the subject of peace and security, provokes extreme polarization between Jews and Arabs and significant polarization between right-wing and left-wing voters. Previous studies show that specific questions on the subject of Jewishness and democracy, such as those referring to religion and the state, also produce significant polarization.

Despite the broad common denominator that characterized the general public (and in other cases most of the Jewish public) on certain issues, we find clear signs of schism. The existence of cleavages and polarization is to a great extent bound up with the developing constitutional framework and the 'tribal' and partisan past of political parties in Israel. These two subjects will occupy us in the following chapters.

2
The Constitutional Revolution and the Breakdown of Balances between the Branches of Government

THE JUDICIARY: 'MAKE US A KING TO JUDGE US'

In the past 20 years Israel's formal and operative constitutional framework has undergone unprecedented change. In large measure, this revolution was wrought by a few Supreme Court justices, and first and foremost by Chief Justice Aaron Barak. Though it is customary to describe what happened in terms of various normative principles, the more important result was a significant accumulation of power and authority in the judiciary vis-à-vis the executive and legislative branches of the government. Some stages in this process were backed by the legislator. Others were based on new Supreme Court interpretations of old constitutional issues. In certain major areas, these new interpretations were entirely at odds with previous Supreme Court positions.

The constitutional revolution seriously undermined the established and normative basis of Israeli democracy, including the lines that separate the branches of government. More specifically, the social dilemma described in Chapter 1 was transplanted from the realm of social, political, and party relations into the sphere of relations between the branches of government. And in that case, as in the Prisoner's Dilemma model, the relationship of the parts threatens the existence of the whole.

The revolution in relations between the judicial branch and the executive branch was sparked first and foremost by the Supreme Court's new interpretation of its own powers when hearing petitions as a High Court of Justice ('Bagatz'). This interpretation did not rest on new legislation but was inspired by the 'activist' approach that developed among Supreme Court justices over the past 20 years under the stewardship of the last two chief justices. The increase in the powers of the Court can be seen mainly in two areas: the right of standing, and the scope of reviewability.

In the past the Court examined the standing of petitioners with a fine-tooth comb. In this respect it based itself on British equity law and on strict and long-standing Israeli precedent. Today such examinations are no longer made and the Court does not hesitate to involve itself in controversies revolving around the activities and decisions of the executive branch, even in cases where the standing of the petitioners is quite doubtful.

As for the subjects in which the Court is prepared to intervene, there has been an increasing tendency to regard everything as subject to judicial review. If in the past the Court tended to shy away from intervening in clear-cut political issues, its approach, in principle, has turned completely around. Since this change is not founded on legislation, the dividing line between the authority of the judicial and executive branches has been considerably blurred. Moreover, this approach has alienated broad sectors of the public from the judiciary as a whole and from the Supreme Court in particular.

The fact that the Court now intervenes in public affairs so frequently has not increased its stature in the eyes of the public. After all, this broadening of the Court's powers comes at a time when cases coming before the courts tend to drag on interminably under a growing backlog. Moreover, the intervention of the Court in controversial issues involving values and ideologies encourages resentment on the losing side. Most vocal in their protest against the Court's approach and its authority to render judgments has been the ultra-Orthodox religious community. But liberal circles as well, which the present Chief Justice once saw himself as representing (when he styled the Court 'the representative of the enlightened public'), have become more critical than before.

This latter criticism is directed mainly against the turnabout in relations between the judiciary and the legislative branch (but not the executive branch). It is spearheaded by legal scholars such as retired Chief Justice Moshe Landau and Prof. Ruth Gavison, and it is sparked by debate over the Basic Laws in general, and the status of the new Basic Laws passed by the Knesset in the 1990s in particular.

Israel's first general elections in January 1949 were for a 'constituent assembly', namely a body mandated to frame a formal constitution that would stand above primary legislation and restrict it. The aim of creating a formal constitution was already stated in the operative part of the Declaration of Independence. A draft of the constitution had been prepared by a committee appointed by the governing bodies of the State-in-the-Making and headed by Dr Zerah Warhaftig, a representative of the Mizrachi movement (and later of the Religious Front in the Constituent Assembly). Within the Constituent Assembly, which changed its name to 'First Knesset' already in the first law it passed—the Law of Transition, 1949—the constitution became a subject of debate. The change of name in itself was evidence of the intention to limit Knesset activities to the legislative function, postponing the framing of a constitution to some time in the future.

The reasons for the postponement were political and valuational. Opposition parties on the right and the left were for the immediate ratification of a constitution. The coalition under the leadership of the Mapai Party and Ben-Gurion was inclined to back off. Most vociferously opposed to a constitution was the Religious Front, and mainly the ultra-Orthodox members of this Knesset faction. On 13 June 1950 the Knesset adopted the Harari Resolution, named after Member of the Knesset (MK) Yizhar Harari of the Progressive Party:

> The First Knesset assigns the Constitution, Law and Justice Committee with the task of preparing a constitution for the country. The constitution will be made up of chapters, each of which will constitute a separate Basic Law. The chapters will be brought to the Knesset after the Committee has completed its work. The chapters will together form the Constitution of the State.[36]

The Knesset thus decided not to adopt a constitution immediately, intending that the status of Basic Laws would be identical to the status of ordinary laws until such time as their legislation was completed and they were incorporated into the constitution. This intention was clear to everyone at the time but is not entirely persuasive to the Supreme Court today. The first Basic Law[37] was only passed by the Third Knesset (in 1958). However, it was clear that the Knesset intended to continue to legislate constitutional laws that do not enjoy formal superiority over 'regular laws'. That is to say, the intention was to accept laws and basic laws stipulating relations between the branches of government and between the government and citizens, as it had occasionally done in the past with such legislation as the Law and Administration Ordinance, 1948, or the Law of Transition, 1949. The upper stratum in the pyramid of legal norms thus included various pieces of legislation whose precedence followed the principle of 'whichever comes later'. The norms embraced (equally, in terms of status) regular Knesset laws, Basic Laws, ordinances of the Provisional Council, and most of the British laws operative in the State of Israel on the day of its establishment. Most mandatory norms were adopted in the Israeli system on the principle of 'the continuity of the law', guaranteed by the 'Minshar'[38] and by the fourth chapter (Art. 11–16) of the Law and Administration Ordinance, 1948.

Among the norms given priority in this pyramid, even before the constitutional revolution of the 1990s, were a few articles (and, from a certain standpoint, a few laws) accorded formal precedence. First, six of the Basic Laws and the Knesset Elections Law were shored up against emergency regulations. Secondly, it was determined that a limited number of articles could be amended only by a special majority of Knesset members. In all cases but one, these articles dealt with the immunity of the law vis-à-vis emergency regulations. The one exception is Article 4 of the Basic Law: the Knesset, which relates to the system of Knesset elections in the following language:

> The Knesset will be elected in general, national, direct, equal, secret and proportional elections in accordance with the Knesset Elections Law; this article shall not be amended save by a majority of Knesset members.[39]

In 1969 there was a new turn of events. A private citizen, Aaron A. Bergman, petitioned the High Court of Justice against the Finance Minister and the State Comptroller, arguing that party financing should not be allowed in accordance with a particular law passed by the Knesset prior to elections to the Seventh Knesset, because that law violated the principle of equality set forth in the same Article 4 mentioned above. The Court upheld this petition, declaring that the term 'equality' in the above article must be understood in its broadest sense, that is, also in the sense of giving an equal chance to each of the political parties. The financing arrangement was indeed passed as a law, but not by a special majority (61 members). Only 24 Knesset members had supported the law after the first reading and it was doubtful whether 60 members had voted for it after the second and third readings. Another of Bergman's arguments, that laws entailing a financial burden could not be tabled as private members' bills, was not upheld by the Court. The Court was aware of the far-reaching significance of its decision. Consequently, it suggested to the Knesset that it might restore the Financing Law by passing that law by the required majority or by amending it as recommended by the Court (retroactive payment to new parties) in order to rectify the violation of the principle of equality.

The Bergman decision was the first in which the principle of judicial review was applied to a Knesset law. The formal reason for upholding the petition was the Court's determination that Article 4 of the Basic Law: the Knesset took precedence over other primary legislation. Judicial review of Knesset legislation was indeed something new, but it was at least limited here to cases where amendments to laws required a special majority. As we shall see, however, the formal precedence of Article 4 (and articles protecting laws from emergency regulations) was subsequently extended to other laws as well.

Oddly enough, efforts in the Knesset to accord formal precedence to all Basic Laws, mainly by passing the Basic Law: Legislation, have been blocked time and again.[40] Nevertheless, despite the continued formal status of Basic Laws as regular laws, the Supreme Court today sees them as taking precedence. This position has no legislative basis and is opposed to the view prevailing among Supreme Court justices until recently. In other words, the Court on its own initiative has broadened its own powers of judicial review to an unprecedented extent, without the license of the legislature to do so.

A far-reaching statement by Justice Aaron Barak is part of the decision in the petition of the LAOR Movement against the Knesset Speaker over the question of increasing election allocations and applying the increase retroactively. In this decision, Barak argued that in exceptional cases the Supreme Court has the power to annul laws (even when they do not contravene a law that takes precedence) if they clash with the 'basic principles' of the system. Since such basic principles are not protected in Israel by an established constitution, implementation of this decision would mean that it would be the Court that determined the content of the principles that stands at the top of the legal pyramid. It is no wonder that the other two justices sitting on the petition criticized Barak's assertion. Academic circles were also critical.[41] However, this criticism did not persist for long, because some critics (including academics, such as Prof. I. England, who later joined the Supreme Court[42]) changed their views and the Knesset itself broadened the powers of the Supreme Court to an extent probably not found in any other country.

With the passage of the new Basic Laws of 1992, and even more so following the amendments of 1994, Israel officially lost its place as one of the countries with the smallest amount of judicial review and became just the opposite. This time, the change was sanctioned by the legislator, but there is much to the argument that most Members of the Knesset were not aware of the real meaning of the new Basic Laws. What is more, the Court played a central role in the enactment process and exerted both direct and indirect pressure on the legislature.

In March 1992 the Knesset passed three new Basic Laws—the Basic Law: the Government;[43] the Basic Law: Human Dignity and Freedom; and the Basic Law: Freedom of Occupation. These three laws took precedence over regular laws, owing to the inclusion of two provisos: the possibility of amendment only by an absolute majority (61 Knesset members) and/or inclusion of a 'limiting clause' stipulating that other laws can contravene the relevant Basic Law only under special conditions.

The new Basic Law: the Government, also known as the Direct Elections Law, enjoyed a preferred status for the first of the above reasons. Article 56 (a) of the Law states:

> This Basic Law may not be amended unless by a majority of Knesset members; however, a provision prescribing that Knesset decisions must be adopted by a specified number of Knesset members will not be amended unless by at least the same number of Knesset members; the required majority under this subsection will be required during first, second and third readings; 'amended' for the purposes of this Article means specifically or by implication.[44]

It should be noted in this context that Article 27 of the same Basic Law concerns itself with Knesset decisions based on a majority of at least 80 members. The proposal to change another article (Article 19) elicited an opinion by Attorney General Eliakim Rubinstein stating that the majority required to amend Article 19 is 80 Knesset members, since it involves an 'implied amendment' to Article 27 in the language of Article 56(a). This protection of the law is truly far-reaching and, given the problematic content of the law, which we shall discuss below, if it had not later been challenged, could have destroyed the country's democratic system. Moreover, the Basic Law: the Government was not passed by an absolute (61) majority, yet the Court nonetheless confirmed its special status. This means that according to the logic of the Knesset, followed by the Court, a simple majority in the Knesset will suffice to give any law the protection of any given special majority (including a majority of 120 Knesset members). This is a peculiar way of looking at things that goes beyond anything a reasonable constitutional mind can accept. The peculiarity of this decision becomes even more apparent when one considers the fact that crucial articles in the Basic Law (3 (c) and 3 (d)) were passed at the last minute as riders and are clearly opposed not only to the spirit of the Law but to the direction of many of its other articles.

The Basic Law: Human Dignity and Freedom can be amended by an ordinary majority, but it includes a limiting clause in Article 8:

> There shall be no violation of rights under this Basic Law except by a law befitting the values of the State of Israel, enacted for a proper purpose, and to an extent no greater than is required or authorized.[45]

The Basic Law: Freedom of Occupation is surprisingly the most elevated from the formal point of view, since it is protected both by the limiting clause mentioned above (Article 4) and the shield created by Article 7:

> This Basic Law may not be amended except by a Basic Law passed by a majority of Knesset members.[46]

In 1994 the Basic Law: Freedom of Occupation and the Basic Law: Human Dignity and Freedom were amended. The main change in both was expressed in the identical preambles to the laws:

> Fundamental rights in Israel are founded on the recognition of the value of the human being, the sanctity of human life and the principle that all persons are free; these rights shall be upheld in the spirit of the principles set forth in the Declaration of the Establishment of the State of Israel.[47]

The Chief Justice of the Supreme Court lobbied strongly in favor of this amendment. The Prime Minister at the time, Yitzhak Rabin, was vehemently opposed to it. Speaking to the members of his Knesset faction prior to the critical vote on this amendment and discovering that he had little chance of persuading them to vote against it, he labeled them 'idiots'.

Including the principles of the Declaration of Independence in these two pivotal basic laws clearly runs counter to the traditional tendency of the Court not to regard the Declaration of Independence as a binding document. This tendency can be seen in its best-known decisions from the early years of statehood. Caution in this regard long seemed advisable because the Declaration's principles are decent but not always practical, inspiring but not always consistent. Under the circumstances, it is possible and even desirable to use these principles for purposes of interpretation but not for more than this.

These are the words of the Declaration:

> The State of Israel will be open to Jewish immigration and the ingathering of exiles. It will devote itself to developing the Land for the good of all its inhabitants. It will rest upon foundations of liberty, justice and peace as envisioned by the Prophets of Israel. It will maintain complete equality of social and political rights of all its citizens, without distinction of creed, race or sex. It will guarantee freedom of religion and conscience, of language, education and culture. It will safeguard the Holy Places of all religions. It will be loyal to the principles of the United Nations Charter ...[48]

What, therefore, is the significance of this neat formulation as adopted (by a minority) in the Knesset at the prompting of activist members of the Supreme Justice?

Since every law directly or indirectly affects freedom of occupation or the rights protected by the Basic Law: Human Dignity and Freedom; since the restriction of rights is permissible under the conditions set forth in the limiting clause; since all the conditions of the limiting clause ('values of the State of Israel', 'proper purpose', 'no greater than what is required') are phrased in the vaguest way; and since the Court is the arbiter of whether other laws conform to these two Basic Laws, it may be said that the laws under discussion are animated by two general ideas: (1) a general and vague affirmation of basic principles worthy of an enlightened regime; and (2) the unlimited power of the Court to exercise judicial review.

The Court foresaw this kind of criticism. Therefore it took the trouble, in a number of recent decisions, to clarify the guidelines by which the Court will interpret the far-reaching powers that have fallen to its lot. Moreover, the Court has thus far exercised these powers only in two marginal cases. All this is of course binding on the lower courts, but as the proponents of reform have themselves demonstrated, rulings of the Supreme Court are not binding on itself, and certainly not on future Courts. As we have seen, the Supreme Court has in recent years exercised this absolute freedom in a series of decisions distinctly opposed to rulings made by previous Courts.

THE LEGISLATIVE AND THE EXECUTIVE: THE COURAGE TO REPENT BEFORE THE FALL

An even more striking change in the constitutional arena was the move to direct election of the Prime Minister in the Basic Law: the Government, of 1992, and its application in the elections of 1996 and 1999.[49] Much that could be said in its condemnation was already said before it became operative. For example, in April 1995 the Movement for Better Government asked a number of scholars, commentators, and activists to analyze the new arrangement before it would be applied in elections to the Fourteenth Knesset. The opinion of the present author (based on research done together with Hanna Diskin) was then published by the Movement, whose leaders had previously been among the most ardent supporters of the reform, under the title 'The Courage to Repent before the Fall'. It is given below in its entirety.

> The Basic Law: the Government in its 1992 version is the greatest constitutional and governmental calamity that has stricken Israel since the founding of the state. Despite the great amount of thought invested in formulating this legislation, the final result has been rightly defined (by an MK who actually voted for it) as 'monstrous'. The reason given by this MK [the reference is to Yossi Beilin—A.D.] and many others who voted like him was that the law was passed from lack of choice, in surrender to popular pressure provoked by an expensive and aggressive campaign and in anticipation of the approach of elections to the

Thirteenth Knesset. This situation produced a desire to pass a law 'at any price', at whose heart would be the direct election of the Prime Minister. I [A.D.] make these remarks in great sorrow, for I had the privilege to accompany the law from its inception and proposed, directly or indirectly, certain central ideas that are part of it.

Notwithstanding Montesquieu's opinion in *The Spirit of the Laws* that the branches of government should be separate, only American politics adopted his advice for any length of time. Most stable democratic regimes use a parliamentary system under which the executive branch and its head are bound to the confidence of parliament. In the parliamentary system, voters do not choose the executive and its head officially in general elections. An elected president in parliamentary systems sometimes indeed has powers little different from those of a constitutional monarch, but basically the head of government (usually a Prime Minister) is appointed directly or indirectly by parliament and depends first and foremost on the confidence of the legislative branch.

Almost every attempt to copy the American model or realize the principle of separation of powers through direct election of the head of the executive branch has failed in other countries, and sooner or later has resulted in the collapse of the democratic regime. One of the reasons has to do with the excessive concentration of power in the hands of the head of government. However, the main reason for the collapse of presidential regimes (for example, in almost all the former democracies of Latin America) was the built-in conflict between the executive and legislative branches of government. Accordingly, soon after the onset of the third wave of democratization, we are witnessing the faltering of new democratic regimes in former Communist countries and Latin American countries because of their inability to bring the ideas of Montesquieu and Madison to fruition and because of clashes between their executives and legislators.

When the executive branch is paralyzed by a 'hostile' parliament, it can ignore it or even dissolve it. Alternatively, if it gives in to a hostile parliament, paralysis in the executive branch may evoke anarchy. Whichever the response of the executive branch to such a situation, mutual hostility over a prolonged period of time guarantees the regime's collapse.

Under such circumstances we often witness seizures of power by undesirable or unauthorized elements like the army. Sometimes these illegal bodies intervene in spite of themselves, when there is no legal alternative to a framework that contains within itself the seeds of its own destruction—a framework of the sort that the Knesset obligingly created for the reasons described above.

It is important to remember that the clash between the executive and legislative branches is not the only reason for the fall of democratic regimes. Still, it is a frequent one, as is shown by many examples, not only in Latin America but also in Europe (in the period between the two world wars) and in post-Communist countries of today. A necessary remedy (but not a complete one) for this widespread and fatal disease is to avoid the direct election of candidates for head of the executive branch. It will suffice to point out in the present context that the statistical correlation between the collapse of democracies and the direct election of the head of the executive branch is much stronger than the connection between heavy smoking and lung cancer. In fact, a systematic examination of the history of crises in democratic regimes shows that the chances of survival of a parliamentary democracy are at least 20 times greater than the chances of a non-parliamentary democracy. It is amazing that men like Walter Bagehot[50] and Simon Bolivar[51] understood this before the historical experience was there.

Many point to the Fifth French Republic as a second successful example, alongside the United States, of the power of survival of a presidential or 'semi-presidential' regime. Unfortunately, this example is not at all relevant to the Israeli experience. Twice since 1958 the French regime was shaken by clashes between the branches of government because of the existence of a right-wing majority hostile to the left-wing president Francois Mitterand. In each case the famous *cohabitation* was made possible by Mitterand's surrender. He appointed Jacques Chirac and Edouard Baladur as right-wing prime ministers enjoying parliamentary majorities. [Since these lines were written the opposite situation has also arisen, of a left-wing French government operating alongside a right-wing president—A.D.]

In other words, the strongman in the French executive branch is always the one who can win a vote of confidence in parliament under a parliamentary regime. As long as the president has a majority in parliament, he stands at the helm, but the moment he loses it, the prime minister takes things in hand as a parliamentary surrogate and the president is in effect left with largely ceremonial functions. However, the Basic Law: the Government of 1992 does not permit such compromises. Even if the elected Prime Minister wished to do so, this monstrosity of a law does not enable him to surrender to an opposition Knesset.

The American example is too complex to be treated adequately within the present framework. Its success stems from unique historical and cultural circumstances. At the same time, we should remember that in this case, too, success is partial. It would seem that precisely the president of the United States, standing at the head of the leading democratic power in the world, and chosen by the largest possible electoral body in the Western-liberal-democratic world, is the weakest element in the system in his capacity as head of the executive branch. This can be seen, for example, in the poor legislative records of American presidents—an 'axiomatic' situation that the Clinton example only underscores.

On the limits of presidential power in determining military policy, a sea of ink has been spilled. Among other cases, that of Lincoln underscores the problem of 'overbalance' between the Federal government and state governments. The American Civil War revolved around this latter issue more so than around the issue of slavery. Yet how did the American people view the presidency after the assassination of Lincoln? A clear indication can be inferred from Woodrow Wilson, then a professor of political science, who called American government of the 1880s 'Congressional government' in a book by the same name published 110 years ago. Later, we know, the last days of Wilson's presidential administration demonstrate the great weakness of the head of the executive branch in America.[52]

It is to the credit of the four MKs who introduced the law— David Libai, Uriel Lin, Yoash Zidon and Amnon Rubinstein— that they recognized some of the problems mentioned above. Thus they tried to fashion a solution to the problem of direct elections by boldly facing the problem of the clash between the branches of government. Unfortunately, their efforts did not bear fruit. Anyone who tracked the legislative process will be reminded of the contortions of a juggler trying to keep too many balls in the air at the same time. Thus, for example, the problem of succession produced the expedient of 'special elections' in which the Prime Minister would be elected without the election of the Knesset at the same time. At first glance, this change seems trivial, but in fact it eliminated the 'balance of terror' that, as a fail-safe device, was meant to keep the two branches of government from running to the sovereign power, that is the people, whenever they came into conflict. In other words, elimination of a small evil produced an infinitely greater one. [These lines were written nearly six years before special elections in 2001 installed a Prime Minister elected two years after the sitting parliament—A.D.]

It is easy to point to many additional defects in the law. Some relate to such major issues as the mechanisms of the election, the sanctions that the executive and legislative branches can bring to bear against one another, and the balances operating between these two branches and other major branches of government. Israel is today in any case in the midst of radical changes relating, among other things, to the standing of the judiciary, the nature of the political parties, the status of the president of the state and the connection between voters and the elected. To all these, implementation of the law will add a series of incidental upheavals. Some of these are bound to lead to results diametrically opposed to what the architects of the law originally had in mind. Thus, for example, it is not hard to show that the political and electoral position of the religious parties will improve after the election law is in place. Some of the law's defects came to light during the second reading, when amendments were passed as proposed by the majority in the Constitution, Law and Justice Committee. However, the rectification of the two defects in question through the efforts of the Minister of Justice [at the time, David Libai—A.D.] is like giving aspirin to a heavy smoker whose lungs are already riddled with pre-cancerous growths.

Some will argue that the Basic Law: the Government aims to solve serious problems in Israel's democratic system. These problems showed their ugliest face in the government crisis of March–June 1990. It is not by chance that proposals for the Direct Elections Law passed their preliminary reading just four days after an Israeli government fell for the first time on a no-confidence vote. But it is important to remember that the crisis could have been avoided by introducing simpler and more effective changes. Such changes, which would have left Israel's 'normal' parliamentary system as it was, had already been proposed in the Knesset and outside it in the summer of 1989.

One proposal, immeasurably simpler than the clumsy and dangerous law passed by the Knesset, was to have 'constructive' no-confidence votes instead of the kind sanctioned by the Law of Transition, 1949, and the Basic Law: the Government in its 1968 version. According to this proposal, governments cannot be removed without a simultaneous motion to form another government or to hold early elections. The framers of the proposal were prescient. Had it been accepted the country would have avoided the disgraceful events of the 1990 crisis [what is termed in Israel, in Yitzhak Rabin's phrase, 'the dirty trick'—A.D.].

Another proposal [made by the author and combined with the proposal mentioned above—A.D.] was to appoint as prime minister the leader of the biggest Knesset faction immediately following Knesset elections. Such automatic appointment (which could be contingent, for example, on a minimum number of seats won by the biggest party) would considerably curtail the ability of individual Knesset members or small factions to 'blackmail' whomever is forming the government. This change too would have left the main lines of the system intact, for it would still have been possible to pass a (constructive) no-confidence motion against the prime minister when there was a clear majority favoring formation of a government under a different prime minister.

The combined proposal of 'constructive no-confidence' and 'automatic appointment' was laid before the Knesset as a private member's bill by a group of Labor and Likud MKs. Among them were at least two members serving as ministers in the present government [the Rabin government—A.D.]. A similar mood prevailed in the Likud. Over 70 percent of the Likud Party's Central Committee voted against the institution of direct elections a few months before the matter was decided in the Knesset. The above proposal was struck down because of the spirited opposition of the small parties, who understood that it would limit their bargaining power as well as strengthening the two big parties at the polls.

It should be emphasized that the electoral damage inherent in the law could easily have been avoided with a few small changes. For example, automatic appointment as Prime Minister could have gone to the leader of the biggest faction in the biggest bloc of party lists, and participation of parties in a bloc could have been linked to the possibility of entering into multi-party surplus-vote agreements. All the dangers inherent in the new Basic Law: the Government would have been avoided if such a proposal had been adopted. But, as mentioned, populist considerations, the approach of elections, and the veto of the small parties (misguided even from their own point of view) all stood in the way, not to mention the personal interests of such leaders as Yitzhak Rabin, Binyamin Netanyahu, Shimon Peres and Ehud Barak, for whom the expedient of direct elections was perfectly suited.

Today we face a moment of truth [written, as mentioned, before the implementation of the law but true up to the moment the law was rescinded—A.D.]. There are a number of alternatives. The worst is to apply the law in its current form already in the elections to the Fourteenth Knesset, or with minor changes like the ones proposed by the Minister of Justice. Adopting one of the two alternatives that he proposed will not necessarily yield immediately tragic results. But sooner or later a scenario that could involve the collapse of the system will be played out. Therefore it is imperative to act with far greater courage. Under existing circumstances, it would appear that the optimal solution is the abrogation of direct elections and implementation (even on a trial basis) of the alternatives described above. Another possibility is to go back to the old system, or to postpone implementation of the new Basic Law: the Government in order to allow for more extensive debate in the next Knesset.[53]

Once the Prime Minister was directly elected in 1996, there emerged another evil of the new arrangement, i.e., its tendency to fragment the political map. If in the past it was customary to blame the existence of so many political parties not on the nature of Israel's political and social system but on the system of proportional representation and the low threshold required to win representation in the Knesset, today the blame may be laid at the door of direct elections. In truth, fragmentation of the political map does not necessarily yield dire results. As opposed to what is frequently argued in the professional literature, the more stable a democracy is, the more likely it is to have more political parties. There are of course opposite examples, the Weimar Republic on the one hand and the United States on the other. It is nevertheless clear that the atomization of the political system represents a real danger. Supporters of the law argue today (like many other prophets blessed with the wisdom of hindsight) that they foresaw the danger and sought to forestall it by such means as raising the threshold. However, it is precisely this kind of solution that can make the situation worse, if special-interest groups were to join hands and thus increase their influence. What is more, when the argument of fragmentation was raised before supporters of the law, they denied that such a problem existed. In a public statement just before the law was enacted they argued the following:

> Will direct elections lead to further fragmentation of the Knesset? The *opposite* is true [my emphasis—A.D.]. Today the citizen is required to vote only for the party of his choice. He does so because he personally identifies with one of the lists of candidates. But deciding which party to vote for is now only one of his decisions. Tomorrow he will have to decide whom he wishes to see as Prime Minister. From this day forth he will have to weigh the ability of the Prime Minister to function and he will wish to strengthen his hand. In mayoral elections it has been proven that when a candidate wins by a big majority he usually takes along his party [this is factually false—A.D.]. On the other hand, the citizen will be able to continue voting for the small parties.[54]

Was it possible to foresee the splintering of the Knesset? Many claim today that they did, but only in one document did anyone go out on a limb and say so at the time. The following was written in 1991 by A. Diskin and H. Diskin under the title 'The Coming Power of the Small Parties':

> The probable result of the proposed reform will be a split of the vote. It is almost certain that in the Knesset elections many voters will not vote for the party headed by the candidate they voted for in the elections for Prime Minister. This can be demonstrated by sample findings in Israel and by the experience of other countries.
> The split in the vote will already be sharp in the first round because of the fairly strict conditions limiting candidacy. It goes without saying that if there is a second round, there will be no

similarity between votes for the Knesset and votes for the Prime Minister.

It is hard to imagine a split of votes in any country, and especially in Israel, not serving to increase the representation of special interest groups in Parliament. Even if the winning candidate for Prime Minister comes from one of the two big parties, the number of seats gained by these two parties in the Knesset will probably drop (and probably by a lot) compared with elections under the existing system. The electoral gains of the various small parties will not be identical. Many studies in Israel and abroad indicate that vote splitting involves additional factors, and according to available data the damage to the parties will also not be equal. Ironically, it is conceivable that it is precisely the most enthusiastic supporters of the law who will be its principal victims. [And this is precisely what happened when the law was first implemented in the 1996 elections: the Labor Party—the prime mover in getting the law passed—fell from power, and Likud's Netanyahu became Prime Minister—A.D.]

The combination of vote splitting (and increased representation for the small parties) and the numerous measures enacted by the legislator to increase the authority and powers of the Knesset, can lead to cases of 'blackmail' more serious than under the present system. This was hardly the intention of the legislator.

Whoever thinks that directly electing the Prime Minister will reduce the power of the small parties, especially when these parties hold the balance of power [the reference is to the ultra-Orthodox parties—A.D.], will find himself actually increasing their electoral strength [as was the case in the 1996 and 1999 elections; see discussion below—A.D.]. Furthermore, it is easy to imagine situations where the Prime Minister will be dependent on small parties that are not in the center of the political spectrum. In fact, the law, in its present form, will increase the dependency of the Prime Minister on the Knesset and the small parties despite his being elected directly by the people. The response of a Prime Minister finding himself in such a situation and knowing that he has the support of a majority of the people is liable to upset the legally binding constitutional order (and we do not necessarily have in mind the Fourth Republic of France). It is not unlikely under such circumstances that the judiciary as well will be drawn into the eye of the storm.[55]

Nine years after the above lines were written and after two election campaigns under the new system, it appears that every word is that much more true.

In a statement of support published in 1991 by the bridegrooms of the law prior to its passage, the 'advantages of the law for the country and the citizen' were highlighted in a boxed-off section that opened with the following words:

> The government will be accorded stability and the ability to function from one election to the next. The existence of the government will not be continuously threatened. Persistent efforts to undermine and bring down the government will cease ...[56]

It would be hard to argue that this was in fact the result of the legislation. It would be easier to show that there has never been a time when the government experienced more frequent crises than since 1996.

What is the linchpin that kept the new system from collapsing? It appears that it is based on the language of Article 19 of the Basic Law:

(a) The Knesset may, by means of a majority of its members, adopt an expression of no confidence in the Prime Minister.
(b) An expression of no confidence in the Prime Minister by the Knesset will be deemed a Knesset decision to disperse prior to completion of its term of service.[57]

This is the famous 'balance of terror' that restrains the Knesset from acting too decisively against the Prime Minister. The idea behind this article is double-edged. First, in the case of a clash between the two directly elected branches of government, the deciding voice belongs to the sovereign, namely the people. Secondly, Knesset members at odds with the Prime Minister will not hurry to depose him if doing so may cause them to lose their seats. This linchpin is especially effective early in the term of a new Knesset. It can of course be removed by a pre-emptive change in the law by those who wish to remove the prime minister.[58] The 'balance of terror' was proposed exclusively by the writer of these lines, a staunch opponent of the concept of direct election of the Prime Minister, in an effort to forestall the general collapse of the system in the event of the law being passed. It was presented to the Constitution, Law and Justice Committee of the Knesset and in seven of the eight informal meetings held by the four initiators of the law before combining their proposals. At the same time it was also suggested that the Prime Minister might be allowed to call for early ('double') elections. This possibility too was incorporated into Article 22 of the law (though distorted by requiring the cooperation of the president).

During the second reading of the law an amendment was attached to Article 3. The amendment was sponsored by the Mafdal, which very much wished to limit the powers of the Prime Minister and increase his dependence on his coalition partners. In contrast to the original proposal passed in committee, according to which the Prime Minister need not present his government to the Knesset for confirmation, subsections (c) and (d) stipulate the following:

(c) Ministers will be appointed by the Prime Minister; appointments will be contingent on confirmation by the Knesset.
(d) Rejection by the Knesset of the Prime Minister's proposed government would be deemed a vote of no confidence in the government in accordance with Article 19 (b).[59]

These subsections empty the idea of direct election of its content. The problems Binyamin Netanyahu and Ehud Barak faced immediately after their election proved the point in the clearest possible way.

When the idea of direct election of the Prime Minister was broached in the late 1980s and early 1990s, some people rejected it for reasons different from the ones discussed above. Thus it was claimed that someone like Ariel Sharon might exploit the new system in a way that would endanger democratic principles. Prime Minister Begin was quoted as saying that he had hesitated to appoint Sharon as his Minister of Defense because he was afraid that Sharon would 'surround the Prime Minister's office with tanks'. Be that as it may, when Sharon was elected, he took the opposite tack, insisting before he presented his government to the Knesset that the entire system of direct election must be scrapped and the old, purely parliamentary system restored. He also insisted on postponing the debate on the conscription of the ultra-Orthodox into the army (the 'Tal Law') and called on the Knesset to approve a new budget. The Knesset acceded to all his requests on 7 March 2001, prior to the presentation of his new government.

The new Basic Law: the Government, 2001, adopted most of the ideas of the Basic Law: the Government, 1968, and the Law of Transition, 1949.

Article 7 (a) of the new law states:

> When a new Government has to be constituted, the President of the State shall, after consultation with representatives of party groups in the Knesset, assign the task of forming a government to a Knesset Member who has notified him that he is prepared to accept the task; the President shall do so within seven days of the publication of the election results, or should the need arise to form a new government; and in the case of the death of the Prime Minister, within 14 days of his death.[60]

According to Article 13 (c), 'The Knesset Member who has formed a Government shall head it.' And Article 13 (d) states:

> When a Government has been formed, it shall present itself to the Knesset, announce the basic lines of its policy, its composition and the distribution of functions among the Ministers, and ask for a vote of confidence. The Government is constituted when the Knesset has expressed confidence in it, and the Ministers shall thereupon assume office.

A major change in the new law was the introduction of 'a constructive vote of no confidence' in the spirit of proposals that had been made since 1989. The procedure in such a vote is mapped out in Article 28:

> (a) The Knesset may adopt an expression of no confidence in the Government.
> (b) An expression of no confidence in the Government will be a decision adopted by the majority of Members of the Knesset to request that the President charge one of its members with the task of forming a Government
> (c) If the Knesset has expressed no confidence in the Government, the Government shall be deemed to have resigned on the day of the expression of no confidence. The President will, within two days, charge the Knesset Member named in the Knesset vote with the task of forming a Government.[61]

Another provision of Basic Law: the Government, 2001, already included in the Basic Law: the Government, 1992—but not part of parliamentary procedure until its implementation of the new system in 1996—is the power given to the Prime Minister to dissolve the Knesset under certain conditions. This power is described in Article 29:

> (a) Should the Prime Minister ascertain that a majority of the Knesset opposes the Government, and that the effective functioning of the Government is prevented as a result, he may, with the approval of the President of the State, dissolve the Knesset by means of an order to be published in *Reshumot*. The order will enter into force 21 days after its publication, unless a request is submitted under subsection (c), and the Government will be deemed to have resigned on the day of the order's publication.[62]

There is no contradiction between this power given to the Prime Minister and the idea of a constructive vote of no confidence. This is because the power to dissolve the Knesset is removed when there is a 'constructive' Knesset majority that opposes the Prime Minister. This is stated in the subsequent subsections of Article 29:

> (b) Within 21 days of the publication of this order, a majority of Knesset Members may request that the President charge one of its members, who has so agreed in writing and is not the Prime Minister, with the task of forming a Government.
> (c) Where a request as aforesaid has been submitted to the President, the President shall inform the Speaker of the Knesset. The President shall assign the task of forming a Government to the Knesset Member named in the request within two days.
> (d) A Knesset Member to whom the task of forming a Government has been assigned under this article shall have a period of 28 days to carry it out. The President of the State may extend the period by additional periods not exceeding 14 days in the aggregate.
> (e) Should no such request be submitted under subsection (b), or if the period defined in subsection (d) should expire, and the Knesset Member did not inform the President that he had formed a Government or that, having presented a

Government, the Knesset rejected his request for confidence under Article 13 (d), it will be deemed a Knesset decision to disperse prior to the completion of its term of service, and elections to the Knesset will be held on the last Tuesday before the end of 90 days from the President's announcement or from the rejection of the request for confidence in the Government, as the case may be.[63]

As described above, most of the constitutional reforms of the 1990s were very problematic. Hence the March 2001 step 'backwards' seems to be a big step forward. It is doubtful, however, whether further remedies for other questionable results from these reforms will be undertaken in the foreseeable future.

3
The Party Map

ROOTS AND DEVELOPMENT, 1949–92

A number of features distinguish Israel's political system and party map from other democratic systems in the West. Some blame these features, at least in part, for the ills and evils of the Israeli system. Nonetheless, in some ways Israel is very much like other, more stable democracies.[64]

In Israel, as in most of these countries, a system of proportional representation by and large prevails. The Israeli Parliament, the Knesset, is the elected body. Until 1996, and since February 2001, a clear-cut parliamentary system was in place. The Parliament was responsible for appointing the government and could dismiss it with a vote of no confidence. Ideological and social cleavages, taken together with the electoral system, produced, as in most Western countries, a multi-party system.[65] Until today no single party has ever won a majority of Knesset seats, so that governments have had to rely on coalitions made up of a number of parties. In most cases, the coalitions consisted of parties fairly close to one another ideologically, with the structure of the coalition determined to a large extent by the identity of the 'pivotal party', that is, the party occupying a 'median' position in parliament.[66]

Israel's party system did in fact have unique features. The issues dividing the parties often differed from those on the agenda of most Western countries. Prominent among these issues were defence and foreign policy.[67] Moreover, the roots of most Israeli political parties can be traced back to movements founded decades before the establishment of the state. Some were set up abroad, mainly in Eastern and Central Europe, and many had branches and centers in Jewish communities throughout the Diaspora. Given the fact that most of these parties arose under foreign governments that provided few public services, some of them took on social and other functions generally not associated with political parties in democratic countries.

What are the political organizations in Israel that constitute 'political parties'? For purposes of discussion here, they are entities elected to the Knesset. This is in accordance with the view that sees parties as organizations contending for the reins of government or for a share in government. In actuality, Israeli parties lacked a formal definition or status until at least 1969. Competition in elections until then was not between parties but between 'lists of candidates'. These lists could be composed of party members or ordinary citizens. With the passage of party financing laws, first as a temporary measure in 1969 and afterwards, in 1973, as a permanent arrangement, standing of the parties was institutionalized, though financing and radio and television time before elections were still not allocated to 'parties' but to 'Knesset factions' and 'lists of candidates'.

Only in March 1992, in parallel with the 'constitutional revolution' and passage of the three special Basic Laws, was the Law of Parties, 1992, legislated. The Law of Parties stipulated that a party is 'an association of individuals joining together to advance political and social causes in a legal manner and seeking representation in the Knesset through elected candidates'. To be accorded the status of a party, the association was required to register with the Registrar of Parties and receive its approval (decisions of the Registrar could be appealed in the Supreme Court). Some of the parties thus registered never won Knesset representation and will not be part of the discussion below. On the other hand, many of those to be mentioned disappeared from the political scene before the Law of Parties was enacted.

The parties in general may be viewed in a number of ways. It is possible, for example, to classify them by their political and ideological positions, by their inclinations toward radical or moderate positions, by their size, by the composition of their voters, by the composition of their elected representatives, or by their political activity within coalitions and other frameworks. Some of these features will be discussed below. However, the most convenient way to chart out the development of Israel's party map is probably in the dimension of time.

Thus we shall begin by focusing on party representation in the Constituent Assembly, namely the First Knesset. The election to that

Knesset determined the nature of the transition from the Yishuv to a state, as well as the implications of this transition for the political parties. To the parties active in the Mandatory period, new parties were now added that play a leading role in Israel to this very day.

We shall then deal with the period commencing with the elections to the Second Knesset (1951) and ending with the elections to the Fifth Knesset (1961). During this period, mass immigration produced unprecedented demographic changes; but, despite these changes, the party map remained fixed, with some upheaval only during the so-called Lavon Affair during the Fourth Knesset.

Starting with the elections to the Sixth Knesset (1965), Israeli parties began changing significantly. These changes affected the party map in the 1965 elections and in the 1969 and 1973 elections. Accordingly, these three elections constitute a distinct era of parliamentary transition.

What came next was a period of struggle between the two major party blocs. This period commences with the 1977 election upheaval and ends with the reversal of fortunes in the elections to the Thirteenth Knesset (1992)

And finally, as we shall see, beginning in 1996 Israel entered a new constitutional and political era, with consequences for the political parties as well. The number of parties grew to an unprecedented extent and on the eve of the 1999 election even further fragmentation was experienced.

Between the establishment of the state and its first elections, the Provisional State Council served as a provisional parliament. The name Provisional State Council replaced the earlier National Council, which had consisted of 37 representatives. The composition of the provisional parliament was based on results of the elections to the Fourth Elected Assembly of 1944 and on negotiations between the parties active at the end of the Mandatory period. The special feature in this arrangement was the inclusion of parties that had distanced themselves from official Jewish institutions under the Mandate. Centrist parties such as Mapai, the General Zionists, and Mizrachi wished to co-opt more radical parties in order to broaden a national consensus they regarded as necessary in the struggle for independence. Thus the Revisionist movement, the Communist Party, and Agudat Israel had representatives in the Provisional State Council. The 37 members of the Council were the ones who signed the Declaration of Independence and devised such important documents as the *Minshar* and the Law and Administration Ordinance, 1948.

The first elections, held in January 1949 at the end of the War of Independence, were to the Constituent Assembly rather than the 'Knesset'. As we have seen, the intent was to frame a constitution, but, in its first legislative measure, the Law of Transition, 1949, the Assembly changed its name to the 'First Knesset'. As we have already noted, the First Knesset decided, on 13 June 1950, not to adopt a constitution but to enact instead, in stages, a series of Basic Laws.

The largest winning party in the first elections was Mifleget Poalei Eretz Yisrael—Mapai—which took 46 seats. Another two seats were won by the minorities' list affiliated to Mapai. These results reflected the balance of political power over the course of many years. Mapai was the dominant party, far larger than any of the other parties, but it never won an absolute majority of votes or Knesset seats. Mapai had controlled the institutions of the pre-State Yishuv almost from the time the party was founded in 1930 as a merger between (the 'historical') Ahdut ha-Avodah and Ha-Poel ha-Tzair.

Mapam (Mifleget ha-Poalim ha-Meuhedet), the second party in size after the first elections, was somewhat to the left of Mapai. It was a new party created through a merger of three entities: Siah Bet ('Faction B'), a left-wing Mapai breakaway group (formed in 1944); Ha-Shomer ha-Tzair; and Leftist Poalei Tziyyon (founded in 1923 and merging first with Ha-Shomer ha-Tzair in 1944 and afterwards with Siah Bet). Many regarded Mapam as the party most closely associated with the Palmach, which was the main fighting force at the end of the Yishuv period and during the War of Independence. This identification was naturally one of the reasons for the popularity of Mapam, which won 19 seats.

The Communist Party, to the left of Mapam, would adopt the name Maki (Ha-Miflagah ha-Kommunistit ha-Yisraelit). Maki was thought of as a 'leper' and never considered a potential coalition partner. Nonetheless, it is worth noting that all the left-wing parties did well in the first elections. Together, including Mapai, they won 71 seats. This so-called camp could block any other, underscoring the considerable strength of Mapai as a pivotal party.

The religious camp was made up of four parties when the state was established. Two were Zionist parties while two had ultra-Orthodox roots. Mizrachi, the premier party of religious Zionism, had been founded in 1902. Agudat Israel arose as an anti-Zionist religious opposition party to Mizrachi in 1912. In 1922, Ha-Poel ha-Mizrachi and Poalei Agudat Israel seceded from their parent organizations.

The religious parties ran for the Constituent Assembly on a joint list called the United Religious Front. The list won 16 seats. This was the only time that all the religious parties were able to unite in a single list.

The biggest setback in the 1949 elections was suffered by the General Zionists. Until the 1930s they had controlled the institutions of the Yishuv and they were the senior partners of Mapai when the latter took over leadership later on. Now they won only seven seats. Their strength lay mainly in the old-time settlements of the First Aliyah.

The most surprising success in the first elections was scored by a party founded in June 1948—the Herut Movement established by the IZL (Irgun Zvai Leummi or Etzel). Immediately after its formal establishment, its leaders became embroiled in the bitter clash over the sinking of the IZL ship *Altalena*. Herut won 14 seats. This success was all the more striking in view of the failure in the elections of the Revisionist Party, the parent organization of the IZL. The Revisionists, who had founded their movement in 1925 under Ze'ev Jabotinsky, did not win a single seat and were fated to be swallowed up by Herut before the elections to the Second Knesset. The Herut Movement can be seen as representing the 'nationalist right' while the 'social and economic right' was represented by the General Zionists.

The more moderate right was represented by a new party, the product of a merger between General Zionist 'Faction A', leaders of Central European immigration organized in Aliyah Hadashah, and Ha-Oved ha-Tziyyoni. These three groups founded the Progressive Party in 1948, winning five seats in the Constituent Assembly.

Seven additional seats were divided between parties destined to disappear quickly from the political map: the Sephardi List, which won four seats, and the Fighters' List, WIZO, and the Yemenite Association, each with one seat. In elections to the Elected Assembly under the Mandate the ethnic lists did quite well. But, in elections to the Second Knesset, the Sephardim won only two seats while the Yemenites retained one.

The Fighters' List was composed of Lehi members (the 'Stern Gang'). They hoped to secure the release of Nathan Friedman Yellin-Mor, who had been convicted under the Prevention of Terror Ordinance after the assassination of Count Bernadotte. After his election he was indeed released from prison and served in the First Knesset.

The first two governments formed during the term of the First Knesset were based on coalitions including Mapai, the minorities, the Religious Front, the Progressive Party, and the Sephardi List.

The number of eligible voters in 1949 was 506,567. For elections to the Fifth Knesset, held in August 1961, the number was 1,271,285. This rapid growth derived mainly from mass immigration during the early years of the state.

Given the big demographic change, the electoral stability of the three main political camps is surprising. Four elections were held between 1951 and 1961. The leftist camp (including the minority lists and Maki) won between 68 (1961) and 71 (1959) seats in these elections. The right-wing parties won between 31 (1959) and 34 (1961), and the religious parties won between 15 (1951) and 18 (1959, 1961). Parties not clearly identified with any of these three camps[68] were not represented in subsequent Knessets.

This stability in the face of dramatic population growth produced many theories about the behavior of the parties, the political establishment, and the voters. One argument, partly refuted by later studies, maintained that voters during this period were prepared to shift their votes only between parties belonging to the same political camp. Thus, while individual parties may have had marked ups and downs, these were 'balanced' by the tally for other parties in the same camp.

Another argument was that immigrants were put in charge of bodies connected with specific political parties in proportion to the relative strength of these parties. Consequently the political co-option of these immigrants maintained the relative strength of the existing political camps.

It should be pointed out that in this period prominent political leaders did not tend to switch camps, though there were cases where politicians jumped from one party to another within the same camp. The only exception was Moshe Sneh, one of the most prominent leaders of the General Zionists in the pre-State period, who went over to the left and ultimately became the head of Maki.

Internally, the biggest change in the leftist camp came about in 1954 when Siah Bet and a faction of Leftist Poalei Tziyyon broke away from Mapam and established the Ahdut ha-Avodah—Poalei Tziyyon Party. Remaining in Mapam were members of Ha-Shomer ha-Tzair and of another faction of Leftist Poalei Tziyyon. Beginning with the elections to the Third Knesset (1955), these two parties ran separately, winning more or less the same number of votes. Mapai always succeeded in controlling at least a third of the seats in the Knesset, hitting a low point of 40 in 1955 and a peak of 47 in 1959. At the same time, minority parties took five seats in all three elections of the 1950s.

On the right during this period Herut dropped to eight seats in the elections to the Second Knesset (1951) but recovered to reach a high-water mark of 17 in 1959 and 1961. The General Zionists tripled their strength in the elections to the Second Knesset, winning 20 seats, but in the last elections in which they appeared as an independent list (1959) they suffered a stinging defeat, winning only eight seats. Consequently, on the eve of elections to the Fifth Knesset (1961) the General Zionists and Progressives merged into the Liberal Party.

The religious camp split itself up into its four constituent groups for the elections to the Second Knesset. Mizrachi and Ha-Poel Mizrachi cooperated in elections to the Third Knesset, first on a joint list (the National Religious Front) and subsequently as a single party (the National Religious Party, or Mafdal). Overall the strength of the religious Zionist parties varied from ten to twelve seats. The two Agudah lists won five seats in the Second Knesset, rising to six from the Third Knesset on. In 1955 and 1959 the Agudah parties ran on a joint list as the Religious Torah Front but in 1961 they went back to running on separate lists.

Mapai continued to dominate government coalitions at this time. Only two parties, Herut and Maki, were never partners in any coalition. Both these parties were regarded as extremist by David Ben-Gurion, who headed the government during most of the period, and by most of the other parties. Agudat Israel too ceased being a partner after leaving the government at the end of 1952[69] and thus joined ranks with the extremists.

Elections to the Fifth Knesset in 1961 marked the end of an era. They were held early because of the Lavon Affair and the rift between Ben-Gurion and most of his coalition partners. Following the elections, the newly formed Liberal Party, the Mafdal, Mapam, and Ahdut ha-Avodah, all traditional partners of Mapai, created a bloc ('the Foursome Club') representing relatively moderate parties from all the political camps and controlling 46 seats in the Knesset compared with 42 for Mapai. This bloc made big demands as its price for joining the government but in effect it would have been impossible to form a government without Mapai, which was the biggest of them all and for all practical purposes the pivotal party. In the end the Foursome fell apart and Levi Eshkol, who conducted negotiations on Ben-Gurion's behalf, succeeded in forming a new government. The criticism leveled against Ben-Gurion and his party, and the rancorous feelings provoked in the public and among political leaders by the events of 1960–61, were the background to dramatic changes in the structure of the party map prior to elections to the Sixth Knesset (1965).

Levi Eshkol, who replaced Ben-Gurion as Prime Minister in 1963, had hoped to form a joint list with Ahdut ha-Avodah for the new elections. Mapai's 'Young Guard' opposed that combination. Eshkol also refused to accede to Ben-Gurion's demand that the 1954 spy fiasco connected with former Defense Minister Lavon be reopened for investigation. Consequently Ben-Gurion, the Young Guard, and others left Mapai and founded Rafi (the Israel Workers List), winning ten seats in the 1965 elections. At the same time, Mapai under Eshkol set up an 'Alignment' with Ahdut ha-Avodah and easily kept its position as the pivotal party with 45 seats.

Menachem Begin, leader of Herut, proposed an electoral alliance with the Liberal Party under the name of Gahal (Herut–Liberal Bloc). Most members of the Liberal Party, including most General Zionists, joined it. Some, on the other hand, mainly from the Progressive Party, refused to join and founded the Independent Liberal Party. The new Gahal list divided its first 22 places equally between the two partners, with Herut given more weight only further down the list. Apparently Begin had grown tired of being a political outcast and was prepared to pay the price of legitimization through this and other political agreements that were to come. Gahal won 26 sets in the 1965 elections. This was the first time any party other than Mapai had won so many seats. For the Alignment this was perhaps the first inkling of what was to come 12 years down the road.[70]

The 1965 elections saw a new party, Ha-Olam ha-Zeh–Koah Hadash, win a seat for the first time since the establishment of the state.

Two years later, the Six-Day War left a watershed imprint on the party map.[71] Just before the war, three new ministers joined the Cabinet as it transformed itself into a National Unity Government. Moshe Dayan of Rafi was given the defense portfolio, while Menachem Begin and Yosef Sapir of Gahal became ministers without portfolio. Gahal's low-key representation notwithstanding, this broke a long-standing taboo by bringing Herut into a governmental coalition for the first time.

The success of the war and the coalition also made far-reaching party changes possible on the left. In 1968 the Alignment of Mapai and Ahdut ha-Avodah merged with most of Rafi (including all of its Knesset members with the exception of Ben Gurion) to create the Labor Party. This was in fact Mapai with the accretion of those who had left it in 1944 and 1965. The new Labor Party ran together with Mapam as the 'big' Alignment in the elections to the Seventh Knesset (1969). Ben-Gurion and his followers kept aloof and ran on their own State List.

The elections mirrored the country's satisfaction with the leadership and its achievements. The Alignment scored the biggest election victory ever, taking 56 seats. With the minority lists affiliated with the Alignment (four seats), it controlled half the seats in the Knesset. Only a single change occurred on the right. Renegade members of Gahal, under the leadership of Shmuel Tamir, formed the short-lived Free Center Party, which won two seats.

As a result of the Yom Kippur War, elections to the Eighth Knesset were postponed from October to 31 December 1973. The atmosphere surrounding the elections differed completely from that in 1969. The sense of failed leadership and anticipation of the yet-unpublished Agranat Commission Report on the war left their mark on the elections. The slogan 'Despite Everything, the Alignment' was based, among other things, on the hope that peace could be achieved via the recently convened Geneva Peace Conference.

The Alignment lost five seats in this election, the minority lists lost one, and a new party sprang up alongside the Alignment. This was the Civil Rights Movement (Ratz), founded by Shulamit Aloni after Golda Meir relegated her to an unelectable position on the Alignment list in 1973. Ratz won three seats.

The extreme left also underwent much upheaval during the period. Maki split in 1965. The more viable faction was called Rakah (the New Communist List), supported in the main by Arab voters and generally more radical in its outlook. The other faction retained the name of Maki and won just a single seat in the 1965 and 1969 elections. For the 1973 elections it joined the new Moked list, which also won just one seat.

Following his retirement from the army in the beginning of 1973, Ariel Sharon joined the Liberal Party. As a condition he demanded that Gahal widen its scope. His efforts, along with the demands of others, led to the creation of the Likud, which included, in addition to Herut and the Liberal Party, members of the Free Center, the State

List,[72] and the Greater Israel Movement, founded among others by former members of the parties constituting the Alignment. The Likud in 1973 made an impressive showing with 39 seats but had to remain in the opposition.

After Gahal left the National Unity Government in summer 1970, the Alignment was left with a narrow coalition, which included the National Religious Party, the Independent Liberals, and the minority lists. Under the Rabin government, formed in June 1974 after the retirement of Golda Meir, Ratz took the place of the National Religious Party, but after five months the latter returned and Shulamit Aloni took Ratz out of the coalition.

Until the upheaval elections of 17 May 1977, Mapai (and its successor, the Labor Party), was the pivotal party in the system. All the parties to the right commanded fewer than half the seats in the Knesset and the parties to the left fewer still. Only with Mapai/Labor as a centrist party could a coalition be formed commanding a majority. This was because a coalition without a pivotal party would require an unlikely partnership between parties on the extreme right and the extreme left to get around the big party in the center.

In December 1976, Prime Minister Yitzhak Rabin called for early elections to the Ninth Knesset, mainly because he wished to keep a new party—the Democratic Movement for Change (Dash)—from getting entrenched. Dash, under the leadership of Yigael Yadin, had quickly become very popular. It was a centrist party made up of prominent figures from the left and the right, from the army and the academic world, from the establishment and from the protest movements that had sprung up after the Yom Kippur War. The Movement's success in the elections was quite impressive. It won 15 seats. But the Likud, which jumped to 43, could now form a government without it, for together the right-wing parties had 63 seats. Consequently neither the Alignment nor Dash could serve as the pivotal party.

Prior to the 1977 election, Ariel Sharon left the Likud and started his own Shlomzion Party. Shortly after the election the two MKs of this short-lived party rejoined the Likud, this time within the framework of Herut. Menachem Begin formed his first government with the support of the religious parties, the personal list of Shmuel Flatto-Sharon, and Moshe Dayan, who left the Labor Party and joined the government as Foreign Minister. Dash joined later on, but some of its members subsequently left the Movement, which ultimately fell apart and disappeared from the political scene. Shinui, a centrist-rightist party on social and economic issues and dovish in matters of defense and foreign affairs, was the only remnant of Dash to endure.

The 1977 elections inaugurated an era of considerable partisan flux.[73] As time passed, both the Begin government and the Likud suffered many defections. Moshe Dayan quit in 1980, running as head of the Telem Party in the 1981 elections together with Yigael Hurwitz, formerly of Rafi, the State Party and the Likud. In the same campaign two MKs who left the Likud, Geulah Cohen and Moshe Shamir, founded the Tehiyyah ('Revival') Movement together with other figures. On the right of the Likud one also encountered Tzomet, founded in 1983 by Rafael Eitan after retiring as Chief of Staff from the army and running jointly with Tehiyyah in the 1984 elections. Starting with the 1988 elections to the Twelfth Knesset, Tzomet ran independently. Tehiyyah disappeared from the political map after failing to reach the minimum vote threshold in the 1992 elections to the Thirteenth Knesset. On the extreme right, even more radical parties made their appearance. The Kach list won one seat in the 1984 elections to the Eleventh Knesset. Subsequently the party was outlawed and kept out of the Knesset in conformity with the Basic Law: the Knesset and the Elections Law as quoted above with reference to racist parties. Moledet made its first appearance in the 1988 elections.

The 1980s saw the birth and demise of a number of parties in the religious camp. In 1981, Aaron Abu-Hatzeirah, a defector from the National Religious Party (Mafdal), founded Tami and won three seats in the Tenth Knesset and one in the Eleventh. Subsequently Abu-Hatzeirah joined the Likud. The elections to the Eleventh Knesset also saw the appearance of Morashah, which won two seats and then disappeared from the map; and Shas ('Sephardi Torah Guardians'), which increasingly gained in strength. Degel ha-Torah, Shas's 'Ashkenazi' ally, made its appearance in the elections to the Twelfth Knesset (1988), joining Agudat Israel in the next elections under the party banner of Yahadut ha-Torah.

Two right-wing groups made a one-time appearance in the 1984 elections and immediately affiliated themselves with the Alignment. These were Yahad with three seats under Ezer Weizman, and Ometz with the single seat held by its leader, Yigael Hurwitz. These defections produced a 60–60 standoff between the left-wing and right-wing parties. This state of affairs led to the creation of a National Unity

Government that lasted until March 1990 (even surviving the 1988 elections) under the leadership of the two big parties and with the participation of other right-wing, centrist and religious parties. The decision of the Labor Party to join the National Unity Government caused a rupture with its Alignment partner, Mapam, which ran independently for the first time since 1965 in the elections to the Twelfth Knesset in 1988. In the elections to the Thirteenth Knesset (1992), under the name of Meretz, Mapam ran on a joint list with Ratz (the leading party on the list) and Shinui.

Numerous changes also took place on the extreme left during this period. Rakah formed an alliance with non-Communist elements and ran as Hadash (Democratic Front for Peace and Equality) beginning with the 1977 elections to the Ninth Knesset. Moked was supplanted by Sheli, which lost its place in parliament in the elections to the Tenth Knesset; and by the Progressive List, which lost its place in the elections to the Thirteenth Knesset. The 1988 elections also saw the arrival of Mada on the scene (Arab Democratic Party), led by Abd el-Wahab Darawshe, who had previously represented the Labor Party in the Knesset.

The victors in the 1992 elections to the Thirteenth Knesset, by a slim margin, were the parties to the right of Labor.[74] However, many right-wing votes were wasted on parties that did not receive the minimum number of votes required to win a seat. This once again turned Labor into the pivotal party, controlling 61 seats together with Meretz, Mada, and Hadash, and thereby blocking the right. Consequently, Rabin formed a government with Meretz and Shas. When Shas left the government in September 1993, the Rabin administration stayed in office as a minority government, counting on the Knesset votes of the two Arab parties.

THE NEW PARTY MAP, 1996–99

In March 1990, for the first time in Israel's history, a government fell on a vote of no confidence. Yitzhak Shamir did in fact succeed in forming a new government within a few months. However, many argued that it was imperative to alter the constitutional framework in order to curtail the power of small parties (especially the ultra-Orthodox parties) and individual Knesset members to blackmail or destroy government coalitions. This was the main consideration behind the revision of the Basic Law: the Government (the 'direct-elections law' discussed above). The law passed its second and third readings in March 1992. It was put into effect for the first time in the 1996 elections and fulfilled the prediction of fragmentation that I made in 1991.

With respect to political parties, the salient feature of elections to the Fourteenth Knesset was a drop in strength for the big parties. In 1996, Labor won only 34 seats. The Likud was even less successful. In the Likud–Gesher–Tzomet bloc of 32 seats, the two small parties—Gesher, newly founded by David Levi, and Rafael Eitan's Tzomet—controlled ten. The Likud had been forced to concede these latter seats to their partners when Levi and Eitan threatened otherwise to run independently in the direct elections for Prime Minister

Two new parties made their debut in the center of the political map. Yisrael ba-Aliyah under Nathan Sharansky won seven seats and the Third Way, started by Labor Party defectors and others, took four. With the exception of Dash, this represented the greatest success among new lists since the first election. The religious parties increased their strength, winning a combined total of 23 seats, compared with a previous peak of 18. The Arab parties came out in new dress. Hadash appeared jointly with Balad (National Democratic Alliance) and Mada ran with Ra'am (United Arab List). These last two parties increased their representation from five in 1992 to nine in 1996. The strength of two small parties was reduced. Meretz dropped from twelve to nine seats and Moledet from three to two. However, both did better than the polls predicted.

With the approach of elections to the Fifteenth Knesset (1999), numerous changes occurred in the look of Knesset factions. Many Knesset members left their parties and founded new factions, hoping to get in on the ground floor of the political alliances but also to get a share of party financing and broadcasting time on radio and television that was to be allocated to existing Knesset factions for the coming campaign. Knesset members also left the newly formed factions, generally for similar reasons. The survey of events sketched out below gives a good indication of the prevailing instability, much of it due to a pursuit of personal interests and short-sightedness bordering on opportunism.

On 20 January 1999 the Knesset Committee approved a split in the Meretz bloc and recognized Shinui as a faction with a single member, Avraham Poraz. Poraz had been operating for some time as a one-man faction, owing to his opposition to the full merger of Ratz, Mapam, and Amnon Rubinstein of Shinui.

On 23 February 1999 the Likud–Gesher–Tzomet bloc split into four separate factions: Likud–Tzomet with 22 seats; Gesher with three members (David Levi, Maxim Levi, and Yehudah Lankri); Herut with Benny Begin and David Re'em and former Gesher member Mikhael Kleiner; and Yisrael ba-Merkaz Bet with Likud renegades Yitzhak Mordechai and Dan Meridor, former Gesher member David Magen and former Tzomet member Eliezer Zandberg.

On the same day the Labor faction also split in two: Labor with 32 seats and Yisrael ba-Merkaz Aleph with two (MKs Nissim Zvili and Hagai Merom).

Immediately following their recognition as official Knesset factions, Yisrael ba-Merkaz Aleph and Yisrael ba-Merkaz Bet merged into a new faction, Yisrael ba-Merkaz, with six seats.

Also on 23 February 1999 the Knesset Committee approved a split in the Yisrael ba-Aliyah and Yahadut ha-Torah factions. MKs Mikhael Nudelman and Yuri Stern, leaving Yisrael ba-Aliyah, started the Aliyah faction with the idea of joining Avigdor Lieberman's new party. MK Avraham Ravitz of Degel ha-Torah split with Agudat Israel, probably hoping to improve his party's bargaining position in the negotiations between these two ultra-Orthodox parties before the coming Knesset elections.

On 4 March 1999 the three members of Tzomet still in the Likud–Gesher–Tzomet bloc—Rafael Eitan, Moshe Peled, and Chaim Dayan—left the joint list and reconstituted their independent Tzomet faction. The Likud was thus left with only 19 seats. On the same day MK Peled left the Tzomet faction and started the Mekhorah faction, immediately thereafter joining his one-man faction to Moledet, which would now have three members.

Another move paving the way for the creation of a new list called National Unity was the resignation of MKs Hanan Porat and Zvi Hendel from the National Religious Party and their creation of a new faction, Emunim.

On 8 March 1999 the Hadash–Balad faction split with the resignation of MKs Hassem Mahmid and Azmi Bishara. The new faction took over the name Balad and Hadash remained with three seats: all this despite the fact that Hassem Mahmid was originally a member of Hadash.

On 17 March 1999 David Zucker bolted from the Meretz faction. On 22 March 1999 Yisrael ba-Merkaz split. Eliezer Zandberg left and started the Young Guard faction. On 25 March 1999 the Labor faction again split. This time MKs Amir Peretz, Adiso Masala, and

Rafiq Haj started the One Nation faction, thus leaving Labor with just 29 seats.

On 29 March 1999 the two one-man factions of Avraham Poraz and Eliezer Zandberg merged. On the same day MK Emmanuel Sussman of the Third Way announced his resignation from that faction. Another of the faction's MKs, Alex Lubotsky, had in effect left it long ago, but without formally changing his status.

All this jockeying for position set the stage for the elections to the Fifteenth Knesset in 1999. Of the 33 lists of candidates registered with the Central Elections Committee, 13 were by and large based on veteran factions in the outgoing Knesset or on partners in these factions that had once operated as independent parties (One Israel, the Likud, Shas, the National Religious Party, Meretz, Yisrael ba-Aliyah, Yahadut ha-Torah, Tzomet, the Third Way, Hadash, Ra'am, Balad, and Shinui). One list (National Unity) was based on one faction in the outgoing Knesset and on members who had left two other factions. Five new lists included MKs who had left their factions in the outgoing Knesset (the Center Party, One Nation, Yisrael Beitenu, Green Peace, and the Negev Party). Two other lists (Pensioners and Moreshet Avot) were led by former MKs, from Knessets preceding the Fourteenth. An additional 12 new parties filled out the lists.[75]

In the past it had seemed that Israel's party map was a solid rock countenancing only marginal changes. The results of the elections to the Fifteenth Knesset, described further on, show that this situation had changed completely. But first let us consider the role of the 'political center' on both the macro and the micro political levels.

THE POWER OF THE POLITICAL CENTER

Recent developments in Israeli politics are to a great extent related to the weight of the political center. Where a rough balance of power exists between the right and left, those occupying the center of the map electorally and politically will assume decisive importance. Thus, as mentioned, the change in Israel's electoral system derived in part from dissatisfaction with the parties and individual Knesset members who appeared to have gained control of the center. In fact, the swing vote in the center decided elections not just in the 1990s but in every single one since 1977. In that year of election upheaval, a new party, Dash, attempted to dominate the center as a pivotal party but failed. More recent elections have witnessed the appearance (and disappearance) of centrist parties that played a leading electoral role in the Knesset and the government. Among such parties were the Center Party, Shinui, Yisrael ba-Aliyah, and the Third Way. It is therefore worth taking a theoretical and historical look at the political center.

Over 200 years ago Jean Charles de Borda discovered the famous Voting Paradox, which has occupied some of the leading scholars of the Western world ever since, from Charles Dodgson[76] to Kenneth Arrow,[77] who won the Nobel Prize for Economics in 1972 mainly for his work on subjects related to the Paradox.

The Paradox may be illustrated by the following example: 30 voters must choose from among candidates A, B, and C the person they prefer for a particular position. Nine prefer A over B and B over C. Ten prefer C over A and A over B. Eleven prefer B over C and C over A.

All the voters are 'rational' in the sense that their order of preference is 'transitive', that is, whoever preferred A over B and the latter over C will also prefer A over C, and so on for the other voters. However, despite this 'transitive' preference of each voter, the order of preference of the voting body as a whole is not transitive, and a 'circular' order of preference is created. Nineteen voters (belonging to the first and second groups) prefer A over B. Twenty (belonging to the first and third) prefer B over C. But, strange to say, C wins with 21 votes (from the second and third groups) when put up against A. On the practical level, no rules of voting can be devised (aside from a 'mixed' solution by lot, rotation, etc.) that will offer a satisfactory solution to the Paradox. The same holds true for the mutual neutralization of orders of preference by the recently popular 'symmetric' solution. In certain senses it may be said that the birth of centrist parties in Israel and elsewhere is often related to problems of preference connected to this Paradox.

Borda himself proposed solving the Paradox by awarding points to the various candidates, as is done in the Eurovision Song Contest. Despite its recent popularity due to its 'symmetry' advantages, this is an 'incorrect' solution that is liable to produce untoward results, as was pointed out by Borda's colleague, the Marquis de Condorcet, secretary of the French Academy of Sciences at the time. Condorcet proposed, as a partial solution, choosing the candidate that wins a majority of votes against each of the other candidates. The winner here is known as the 'Condorcet winner' and is generally recognized by scholars as a valid winner. Often (as in the above example) there is no Condorcet winner, and we may ask whether such a winner should be considered the proper one under all circumstances. The problem can be brought home in the following example:

Candidate A represents the 'right', candidate B the 'center', and candidate C the 'left'. In this field of candidates, right-wing voters, supporters of A, prefer B over C. Left-wing voters, supporters of C, also prefer B, this time over A. Let us assume that right-wing candidate A is supported by 49 percent of voters, as is left-wing candidate C. Candidate B, who is supported originally by only 2 percent of voters, is the 'Condorcet winner'. A majority of 51 percent will prefer him over A and a majority of 51 percent will prefer him over C.

If we move on now to the events that occupied the Israeli public in the 1999 elections, we can see how the old paradox we have just described went a long way toward determining the look of the new political map of Israel. Yitzhak Mordechai was considered right up to election day the least popular 'first preference' among the three main candidates for Prime Minister. According to all the polls he was behind both Binyamin Netanyahu and Ehud Barak. Nonetheless, like several other candidates from the center, he was believed to have the best chance of winning the election in a second round, where only two candidates would remain. A poll gave him the edge over Amnon Shahak and Dan Meridor, fellow members of the Center Party, as the potential 'Condorcet winner', and, though his victory in the poll was slight, it was enough to crown him as the party's candidate in the race for Prime Minister.

Let us further assume that the position of each of the three candidates of the Center Party was equal to those in the example of the Borda Paradox. Under such circumstances the candidate joining the race last has, theoretically, the biggest advantage. A (Amnon) defeats B (Dan). But, after B drops out, C (Yitzhak) will defeat A. C thus guarantees his victory by his late entry into the race. If C had been pitted against B earlier, B would have defeated C but lost to A in a second face-off. In this case A would win by virtue of his late entry. We have no precise data concerning the reasons why poll respondents preferred Meridor, Shahak, or Mordechai, but there are grounds for believing that Shahak and even more so Meridor were hurt by their entry into the race before Mordechai. Furthermore, another Center Party candidate for premiership, Roni Milo, was the first to announce his candidacy. No wonder that he found himself in the fourth place on the Center's list, following Meridor (third place), Shahak (second), and Mordechai (first on the list and its candidate for premiership). This kind of paradox encouraged yet other candidates for Prime Minister right up to the eve of the elections (Binyamin Ze'ev Begin and Azmi Bishara).[78]

The power of the centrist candidates and parties has been a known factor since at least the end of the 1960s. All along, polls have requested voters to indicate their second choice of a party after their own. It turns out that parties in the center are usually the second choice. The Progressives and their successors the Independent Liberals, for example, were the second choice of approximately 20 percent of respondents and the first choice of approximately only 5 percent or fewer. The big problem of the centrist parties was therefore how to capitalize on their potential and win the support of voters who saw them as a second choice. There were exceptional cases where centrist parties were strikingly successful, such as Rafi in 1965 and Dash in 1977. But these successes were short-lived and each of the parties that achieved them fell apart without succeeding again. One reason for such ups and downs is the vagueness of the positions of the centrist parties. Their weak 'ideological glue' does not stick for very long. Moreover, these parties are often made up of defectors from existing parties who fanned out in every direction after failing to win power.

We should note that the advantages enjoyed by centrist parties and centrist candidates are not only the ones mentioned above. A more distinct advantage is mapped out by A. Downs in his well-known Economic Theory of Democracy.[79] Downs presents a model that had already been proposed by the economist H. Hotelling.[80] Two big parties (as in the United States) are likened in this example to two supermarkets looking for a good location on the main street of an American town. Since most of their potential customers (or voters) are located in the middle (residentially or politically) the optimal strategy would be to locate the supermarket (or party) near the same center (geographic or political). Accordingly, there were periods in which the two American parties became centrist parties, having more in common than separating them.[81]

Another and later example of the success of this strategy in a democratic system is the rightward shift by British Labour under Tony Blair. This move, as with the revival of the idea of the 'third way' in Europe, resulted in a change of governments after a long period of Conservative rule at a time when 'pure leftists' had no chance whatsoever of bringing about such a change. Blair's predecessor, John Major, also attracted the center and left, thanks to his moderate origins (though quite rightist in his views), and achieved a victory in the 1992 general election. Moreover, the rise of a centrist party in Britain in the 1980s under the leadership of David (now Lord) Owen split the leftist vote and pushed certain Labour leaders toward more Conservative positions, which under Britain's nonproportional electoral system guaranteed dominance to the Conservatives for some time.

The attempt to arrive at 'centrist positions' is not new in Israel. For years public opinion polls have unearthed centrist leanings when voters were asked to grade themselves in various ideological configurations.[82] One way to reveal such preferences is by using a scale with an odd number of categories. The respondent might be asked a question such as the following: 'On a scale where 1 represents someone far to the right in matters of security and foreign policy and 5 someone far to the left, where would you place yourself on the scale of 1 to 5?' Similar questions can be asked on other ideological issues, whether social, economic, religious or political. The upshot of these polls was that voters generally revealed a clear-cut gravitation toward the center (3 on the scale) while most 'rightists' and 'leftists' revealed only leanings in their respective directions (2 and 4 on the scale). The exception is on the issue of religion and state. Here we generally find two peaks: the nonreligious peak (5) and the middle-of-the-road peak (3). Thus on major issues the center seems like a good place to look for political clientele (see Table 13). Moreover, most voters see themselves as more centrist than the parties they support.

Notwithstanding these tendencies, it must be said that under certain circumstances voters do move toward the extremes of the political spectrum. Thus, for example, when asked specific questions they retreat from the centrist positions that they expressed in their replies to the general questions. For example, in a survey of support for civil marriage in Israel (on a scale of 1 to 5), many placed themselves at the extremes (1 and 5) as opposed to their centrist response to a general question on the religious-versus-secular issue. Moreover, leanings toward the center weaken as election-day approaches. More and more voters 'return to the fold', and this is reflected in their ideological positions.

Another factor that gives advantage to the center is connected with 'cognitive dissonance' in Israeli politics, reflected on all three

Table 13: Ideological Self-Definition of Voters on Eve of Elections to the 15th Knesset

Policy Dimension	1 Extreme Right	2 Right	3 Middle	4 Left	5 Extreme Left	No.
Foreign Affairs and Security	6.6%	27.6%	29.1%	26.7%	10.0%	967
Social and Economic Issues	6.2%	24.9%	36.8%	23.6%	8.5%	987

	1 Very Religious	2 Quite Religious	3 Traditional	4 Quite Secular	5 Secular	No.
Religiousness vs Secularism	6.6%	11.3%	24.3%	19.2%	38.6%	990

Source: Public opinion survey, 1999.

of the main ideological axes: security and foreign affairs; social issues and the economy; and religion and state. Many voters, for example, say they are willing to give up territories occupied in the Six-Day War. On the other hand, many put little faith in the Arabs and maintain an extremely negative image of the enemy. Other examples are not lacking. Many recognize the advantages of a free economy but at the same time wish to enjoy the advantages of a magnanimous social welfare policy. Many believe in social equality without regard to ethnic origin but also hold racist views. Many who are against mixing religion with politics and affairs of state have traditional religious views. Centrist candidates, centrist parties, and 'supermarket' parties are an escape hatch for these undecided voters, letting them have their cake and eat it too. Sometimes such parties offer compromise positions that show a clear grasp of reality. But in other cases they sow illusion, hiding behind populist clichés devoid of content.

In parliamentary regimes, the advantage of centrist parties derives not only from their electoral attractiveness but also from their ability to maneuver for position when coalitions are being formed. Most democratic countries have multiparty parliamentary systems. Generally no single party has an absolute majority in the lower or single house of parliament and it is the centrist parties that determine the composition of the government. Under such circumstances, a 'pivotal party' may emerge, as we have noted in several contexts.

As we saw, the pivotal party is the one occupying the ideological median point in parliament when neither the left nor the right has a majority. The experience of Western democracies demonstrates that government coalitions do not generally exclude parties within the ideological 'range' of the coalition. It follows that, in the absence of a majority party, the inclusion of the pivotal party in the government is guaranteed. Moreover, the pivotal party sometimes succeeds in dominating the system even when it forms or is part of a minority government, through a 'blocking majority'. For years, for example, the Social-Democrats of Sweden stayed in power with the support of the Communists, who formally did not join the coalition. The Communists were afraid that a 'Red–Green' coalition of Social-Democrats and the Center (Agrarian) Party further to the right would revive if they withdrew their support from the government and undermined the blocking majority.[83] Similarly, as we shall see, the Rabin and Peres governments stayed in power after the exit of Shas in September 1993, despite being minority governments. The reason for this was that the Labor Party was a pivotal party with a blocking majority together with the Hadash and Mada factions.

While surveying the history of Israel's party system earlier, we described the crucial position of the pivotal party in the Israeli political experience. Up to the election upheaval of 17 May 1977, Mapai and its successors dominated the political scene by virtue of its control of the pivotal position. The 1977 upheaval gave religious and other parties a chance to compete for this position, but interestingly enough the bargaining power of the ultra-Orthodox parties, more moderate politically than the ruling Likud party, did not increase after they came to occupy the pivotal position. These parties were able to serve as coalition partners for Labor as long as it remained the pivotal party. But once they themselves occupied this position they had to support a Likud government, because such was the preference of their voters and some of their leaders. The 'dirty trick' of March–June 1990 demonstrated this tension dramatically. There is truth in the argument that Shas, which was then the pivotal party, was not only inclined to join a coalition headed by Peres but was also part of the plot leading to the fall of the Shamir government in the no-confidence vote of 15 March 1990. Nevertheless, it was the rebellion of two Yahadut ha-Torah MKs and the reaction of Shas voters (including pelting the spiritual leader of the movement with tomatoes) that kept Shas away from Labor and enabled Shamir to form a new government.

In many countries one sees sector, religious, ethnic, agrarian, and other parties jockeying for position in the political center in order to become the pivotal party. It is relatively easy for parties of this kind to occupy the center because their political and ideological views on the major issues are not extreme and because they focus on special interests. Often parties calling themselves 'centrist' have such origins. Thus Centrum Party in the Weimar Republic had distinctly religious roots. Similarly, centrist parties in Finland and Sweden were in the past agrarian parties representing first and foremost the rural population.

In Israel, several centrist parties displayed equivocally sectarian features on a number of issues. For example, in the first elections to the Jerusalem municipal council (1950) after the establishment of the state, a Center List was among the contenders. This party, which won 16 percent of the vote and four of the 21 seats on the council, was simply the list representing the General Zionists. The General Zionists can of course be seen as a centrist party in many respects. They always considered themselves 'just Zionists', not religious, not socialist, not nationalist. If we remember that during the pre-State period the General Zionists were the second biggest party (and, at the beginning of that period, the biggest), then it can be said that the history of centrist parties in Israel began as a success story. Nonetheless, it can be argued that the General Zionists had a certain sectoral base. One of their greatest sources of strength was the pioneers of the First Aliyah and their descendants. In many cases, the General Zionists enjoyed enormous success in the old-time settlements.

In the elections to the Constituent Assembly (1949), the General Zionists were routed. Their recovery in the elections to the Second Knesset (1951) and their participation in the governments of Ben-Gurion and Sharet did not restore them to their previous position. From 1955 they were no longer part of the government and subsequently (after an ephemeral alliance with the Progressives in 1961–65) they were swallowed up by Gahal, which was created in 1965, and the Likud, which was constituted in 1973.

One Israeli party serving for many years as a clearly centrist party was the Progressives (from 1965, the Independent Liberal Party). They were located there from many points of view, being to the right of Mapai but nonactivist in matters of security and foreign policy. The Progressive Party too had much in common with European centrist parties. As mentioned above, it was founded with the establishment of the state as an alliance among defectors from the General Zionists, Central European immigrants ('*Yekkes*'), and Ha-Oved ha-Tziyyoni. The Progressives were the only 'right-wing' party allowed to join coalitions led by Mapai. Failure at the polls was what ultimately caused it to disappear from the political map. At its peak in 1959 it commanded just six seats. In 1977 its successor, the Independent Liberals, had one seat and in 1981 they failed to reach the threshold of votes for a Knesset representation. Former MKs later joined the Likud (Hillel Zeidel) and the Alignment (Yitzhak Artzi).

The best-known attempt to create a nonreligious centrist party in Israel belongs to Dash—the Democratic Movement for Change—in 1977. As we saw, the party came out of nowhere in December 1976. The gallery of personalities that stood at its head was undoubtedly one of the most impressive in the history of Israeli politics. Nevertheless, developments after the election caused it to fall. On 18 May 1977, Menachem Begin, leader of the Likud, woke up to discover that he was able to form a government without Dash. Not only had the Alignment lost its pivotal position in the system in the wake of the election upheaval, but Dash too found itself marginalized as several religious parties took center stage. Despite Dash's 15 seats, Begin formed his government without it, and the new party came on board only later, its members fighting among themselves over the question of joining the government and then over the question of leaving it. By the time the Ninth Knesset completed its term, Dash had split into a number of factions. Only a single remnant, the Shinui movement, under the leadership of Amnon Rubinstein, was able to survive electorally, with just two seats in the Tenth Knesset (1981). Another nonreligious centrist party, Telem, under Moshe Dayan, also won representation in these latter elections. However, it too vanished from the scene with the death of its leader.

The elections to the Eleventh Knesset (1984) saw the birth of two other centrist parties, Yahad, led by Ezer Weizman, and Ometz, under Yigael Hurwitz. Both had formerly been members of the Likud. However, opinion polls showed that most of their votes did not come from bona fide Likud voters. Yahad won three seats and Hurwitz became his party's only representative in the Knesset. The two parties subsequently joined the 'blocking coalition' under the leadership of Shimon Peres and the Alignment, giving it 60 seats against the 60 of the Likud and the right-wing and religious parties. This standoff, as we saw, gave birth to government by rotation under Peres and Shamir. Yigael Hurwitz, who returned to the Likud before the 1988 elections, had in the past belonged to centrist parties such as Rafi (ten seats) and the State List (four seats) under Ben-Gurion in the 1965 and 1969 elections, respectively. He was also a prominent member of Moshe Dayan's Telem Party.

Disappointment in the big parties and a steady drop in their strength since 1981 encouraged politicians to start up new centrist parties. What contributed to this phenomenon was not only the intrinsic advantages of these parties (as described above) but also, in 1996 and 1999, the implementation of the new election system which permitted voters to split their vote between a candidate for Prime Minister and another political party. The new parties that tried to occupy the center after 1992 all tried to take advantage of this split in the vote, and some succeeded. Thus after negligible gains for nonreligious centrist parties in the 1988 and 1992 elections, they made an impressive showing in the 1996 elections to the Fourteenth Knesset, in the guise of the Third Way and Yisrael ba-Aliyah. As we shall see, in the 1999 elections too the political center, and the parties who competed to occupy it, most prominently the Center Party, had a decisive influence.

4
Days of Storm and Stress

FROM RABIN TO PERES: 'YES TO PEACE—NO TO VIOLENCE'

Israelis will never forget the fourth day of November 1995. On that day, the bullets of an assassin, Yigal Amir, ended the life of Israel's Prime Minister, Yitzhak Rabin, who had served as Chief of Staff of the Israel Defense Forces in the Six-Day War, as Ambassador to Washington (between 1968 and 1973), and as the country's first native-born Prime Minister (from 1974). The end of his term of office as Prime Minister in 1977 had marked the end of rule by a dominant party in Israel, but in 1992 he had led the Labor Party back to power and had then forged revolutionary and controversial agreements with the PLO (1993–94) and signed a peace treaty with Jordan (1994).

The gestures he made in the last hours of his life symbolized the profound transformation of his outlook. In clear view of the multitudes that had come to say 'Yes to Peace—No to Violence' in Tel Aviv's Kings of Israel Square, the man who shied away from physical contact embraced both his rival and colleague, Shimon Peres, and one of the evening's lead singers, a scion of the country's best-known 'aristocratic' family, who had once mocked Rabin's supposed drunkenness. At the end of the rally he had joined in and sung the 'Song of Peace'.[84] A bloodstained page with the words of this song was later found in his pocket.

The commission of inquiry under Justice Meir Shamgar, and the courts before which the assassin appeared, concluded that no organization had been involved in the murder, other than the three people who had known about it and conceivably abetted the crime. At the same time, tensions between the right and the left, between doves and hawks, had never been so fraught with foreboding as prior to the despicable act.

Emotional reactions to the assassination threatened to tear Israel apart, divided as it already was. Many blamed leaders of the right for creating the atmosphere that prompted Amir to commit his crime.[85] It is doubtful whether this is the case. On the one hand, Binyamin Netanyahu, leader of the Likud, the biggest and most important right-wing party, repeatedly urged party followers not to interfere with the peace rally, including a call issued the previous day. Moreover, the vicious slogans directed against Rabin and used in right-wing demonstrations, where he was also depicted in Nazi uniform, were eventually revealed as the handiwork of Avishai Raviv, an operative of the General Security Services. On the other hand, fingers were pointed at extremist rabbis who in the past had accused Rabin of 'collaboration' with the enemy, using the expression 'fit for execution' with reference to him and asserting that his theological status was the same as that of an 'informer'. Consequently a number of rabbis were investigated, but no criminal proceedings were initiated. Following the murder, the act was condemned by all the prominent political and religious leaders of the settlers in no uncertain terms.

As befits so dramatic an event, the Rabin assassination produced a slew of conspiracy theories, according to which Rabin was murdered by his rivals on the left with the aid of the General Security Services. Notwithstanding such distractions, opinion polls conducted in the months following the assassination revealed a marked drop in the popularity of right-wing leaders and the right-wing parties, while the popularity of Shimon Peres and the Labor Party rose to new heights. This turn of events bred rumors that early elections to the Knesset would soon be held, and such elections did eventually take place on 29 May 1996.

Since the Six-Day War, the major debate in Israel had been over the issue of what policy to pursue as a result of the war.[86] The basic dilemma growing out of the results of the war was already clear in its immediate aftermath. Those with rosy visions were disabused of their notions within a few years, when the terrorist organizations and first and foremost the Fatah movement under Yasser Arafat gained control of the PLO. However, the positions in this debate were originally very different from what they are today. One position, that Israel should extend its sovereignty over all the territories captured in the war, including the Sinai Peninsula, is apparently maintained now by few people. In the center of the political map and particularly in the Labor Party, the debate was between 'territorial compromise' and 'functional compromise'. The view in favor of territorial compromise, whose standard bearer was Yigal Allon, was the one that prevailed. This view maintained that it was in Israel's interests to give up territories with large concentrations of Arab population and to only keep those with few Arabs who were vital to Israel's ('conventional') security needs (such as the Golan Heights, the Jordan Valley, the northern part of the Dead Sea, and areas in Sinai south of the Gaza Strip and along the Red Sea shore toward Sharm el-Sheikh). Evidence suggests that Moshe Dayan, seemingly the prophet of functional compromise, had looked into the possibility of a compromise in the spirit of the Allon Plan even while the fighting was still going on.[87]

The Allon Plan was put into effect under the Eshkol, Meir, and Rabin governments though never officially adopted. Menachem Begin, who was a member of these governments (in the 1967–70 period), went along with the idea, though later, in the Opposition, he would revert to more hawkish positions. As Prime Minister, he went somewhat to the opposite extreme, returning all of the Sinai Peninsula to Egypt and thereby going beyond even what some of the doves in the Labor Party were prepared to do. Only on the extreme left of the political map could anyone be found, mainly among avowed non-Zionists and anti-Zionists, who was in favor of returning all or most of the territories and supported the establishment of a Palestinian state. Some now say that this last view proved most realistic in the course of time. However, the truth is that what generally prevailed in all the camps was blindness to the demographic situation, to the depth of hostility in the Arab world, and to the limits of Israel's power. To some extent, this blindness continues to afflict many people today.

Over the years, basic approaches to the territorial issue have changed as a result of evolving circumstances and major events like the War of Attrition, the Yom Kippur War, changes of government in Israel, the peace agreement with Egypt, the Syrian and Israeli involvement in Lebanon, and the Intifada. But the second term of Yitzhak Rabin as Prime Minister of Israel represented a turning point more meaningful and more far-reaching than anything that had preceded it.

In the 1992 elections Labor under Rabin again won control of the political center, for the first time since the upheaval of 1977. As we saw, Rabin's blocking coalition held a majority of 61 seats in the Knesset despite the fact that the 'left-wing' parties had won a minority of the votes. There is little doubt that the revival of the Labor Party derived from the fact, among other things, that Rabin was perceived as security-minded and hawkish in comparison with other Labor leaders. This image was what tipped the scales in favor of the Labor Party among middle-of-the-road voters.

Already at the Madrid Conference, held a few months before the start of the election campaign that ended with Rabin's victory, it was obvious that the PLO was a silent partner in the talks.[88] Formally, however, Palestinian representation at the Conference was within the framework of the joint Jordanian–Palestinian delegation. Prime Minister Shamir was unbending about the formalities of contact with the PLO.[89] But in the Rabin era the approach to the Palestinians underwent a diametrical change. In parallel to the official negotiations following on the Madrid track, secret and unofficial negotiations were conducted on the Oslo track.[90]

In fact, since the Camp David agreement establishing the framework for peace in the Middle East, signed by Sadat, Begin and Carter (as a witness) on 17 September 1978, and since the peace treaty with Egypt, signed by the two sides on 26 March 1979, no real peace agreement had been signed with an Arab partner until Rabin's second term following on the 1992 elections. An exception was the 'peace treaty' signed by Israel and Lebanon on 17 May 1983, which neither side sees as remaining in force today.

During Rabin's second term, a number of agreements were signed by Israel and the PLO as well as a peace agreement by Israel and Jordan. The breakthrough was the Declaration of Principles signed on 13 September 1993 on the White House lawn. The Declaration of Principles was preceded by a public exchange of letters (10 September 1993) between Arafat, Rabin, and Norwegian Foreign Minister Holst. In his letter to Rabin, Arafat accepted the principles of the 'Shem Tov-Yariv formula', dating back to Rabin's first term (1974–77). This document affirmed Israel's willingness to negotiate with 'any Arab party' prepared to recognize Israel's right to exist and disavow the use of terror. The party that the document had in mind was the PLO. With the exchange of letters and the signing of the Declaration of Principles, the PLO appeared to agree to alter the PLO Covenant and cancel its clauses calling for the destruction of Israel. In his letter to the Norwegian Foreign Minister, Arafat undertook to end the Intifada. In his reply, Rabin recognized the PLO as the official representative of the Palestinian people and praised its decision to join the peace process.

The first paragraph of the Declaration of Principles stipulates that Israeli–Palestinian contacts will take place within the framework of the Middle East peace process with the aim, among other things, of creating an autonomous Palestinian Authority and an elected Palestinian Council operating on the West Bank of the Jordan River and in the Gaza Strip. The Declaration of Principles, which was known as Oslo I since its terms were negotiated in Oslo, was finalized by Uri Savir, Director-General of the Israeli Foreigh Ministry, and Abu Ala, the Palestinian representative[91]. The agreement also goes under the name of 'Gaza-Jericho First', since Article 14 affirmed Israel's intention to withdraw its troops from the Gaza Strip and Jericho. Many Arab leaders condemned the agreement entirely, in part, or because of the veil of secrecy under which it was worked out. Among them, surprisingly, was King Hussein of Jordan, who would soon sign a peace treaty with Israel.

Without a doubt, the Oslo process was a bombshell. In 1986 the Knesset had passed a law prohibiting any contact between Israelis and members of the PLO. In January 1993 the law had been rescinded, a step seen as declarative only and not as a license to conduct negotiations that would result in recognition of the PLO and a preliminary agreement with it within a few months.

It is interesting to note that, after the Oslo process was completed, informal secret negotiations continued between Yossi Beilin and Abu Ala.[92] These negotiations, which took place in Stockholm, produced an understanding on the framework for a permanent settlement of the Israeli–Palestinian conflict. Arafat[93] knew of these negotiations but Prime Minister Rabin did not. What is more, in the early stages of the Oslo and Stockholm talks, not even Beilin's superior, Foreign Minister Shimon Peres, knew about them. The Beilin–Abu Ala agreement came to Rabin's attention only after the talks ended and were rejected by him without any discussion by the relevant government bodies.

As we have seen, Shas left the government before the Declaration of Principles was signed, turning it into a minority government formally supported by 44 Labor MKs and 12 Meretz MKs. Practically speaking, the government was also supported by three MKs from Hadash and two from Mada. In January 1995, the coalition was joined by two MKs from the Yi'ud faction after they defected from the hawkish Tzomet faction. Their elevation to ministerial positions, with the accompanying perks, aroused much anger and did little to increase their popularity, or the popularity of the government. At the same time, members of the Ram faction—Chaim Ramon, Amir Peretz, and Shmuel Avital—who had left the Labor Party in 1994 in order to run against it in the Histadrut trade union elections (in an alliance with Meretz and Shas), also continued to support the coalition. Two other Labor MKs, Avigdor Kahalani and Emmanuel Sussman, sometimes voted with the right-wing Opposition against government positions that were too dovish for their tastes. The two joined the Third Way Movement, founded under the leadership of Yehudah Harel of Kibbutz Merom in the Golan Heights. This Movement became a political party before the 1996 elections and later joined the Netanyahu government. The far-reaching political moves undertaken by a minority government dependent on Arab MKs was a source of considerable irritation to many of its critics.

On 29 April 1994 an agreement was signed in Paris dealing with economic relations between the State of Israel and the Palestinians. On 4 May 1994, another agreement was signed in Cairo, elaborating the details of the transfer of most of the Gaza Strip and Jericho with its adjacent areas to the Palestinian Authority. The signing ceremony was delayed for a few embarrassing moments when Prime Minister Rabin learned that Arafat was refusing to initial the attached maps. Meanwhile, Jordan's basic objections to the Oslo process did not keep it from moving forward in bilateral discussions with Israel. On 25 July 1994 Yitzhak Rabin and King Hussein signed a declaration in Washington bringing to an end the state of war between the two countries.[94] The declaration set forth a number of principles, including mutual commitment to peace; the intention to achieve peace on the basis of UN Security Council Resolutions 242 and 338 and the principles of freedom, equality and justice; recognition of Jordan's special status with regard to the holy places in Jerusalem; and recognition of the sovereignty of all the countries in the region and their right to live in peace within secure borders and based on mutual commitment to refrain from threats and the use of force in the future.

On 26 October 1994 the Prime Ministers of Israel and Jordan, Yitzhak Rabin and Abdul Salam Almajali, signed a peace agreement between the State of Israel and the Hashemite Kingdom of Jordan at the Arava border crossing. President Clinton attended the ceremony and signed the treaty as a witness. The speakers at the ceremony were King Hussein, Prime Minister Rabin, Russian Foreigh Minister Andrei Kozirev, American Secretary of State Warren Christopher, Israeli Foreign Minister Shimon Peres, and President Clinton.

Leaders on the Israeli right welcomed the agreements with Jordan. A total of 105 MKs voted for the treaty in the Knesset. Even the head of Moledet, Rehava'am Ze'evi, did not go so far as to condemn it when he spoke in the Knesset, limiting himself to criticizing a few of its details and mentioning Jordan's past involvement in anti-Israel and anti-Jewish activity, including Jordan's support of Iraq in the Gulf War. In this context it is worth mentioning the secret contacts between Prime Minister Shamir and King Hussein during that war for the purpose of coordinating positions, despite the permission given to Iraq by Hussein to fly over Jordan right up to Israel's border.

Beginning in August 1994 the Knesset approved government plans for the redeployment of Israeli forces and the gradual transfer of authority to the PLO. On 13 May 1995 a document of understanding was signed as a preliminary to the interim agreement known as Oslo II. This agreement, on self-rule in areas of the West Bank of the Jordan River and in the Gaza Strip, was initialed by Foreign Minister Shimon Peres and Yasser Arafat on 24 September 1995.

On 27 September 1995, the government approved the agreement, which was signed the next day in Washington and approved by the Knesset on 5 October 1995, a month before the Rabin assassination. In accordance with the 315-page document Israel agreed to give the Palestinians full control over the six cities on the West Bank (Area A) and civilian control, including responsibility for the maintenance of public order, over 440 villages (Area B). According to the agreement, authority would be transferred from Israel to the council and 'head' of an executive body. The agreement contained five articles: the first dealt with the aforementioned council, the second with security arrangements and the redeployment of Israeli forces, the third with legal issues, the fourth with cooperation between the two sides, and the fifth with miscellaneous items. The agreement also included seven appendices and nine maps.

Oslo II was universally regarded as the first step toward the establishment of a Palestinian state whose future borders had already been preliminarily mapped out. The reaction of the Opposition was much more negative than its response to the Israeli–Jordanian agreements, for a number of reasons.

First of all, suspicion of the Palestinians ran much deeper than in the case of the Jordanians. Among other reasons, this was because of their failure to abrogate the Palestinian Covenant with its blatant call for the violent destruction of the State of Israel, and because of the terrorist past of the Palestinian leaders.

Secondly, the agreement with Jordan had entailed only minor border alterations. It was clear to everyone that the final agreement with the Palestinians would require giving up extensive territory in the heart of the Land of Israel. Many Zionist leaders had favored such a compromise in the past, but after the Six-Day War even certain 'leftists'[95] hoped that Israel would continue to rule 'all the territory of the Western Land of Israel', granting no more than autonomy to those 'local' residents whom Prime Minister Begin insisted on calling 'Arabs of the Land of Israel'.[96]

Thirdly, the territories occupied in the Six-Day War (excluding the new neighborhoods of Jerusalem) contained over 100,000 Israeli citizens. These were backed not only by right-wing parties and their supporters, but in one degree or another by all the governments of Israel. Many of the settlers lived in areas earmarked in the Allon Plan. Many who had devoted their entire adult lives not only to the idea of settlement but to intensive and wide-ranging activity on its behalf now saw their life's work being threatened in arrangements with what they considered the most loathsome of Israel's enemies. The government and its Prime Minister expressed little understanding of their distress. Moreover, even supporters of the Oslo process who criticized parts of it or government policy in other areas[97] met with enormous hostility at the time. Given such polarization, some saw the writing on the wall. For example, the writer himself raised the possibility of a political assassination on a radio program a few weeks before Rabin was murdered. But the indications were abundantly clear even before that time.

The willingness of Palestinian extremists to carry out the most despicable acts of terrorism characterized the entire period of the Rabin government and would continue to make itself felt under Peres. Palestinian terror was a factor from Israel's early years. In fact, Fatah Day commemorates a terrorist attack dating to 1 January 1965, long before the Six-Day War. But extremist Jews too were capable of shocking acts of terror, and they even organized to that end the 'Jewish Underground' in 1980–84.

This Jewish willingness to carry out terrorist acts climaxed in the attack of Dr Baruch Goldstein on Arab worshipers in the Cave of Machpelah in Hebron on 2 February 1994, during Rabin's second term of office. Goldstein murdered 29 Palestinians before he was killed. Nevertheless not a few extremists praised Goldstein's memory. His grave in Kiryat Arba became a place of pilgrimage and Yigal Amir possessed a book commemorating him. After the terrorist act in the Cave of Machpelah, a commission of inquiry under Justice Shamgar was set up. It found that Goldstein had acted alone without anyone knowing of his intentions. The head of the General Security Services, who was forced to resign in the wake of the findings of the Shamgar Commission on the Rabin assassination, had warned long before these events[98] of the potential for terrorism among Jewish extremists.

The polarization of Israeli society has long been widely discussed and not only in the context of the Arab–Israel conflict. Readiness to resort to violence can also be seen in the conflict between the religious and nonreligious populations. For example, attacks on houses of prostitution in Tel Aviv, with a toll in human life, were carried out by religious extremists. Nonetheless, the Arab–Israel conflict is the background to the most threatening outbursts, and the potential for violence is not always the exclusive property of the 'right'. From time to time extremist Israeli Arabs are also arrested and convicted for involvement in acts of terror. In response to the argument that there are 'folds' of black sheep on the extreme Jewish right, others sometimes recall the Jewish-Arab terrorist ring of Udi Adiv and his left-wing associates, who were arrested toward the end of 1972. All the differences notwithstanding, some also point to the implications of the 'post-Zionist' and anti-Zionist ideas of recent years. There is of course no similarity between one thing and the other, but all would seem to point to tensions that are liable to explode again into violence in the future.

FROM PERES TO NETANYAHU: THE SHIFTING SANDS OF PARITY

After the Rabin assassination, Shimon Peres became acting Prime Minister. Two weeks later he formed a new government. Its parliamentary basis was identical to the Rabin government's, that is to say, it continued to be a minority government supported 'from the outside' by the Arab factions. Most of the ministers continued to hold the same portfolios. Nonetheless, a number of changes introduced into the government by Peres are worth noting.

Peres held the defense portfolio, like Rabin before him. Having clashed with Rabin many times in the past and having been described by his rival as a 'tireless schemer' after Rabin's first term in office,[99] Peres was now perceived as Rabin's colleague and direct successor. Their personal and working relations had improved enormously during Rabin's second term. Nonetheless, a third party[100] had always been present in their meetings to take notes and summarize the proceedings.

Peres added to the cabinet Rabbi Yehudah Amital, leader of Meimad, as minister without portfolio. Rabbi Amital, who lived in the 'territories', headed a relatively dovish movement made up of defectors from the National Religious Party. Meimad ran in the 1988 elections but, despite getting proportionately enough votes for a Knesset seat, did not pass the required threshold. The addition of Rabbi Amital to the government was meant to heal the rift with the settlers and the religious public. This was the first time since 1959 that a 'nonpartisan' minister had joined the government. Ironically, the previous 'nonpartisan' appointment[101] had underscored precisely the deep rift between Mapai and the National Religious Party and other religious bodies.[102]

Another new face in the Cabinet was Chaim Ramon as Minister of the Interior. Ramon had to resign his position as Secretary-General of the Histadrut. Amir Peretz, his running mate in the Histadrut elections, replaced him as the new Secretary-General. The appointment of Ramon meant not only his return to the Labor Party but his entry into what would become the party's leadership race in the post-Peres era. On this score, another appointment that would bear on such a future race was the transfer of Ehud Barak from the Interior Ministry to the Foreign Ministry.[103] This was the portfolio that Shimon Peres himself had previously held.

Peres had never been very popular. Even in the 1984 elections, after which he was appointed Prime Minister, public opinion polls conducted on behalf of the Alignment pointed to his distinct lack of popularity. A few days before the elections, only 7 percent of voters wished to see him become Prime Minister while his colleagues in the Labor Party, Yitzhak Rabin and Yitzhak Navon, enjoyed two and three times that amount of support, respectively. In fact, Peres had a long record of losing elections. But after the Rabin assassination his popularity soared, and he seemed to be not only the country's most seasoned politician but also one whose leadership could no longer be challenged. This assessment, however, failed to take into account dissatisfaction with government policy and, perhaps more important, scorn for the new Prime Minister's personality. Even before the assassination, for example, many Israelis remembered Peres as standing on the right in Rabin's first government of 1974–77 and they suspected that his shift to the left was not necessarily a matter of conviction. This was not the only area in which Peres had completely reversed his position. In addition, while in the past Rabin had got the vote in the center because of some of his hawkish views, Peres's image as a dove could become a stumbling block during elections.

Another factor that could militate against the apparent popularity of Peres and the new government was the attitude of recent Russian immigrants to the Rabin and Peres governments. Disappointed by the Shamir government, most had voted for Labor in the 1992 elections. But their struggle to find a place for themselves in the country's life continued. While unemployment and lack of proper housing was less marked among them than among similar waves of immigrants in Israel and other countries, there is no question that many of these newcomers were living under straitened circumstances. What is more, the basic positions of most of the immigrants, both with regard to the Middle East conflict and on economic and social issues (but not on the issue of religion and state), were closer to the right than to the left.

The importance of other issues notwithstanding, the Arab–Israel conflict also continued to dictate the political agenda in the interim period between the Rabin assassination and the 1996 elections. The period was characterized, on the one hand, by additional moves on the political front but at the same time by an increase in hostile acts and mounting Israeli and Palestinian casualties.

On 20 January 1996 the Palestinians living in Jerusalem, the West Bank, and the Gaza Strip chose 88 representatives to the Palestinian Council and the 'head' of the Palestinian Authority. The system of elections was agreed upon by the Israelis and Palestinians in the interim agreement of 28 September 1995.

In the last week of February and the first week of March 1996, Israel was rocked by a number of suicide attacks carried out by members of the extremist Islamic Jihad and Hamas organizations. Jerusalem and Tel Aviv were hit the hardest. In response the Peres government restricted Palestinian travel from Judeah, Samaria, and Gaza into Israel until after the elections. This 'closure' had serious repercussions on economic activity in the territories.

After attacks on Israeli soldiers in the security zone in South Lebanon and a deterioration of the situation there that led to Hizbullah rocket attacks on Israeli settlements, the government initiated Operation Grapes of Wrath. This military operation in South Lebanon commenced on 11 April 1996. On 18 April a large number of Lebanese citizens were killed accidentally when Israeli artillery shelled Kafar Kana. Prime Minister Peres blamed this incident on the Hizbullah, for firing rockets at Israel from inside that Lebanese village and others. The civilian casualties on the Lebanese side produced much criticism and subsequently an 'understanding' was reached that resulted in a ceasefire. The terms of the understanding were published in Beirut and Jerusalem on 26 April.[104] Many Israeli Arabs criticized Peres for the Israeli shelling. Nonetheless, 95 percent of Arab voters cast their ballots for Peres in the elections (as opposed to 5 percent for Netanyhau). However, the percentage of Arabs voting in the elections for Prime Minister was much lower than in the parallel Knesset elections, and this undoubtedly had a major effect on the results.

On 24 April 1996 the Palestinian National Council, the quasi-parliamentary body of the PLO, voted to amend the Palestinian Covenant. The vote was meant to bring about the abrogation of all those articles in the Covenant calling for the destruction of Israel. Many Israelis criticized the way the vote had been conducted, arguing that it was not in accordance with the interim agreement or with what Arafat had guaranteed in his letter of 9 September 1993 to Rabin. Critics pointed out that the National Council had not actually changed the Covenant by its vote but had only laid out a procedure for changing it in the future without specifying when that would happen or which articles it would affect.

Security and foreign affairs were major issues in the 1996 election campaign. Voters regarded these issues as the factor that decided their vote. In a poll conducted on the eve of the elections[105] respondents were asked, 'What in your opinion is the main reason for supporting a political party in the coming elections?' Both Peres supporters and Netanyahu supporters, both Jews and non-Jews, gave security and foreign affairs as their reply (see Table 14). These issues continued to occupy center stage in the 1999 elections, though to a slightly smaller extent.

For all the importance of the Arab–Israel conflict among all voting sectors, it played a bigger role among right-wing voters than among left-wing voters and among Jews than among Arabs. The somewhat lesser importance of the issue in the 1999 elections derived from the relative success of the left and of its candidate for Prime Minister. In 1996 the security and foreign-policy issue was so prominent because of the ongoing negotiations and the incident in Kafar Kana, but also, and mainly, because of terrorist attacks. This prominence of the issue

Table 14: Reasons for Supporting Parties in the 1996 Elections

	Peres Supporters	Netanyahu Supporters	Jews	Non-Jews	All Respondents
Foreign affairs and security issues	43%	53%	53%	22%	48%
Parties' positions on other issues	9%	7%	6%	19%	8%
Party leadership	18%	14%	14%	21%	15%
The party 'represents people like themselves'	21%	17%	18%	33%	20%
Other reasons	9%	9%	9%	5%	9%
No.	451	409	848	178	1,026

Source: Public opinion survey, 1996.

worked in favor of the right and its candidate for Prime Minister. The Rabin assassination also highlighted the issue. The Labor Party decided not to exploit the assassination in its campaign, both because it wished to downplay the country's divisions and because it believed that an all-out attack on Rabin's critics in the context of the assassination would not win the undecided vote but rather send it into the arms of the right.

One of the major issues on which the Likud in 1996 focused its attacks was a possible division of Jerusalem in an agreement with the Palestinians (see Table 15). Opposition to the division of the city was found to be greater than with regard to any other concession, and even among Peres supporters few were in favor of it. Accordingly, 'Peres will divide Jerusalem' became the Likud's chief campaign slogan.

Table 15: Replies to the Question 'Should Israel Agree to a Division of Jerusalem within the Framework of a Peace Agreement with the Palestinians?' in a 1996 Election Poll

	Peres Supporters	Netanyahu Supporters	Others
Absolutely yes	25%	3%	20%
Yes	12%	1%	5%
Maybe	15%	1%	4%
No	19%	9%	8%
Absolutely no	29%	86%	63%
No.	461	427	158

Source: Public opinion survey, 1996.

Labor took a different tack. All of Labor's leaders in recent years—Rabin, Peres and Barak—favored direct election of the Prime Minister. Netanyahu's support of the idea was opposed to his party's position and derived, among other things, from personal considerations. The left was convinced that it would be easier for a left-wing candidate to win in a direct contest with a right-wing candidate than for the Labor Party to regain the pivotal position in parliament. The left thus attacked the 'weak point' of the Likud, the candidacy of Binyamin Netanyahu. 'Bibi [Netanyahu] isn't good enough' was the chief slogan of Labor. This slogan seemed effective because data gathered during the campaign indicated that most voters leaned toward Peres because of his great experience and what they perceived as his suitability for the position. Opinion polls showed Peres in the lead from the day that early elections were announced right up to the day of elections itself.

Furthermore, Netanyahu's lack of experience was also apparent *vis-à-vis* other front-benchers in the big parties, not only Peres. In this respect his candidacy was indeed problematic. Netanyahu had never held a senior government position and had been an MK since only 1988. In Shamir's government he had first served as Deputy Foreign Minister and later, because of tensions with Foreign Minister David Levi, became Deputy Minister in the Prime Minister's Office. Before that time Netanyahu had been Israel's Ambassador to the UN (1984–88). The media were almost all for Peres. Attacks on Netanyahu sometimes boggled the imagination. He was accused, for example, of working for the CIA, under the name of John J. Sullivan, a flight of fancy, which of course had no basis in fact. However, criticism of certain aspects of his character did in fact turn out to have some foundation.

Apart from what Peres and Netanyahu said about each other, the early stages of their campaign disproved the claim that the new system of elections would limit the ability of the small parties to brandish the weapon of 'blackmail'. Two small parties, Tzomet and Gesher, announced their intentions to put up their own candidates for Prime Minister, namely their leaders, Rafael Eitan and David Levi. Since this would have split the right-wing vote and most of all hurt the chances of Binyamin Netanyahu, he did everything in his power to prevent it. Tzomet and Gesher were co-opted into a 'Likud–Gesher–Tzomet' election list. Each won five seats as part of the joint list, leaving the ruling party, the Likud, with only 22 on the day after the elections. Many in the Likud criticized the deal, but it was clear that, if Levi and Eitan had run as independent candidates for Prime Minister, Netanyahu could not have won in the first round.

Netanyahu's victory was confirmed only after four days, mainly when absentee ballots and soldiers' votes were counted (see Table 16). The two major TV networks, which had conducted extensive sample polls outside voting booths, had erroneously declared Peres the winner on election night. It is worth mentioning however that, in view of the high percentage of invalid votes (4.8 percent), Netanyahu failed to win an absolute majority.

Today, political scientists think of the number of parties in parliament in terms of their 'effective' number.[106] Thus it is obvious that in a parliament where ten parties are equally represented there are in fact ten parties. But in a parliament where one party controls 91 percent of the seats, and each of the other nine parties has only 1 percent of the seats, there is really just one party, 'embellished' by insignificant fragments of parties. The count of parties should therefore take into account their relative strength. The effective number of parties may in fact be measured by dividing the number 1 by the sum of the square proportions of the different parties. In this way, even if we take the Likud–Gesher–Tzomet bloc as a single faction, the effective number of Israeli parties will be seen to have risen from 4.38 in 1992 to 5.65 in 1996 elections; this is to say that the hope of reducing the number of parties by means of the new system has not been fulfilled. As we shall see below, the additional idea of getting a better balance between the branches of government has fared no better.

In a poll conducted on the eve of the 1996 elections, respondents were asked to indicate the extent to which they agreed with the following statement: 'It Is Easier to Vote for the Small Parties in Knesset Elections Now That the Prime Minister is Elected Directly'. Only a small minority in all the groups disagreed (see Table 17).

Table 16: Election results from votes for Prime Minister (29 May 1996)

	Votes	% of valid votes	% of all votes
Binyamin Netanyahu	1,501,023	50.5	48.1
Shimon Peres	1,471,566	49.5	47.1

Electorate: 3,933,250
Turnout: 79.4% (3,121,270)
Valid votes: 95.2% (2,972,589)

Source: Based on data supplied by the Central Election Committee.

Table 17: Responses to the Statement: 'It Is Easier to Vote for the Small Parties in Knesset Elections Now That the Prime Minister is Elected Directly'

	Peres Supporters	Netanyahu Supporters	Jews	Non-Jews	All Respondents
Absolutely yes	30%	13%	17%	46%	22%
Yes	25%	34%	33%	17%	30%
Maybe	23%	24%	21%	29%	22%
No	16%	21%	22%	5%	19%
Absolutely No	6%	8%	7%	3%	7%
No.	457	417	860	180	1,030

Source: Public opinion survey, 1996.

Many small parties called on their supporters to split their vote. Some of them indicated a preference among the candidates for Prime Minister. However, in order to maintain their ability to maneuver in coalition negotiations later, small parties in the center refrained from taking sides. Instead, they stressed the importance of voting for themselves in the Knesset elections 'to keep the Prime Minister from being held hostage by the "extremists" in his camp'. It turned out that the public and the small parties understood the new system better than its architects.

As we saw, the Labor Party had a minimal blocking majority in the Thirteenth Knesset (1992). In the elections to the Fourteenth Knesset the parties that comprised this majority won just 52 seats. Had Peres won, his government would have been at the mercy of parties that had not supported him in the past. The incongruity of this situation is perhaps all the more striking given the fact that the Labor Party continued to be the biggest party in the Knesset. It is true that it dropped from 44 to 34 seats. But the Likud too (without its partners) lost ten seats, down from 42 to 32 in 1992.

Among the small parties the drop in the strength of Meretz was especially steep, with a loss of 2.2 percent in its share of the general vote. Neither Moledet nor Yahadut ha-Torah improved its previous showings, either. All the other small parties did.

Two new parties did much better than expected. Yisrael ba-Aliyah under Nathan Sharansky took nearly 6 percent of the general vote and won seven seats. The party was thus the chief beneficiary of the big waves of immigration at the start of the 1990s. Sharansky, like most of his voters, leaned to the center-right with respect to the Middle East conflict. In this sense the shift of the 'Russian' vote from Labor to Sharansky's party was a double-edged loss for the leftist

Table 18: Knesset Election Results (29 May 1996)

	Votes			Seats		
	Number	%	Change since 1992	Number	%	Change since 1992
Labor	818,741	26.8	–7.8	34	28.3	–8.3
Likud	767,401	25.1	–6.2	32	26.7	–6.7
Shas	259,796	8.5	+3.6	10	8.3	+3.3
Mafdal	240,271	7.9	+2.9	9	7.5	+2.5
Meretz	226,275	7.4	–2.2	9	7.5	–2.5
Yisrael ba'Aliyah	174,994	5.7	+5.7	7	5.8	+5.8
Hadash	129,455	4.2	+1.8	5	4.2	+1.7
Yahadut ha'Torah	98,657	3.2	–0.1	4	3.3	–
Third Way	96,474	3.2	+3.2	4	3.3	+3.3
Mada	89,514	2.9	+1.3	4	3.3	+1.7
Moledet	72,002	2.4	–	2	1.7	–0.8
Other Parties	78,550	2.6	–2.6	0	0.0	–

Electorate: 3,933,250
Turnout: 79.2% (3,116,832)
Valid votes: 97.8% (3,052,130)

Source: Based on data supplied by the Central Election Committee.

camp. The success of still another small new party was also potentially problematic for Labor. The Third Way won nearly 100,000 votes, good for four seats. Aside from the two Labor defectors, Avigdor Kahalani and Emmanuel Sussman, its MKs included Yehudah Harel from the Golan Heights and a 'moderate' settler from Efrat, Alex Lubotsky.

In truth, the dire predictions of the opponents of direct elections were not immediately fulfilled in 1996. The new Knesset was not openly hostile to Netanyahu. In forming his government he had a broad margin of safety. Practically speaking, he could have formed a narrow coalition including the 68 members of the Likud–Gesher–Tzomet bloc, the religious parties, the new parties, and even Moledet on the extreme right. Furthermore, there was also the possibility of forming a national-unity government. Nevertheless, in reality things quickly became very complicated.

THE NETANYAHU GOVERNMENT: IN THE ABSENCE OF CHECKS AND BALANCES

Had the hopes of the architects of direct election been realized, the Netanyahu government, the 27th in the country's history, was

96 *The Last Days in Israel*

expected to be one of the most stable Israel had ever known. As a directly elected Prime Minister, Netanyahu had the benefit not only of popular support and the 'balance of terror' guaranteed by Article 19 of the new Basic Law: the Government, but he also benefited from the fact that Labor had lost its pivotal position in the system. The blocking majority that Labor had commanded after the 1992 elections was now reduced to 52 seats. Netanyahu had created a 'closed and winning coalition' that was near to being what is termed in the professional literature 'a minimal winning coalition'; that is to say, the type of coalition most highly recommended by the father of modern coalition theory, William Riker.[107] Netanyahu's coalition included six of the seven parties to the right of Labor: Likud–Gesher–Tzomet (32), Shas (10), National Religious Party (9), Yisrael ba-Aliyah (7), the Third Way (4), and Yahadut ha-Torah (4). Netanyahu also had the safety net of Moledet (2) on the right. Likewise, under certain conditions, it would have been possible to form a national-unity government with Labor.

Despite all this, it became apparent from its first day that the government was on shaky ground. More than anything else the coalition was threatened by personal rivalries, mainly within the Prime Minister's own faction. In addition, a number of ministers came under criminal investigation. Though only one was ultimately convicted (Aryeh Deri), the investigations and suspicions directed against Netanyahu and his ministers produced not only strained relations from within, but unease among broad sectors of the public.

As we have pointed out, Netanyahu lacked experience in government. Conceivably this inexperience too had something to do with his lack of success. For example, Netanyahu had not intended at first to give Dan Meridor a senior portfolio in his government. Meridor was considered by many to be Netanyahu's chief rival for leadership of the Likud. Another threat to Netanyahu's leadership was seen as coming from Binyamin (Benny) Ze'ev Begin, the most prominent of the Likud's hawks. Yet when Begin took the lead in pressing Netanyahu to give Meridor a senior post, the Prime Minister gave in and appointed Meridor to be Minister of Finance. Similar ferment surrounded the appointment of Ariel Sharon. The government was presented to the Knesset on 18 June 1996. Following pressure exerted on Sharon's behalf, primarily by Foreign Minister and Gesher leader David Levi, Sharon was named Minister of National Infrastructures on 8 July 1996.

Tensions between the Prime Minister and members of his party did not abate after the government was formed. This was somewhat surprising given the fact that the Likud held more than 40 percent of the portfolios in the government (7 out of 17 ministers) and the Likud–Gesher–Tzomet bloc held a majority of nine, despite the fact that the Likud itself held only a third of the seats in the coalition (22 of 66) and the Likud–Gesher–Tzomet bloc less than a majority (32 seats). The Likud's overrepresentation in the government did not serve to dull the edge of internal discord. Apparently, the source of the friction was, first and foremost, frosty personal relations (mainly between the Netanyahu camp and other ministers and MKs), as well as also factionalism from within. The latter derived from internal party reforms, and specifically from the way in which candidates for the Knesset and Prime Minister were selected.

On 16 January 1997, Benny Begin, Minister of Science and Technology, handed in his resignation to the Prime Minister. Begin, who opposed Netanyahu on many issues and also decried his personal conduct, resigned over the agreement with the Palestinian Authority on the withdrawal of the army from parts of Hebron. As will be recalled, the agreement on Hebron had already been reached under Peres, but its implementation had been postponed, apparently due to election considerations. Netanyahu had renegotiated the agreement. The events that preceded the negotiation and the approval of the agreement would soon become known as the 'Bar-On for Hebron' affair, which will be discussed below.

On 18 June 1997, Finance Minister Dan Meridor resigned. This time the background was Meridor's differences of opinion with the Governor of the Bank of Israel, Prof. Yaakov Frankel, over a somewhat minor issue.[108] As it turned out, the resignation too was caused by poor personal relations with the Prime Minister. According to one source, the Frankel–Meridor crisis was engineered by one of Netanyahu's intimates, the Director-General of the Prime Minister's Office, Avigdor Lieberman, to induce Meridor to resign.

At the end of 1997, a new crisis erupted between Foreign Minister David Levi and Netanyahu over the state budget. Even before the date fixed by law for the passage of the budget (31 December 1997) it became clear that Levi would soon resign, leaving the government without the support of the five Gesher MKs and turning it into a coalition that could be brought down by any three of its members. Levi resigned on 4 January 1998.

The rift between Netanyahu and his colleagues in the Likud reached a peak in November 1997, with the convening of the Likud

Center and the attempt at a political *putsch* against the Prime Minister. In the end, the party convention approved the cancellation of primaries for Knesset candidates. Apparently Netanyahu's intimate, Avigdor Lieberman, was behind this move, which was intended to give Netanyahu greater control over the Likud faction in the Knesset in the future. The tensions produced by the crisis and its aftermath soon led to the resignation of Lieberman.

The personal (and ideological) rifts in the Likud filtered down to its nonministerial levels as well. In April 1998[109] the mayor of Tel Aviv, Roni Milo, announced that he was leaving the Likud (and resigning as mayor) to run for Prime Minister.[110]

On 23 January 1999, infighting over personnel returned to the major leagues when, somewhat over two weeks after the second and third readings of the Early Elections Law (5 January), Netanyahu dismissed another senior minister, Defense Minister Yitzhak Mordechai. The dismissal followed Mordechai's contacts with members of the Center Party to discuss the possibility of his joining the party as its candidate for Prime Minister.

It was not only strains within the Likud–Gesher–Tzomet faction that cast a pall over the government's existence. Attempts to act on important issues were also stymied, often due to opposition from some of the other coalition partners. A striking example was the attempt of the Ne'eman Commission, which had presented its conclusions at the beginning of February 1998, to solve one of Israel's major problems in the realm of religion and the state. The Commission had tackled the issue of conversion to Judaism, which lay at the heart of the 'Who is a Jew?' controversy that had divided the Israeli public since 1958. The problem had been accentuated by massive immigration from Ethiopia and Russia and by the significant proportion of non-Jews arriving as part of it. Under Ne'eman, an Orthodox Jew himself, the Commission recommended that Reform and Conservative rabbis, and not only Orthodox clergymen, sit on the boards charged with the preparation of candidates for conversion. The recommendation was rejected by the Chief Rabbinate and by the religious parties.

The government's difficulty in raising a majority accompanied all its activities from at least the beginning of 1998 and right up to its demise with the elections to the Fifteenth Knesset. A good example was the defeat of the Likud's candidate for the presidency, Shaul Amor, by Labor's candidate, the incumbent Ezer Weizman, in a 63–49 Knesset vote on 4 March 1998.

Beyond painful defeats, there were also scandals. One of the biggest of these to rock the Netanyahu government was the 'Bar-On for Hebron' affair, which occupied the center of the political stage for months on end in 1997. This affair symbolized the Netanyahu period better perhaps than anything else, linked as it was to the Israeli–Palestinian conflict, to internal political relations, and to the norms of conduct of the Prime Minister and members of his government.

According to Israeli television reports, ministers from the Shas Party promised to vote for the Hebron agreement in exchange for the appointment of Roni Bar-On as Attorney General. Shas appeared to be seeking Bar-On's appointment on the assumption that he would, in office, block the conviction of the Shas leader Aryeh Deri on charges of bribery and other offenses in his ongoing trial in Jerusalem's District Court. Both the Prime Minister and Justice Minister Tzachi Hanegbi spoke out in favor of the appointment when the government met to discuss it. However, public pressure forced Bar-On to resign two days after his being named, and the government appointed Dr Eliakim Rubinstein instead. Following an investigation, the police recommended the indictment of the Prime Minister and Justice Minister for their role in this affair. The recommendation, as is customary, was passed on to the State Attorney's office. On 20 April 1997 the Attorney General, Eliakim Rubinstein, and the State Attorney, Edna Arbel, announced their findings. Rubinstein and Arbel pointedly criticized the conduct of the Prime Minister and Justice Minister but decided not to indict them despite police recommendations.

Deri was convicted by Jerusalem's District Court on 17 March 1999 and sentenced to four years' imprisonment, later reduced to three by the Supreme Court on appeal. The conviction created a deep rift between his many followers, mainly Sephardim, and the legal system. A month prior to his conviction (on 14 February) about 200,000 ultra-Orthodox Jews had staged a demonstration against various Supreme Court decisions.

Despite all these developments, the government continued to be preoccupied by security and foreign affairs during its entire existence. It would appear that its lack of success on this front was caused not only by mistakes made by Netanyahu and his ministers but was mainly a result of Arab responses, which produced endless clashes and the collapse of agreements already reached between the two sides.

On 23 March 1997, for example, the Hasmonean Tunnel was opened in the Old City of Jerusalem on orders from the Prime Minister. The press accused him of opening the tunnel despite the opposition of the General Security Services and other security personnel, though this charge seems to have been without foundation. The day after the tunnel was opened, Yasser Arafat called for strikes and demonstrations. Moslem leaders claimed that the tunnel ran under the foundations of the Al-Aqsa mosque near the Dome of the Rock on the Temple Mount and that excavation there was intended to undermine the holy places.[111] Despite the fact that these claims were false and that repair work in the tunnel had been going on since 1987 with the knowledge of everyone concerned, large-scale rioting broke out on 25 September 1997. During its course, which provided a foretaste of the 'Al-Aqsa Intifada' that started in 2000, 15 Israeli soldiers and settlers and at least 50 Palestinians were killed. The riots were the most violent in the occupied territories since the signing of the Declaration of Principles (Oslo I) in September 1993. In truth, it was the Palestinians themselves who had continued to enlarge the mosques on the Temple Mount in a series of massive excavations that had intentionally destroyed every Jewish artifact of archeological value.

The tunnel affair did not stand alone, because rocky relations between Israel and the Arabs made themselves felt in numerous events during Netanyahu's term of office. These included repeated clashes in Lebanon, the Khallad Mishal affair, the killing spree of a Jordanian soldier in the 'Isle of Peace', the attempted murder of security guards at the Israeli Embassy in Amman, and other incidents.

Many argued before the 1996 elections that Netanyahu was not committed to the Oslo process. They assumed that contacts with the Palestinian Authority and its head were liable to be broken off if he were re-elected, his government having included just one small party (the Third Way) originating in the 'other' camp.[112] In fact, Netanyahu had had his first meeting with Arafat at the Erez check-post on 23 July 1996, just a month after forming his government. The meeting had been approved by the government with just one dissenting vote (Benny Begin). It should be noted that Arafat himself had only been elected Chairman of the Authority on 20 January 1996, after implementation of the interim agreement between the PLO and Israel dating from 28 September 1995. Arafat had received 88.1 percent of the vote in Jerusalem, Judeah and Samaria, and the Gaza Strip.

Following the implementation of the Hebron agreement, and especially after the tunnel riots, the peace process broke down. Its revival under the Netanyahu government seemed unlikely. A significant turning point came in October 1998. Following negotiations at Wye Plantation, Netanyahu and Arafat signed the Wye Agreement in the presence of President Clinton and King Hussein. According to its terms, Israel was to transfer 13 percent of Judeah and Samaria to the civilian control of the Palestinians and another 14 percent, where civilian control already existed, was to fall under their security control. In exchange, the Palestinian National Council was to abrogate those articles of the Palestinian Covenant calling for the destruction of Israel.

The Wye Agreement was approved by the government on 11 November 1998 by a vote of eight to four with five abstentions. The Knesset approved the agreement on 17 November in a 75–19 vote (with nine abstaining). The first stage of the agreement was implemented on 20 November. With President Clinton in attendance, the Palestinians cancelled the relevant articles of the Covenant in a somewhat bizarre and controversial procedure. These events led to the desertion of the coalition by right-wing parties, and first and foremost by the National Religious Party, which meant the loss of Netanyahu's majority in the Knesset. Subsequently, a motion for early elections passed in the Knesset on 14 December 1998. Thus Netanyahu's 'dovish' actions led to the fall of his government, the early elections and the change of governments in May 1999.[113] The passage of the Election Law was quite swift, with its second and third readings on 5 January 1999.

THE 1999 ELECTIONS

Despite dramatic changes in Israel's political party map, the most striking result of the May 1999 elections was in the direct vote for Prime Minister. Ehud Barak won the election by 12 percent (see Table 19).[114] It will be remembered that, in the 1996 elections, the margin of victory had been just 1 percent, representing fewer than half the valid votes. This time the percentage of invalid votes had been even higher (5.3 percent) but Barak had still managed to receive 53 percent. The absentee ballots cast for the three candidates who had dropped out of the race on the last day of the campaign could have counted if they had been cast before the announcement of their withdrawal. But the Central Election Committee disqualified them. In any event, this was just an academic legal point, since Barak's margin made him the winner regardless of how the votes were counted.

Barak's victory cannot be attributed to demographic changes affecting the structure of the electoral body. The Arab population had indeed grown in relative size but the drop in the percentage of Arabs voting balanced this. Rather, the swing away from Netanyahu is attributable to attitudes that had shifted. We shall not go into the reasons for this shift here. It should only be mentioned that the turnaround in the elections for Prime Minister was not paralleled in the party vote. Instead, parties participating in the outgoing coalition took exactly half the seats in the Knesset, which was more than the coalition commanded in the last days of the Fourteenth Knesset. Moreover, the camp represented by the former coalition won slightly more than half the popular vote. Had these parties been in deep disagreement with Barak and his views, and had they been of one mind, we would certainly have immediately witnessed that apocalyptic vision of a Knesset hostile to an elected Prime Minister, a situation that, as we have noted, had caused dozens of democratic regimes to collapse in the twentieth century.[115]

The most noteworthy result of the party vote was a crushing blow received by the two big lists, One Israel and the Likud. Together they won just 45 seats, fewer than Mapai at its peak (47 seats in 1959) or than the Likud alone (48 in 1981). Moreover, within One Israel, three seats had been allocated to other parties (two to Gesher and one to Meimad). This was an unprecedented rout for the big parties. In this context it is worth mentioning that after it was founded in 1973 the Likud won 39 seats (though remaining in the Opposition). Now it had as few seats as Herut had had during much of the 1949–61 period. Herut had won 17 seats in 1959 and 1961, but then it had had at its side the General Zionists (and the Liberals), who would become a major component in both Gahal and the Likud.

Table 19: Election results from votes for Prime Minister (17 May 1999)

	Votes	% of valid votes	% of all votes
Ehud Barak	1,791,020	56.1	53.1
Binyamin Netanyahu	1,402,474	43.9	41.6

Electorate: 4,285,428
Turnout: 78.7% (3,372,952)
Valid votes: 94.7% (3,193,494)

Source: Based on data supplied by the Central Election Committee.

Other parties as well in the outgoing Knesset, like the National Religious Party and Yisrael ba-Aliyah, lost strength. On the whole, however, it can be said that the elections of 17 May 1999 were a great victory for the small parties. Fifteen lists won seats (as opposed to 11 in 1996). The 'effective number' of parties rose to 8.69, one of the highest in the history of Western democratic regimes (see Table 20). Because of the split in the vote and the support of small parties, the number of votes 'wasted' on parties that failed to reach the threshhold for seating in the Knesset grew significantly, amounting to 4.9 percent of valid votes (almost twice as high as in 1996).

The most successful of the small parties was Shas, represented in the Fifteenth Knesset by 17 MKs. Its gains won it admittance into the 'big-party club', heretofore the domain of the two big lists or their constituent partners. Together the religious camp took 27 seats, a high-water mark that few had anticipated.

Until the 1980s the religious parties had controlled 15 to 18 seats in the Knesset. In 1981 the established religious parties had to content themselves with just 13. The appearance of Tami, with three seats, was a sign of things to come. In the 1996 elections, the first with a direct vote for Prime Minister, the old and new religious parties made a great leap forward and together captured 23 seats. It was now unquestionably true that direct elections, which some advocates had hoped would reduce the electoral and political strength of the religious parties in

Table 20: Effective Number of Parties in the Knesset Following Elections, 1949–99

Knesset	Year of Elections	Effective Number of Parties
First (Constituent Assembly)	1949	4.7
Second	1951	5.0
Third	1955	6.0
Fourth	1959	4.9
Fifth	1961	5.4
Sixth	1965	4.7
Seventh	1969	3.6
Eighth	1973	3.4
Ninth	1977	4.4
Tenth	1981	3.1
Eleventh	1984	3.9
Twelfth	1988	4.4
Thirteenth	1992	4.4
Fourteenth	1996	5.6
Fifteenth	1999	8.7

Source: Based on data supplied by the Central Election Committee.

Table 21: Knesset Election Results (17 May 1999)

	Votes			Seats		
	Number	%	Change since 1996**	Number	%	Change since 1996**
One Israel (a)*	670,484	20.3	−6.5	26	21.7	−6.6
Likud (b)	468,103	14.2	−10.9	19	15.8	−10.9
Shas (c)	430,676	13.0	+4.5	17	14.1	+5.8
Meretz (a)	253,525	7.7	+0.3	10	8.3	+0.8
Yisrael ba'Aliyah (d)	171,705	5.2	−0.5	6	5.0	−0.7
Shinui (e)	167,748	5.1	+5.1	6	5.0	+5.0
Center Party (f)	165,622	5.0	+5.0	6	5.0	+5.0
Mafdal (b)	140,307	4.2	−3.7	5	4.2	-3.3
Yahadut ha'Torah (c)	125,741	3.8	+0.6	5	4.2	+0.8
Ra'am (g)	114,810	3.5	+0.6	5	4.2	+0.8
National Unity (d)	100,181	3.0	+0.6	4	3.3	+1.7
Yisrael Beitenu (h)	86,153	2.6	+2.6	4	3.3	+3.3
Hadash (g)	87,022	2.6	−1.6	3	2.5	−1.7
Balad	66,103	2.0	+2.0	2	1.7	+1.7
One Nation (h)	64,143	1.9	+1.9	2	1.7	+1.7
Pnina Rosenblum (i)	44,953	1.4	+1.4	0	0.0	−
Pensioners (i)	37,525	1.1	+1.1	0	0.0	−
Green Leave	34,029	1.0	+1.0	0	0.0	−
Third Way (f)	26,290	0.8	−2.4	0	0.0	−3.3
Greens (e)	13,292	0.4	+0.4	0	0.0	−
Other Parties	41,004	1.2	−1.3	0	0.0	−

Electorate: 4,285,428
Turnout: 78.7% (3,373,748)
Valid votes: 98.1% (3,309,416)

Source: Based on data supplied by the Central Election Committee.
* The letters in parentheses after the names of the lists indicate surplus-vote agreements.
** The comparison with 1996 figures is with the list closest to the current one. In most cases there were changes in the composition or name of the lists.

general and the ultra-Orthodox parties in particular, had had the opposite effect. The success of the ultra-Orthodox parties probably also stemmed to some degree from the aggressive campaigns conducted against them by Yisrael ba-Aliyah and Shinui. Some of those who sought to weaken the religious parties through aggressive anticlerical attacks had in the past been among the advocates of direct elections, so this time, too, they gained the opposite of what they pursued. Yet, even as an anti-Ultra-Orthodox stance characterized both Shinui and Meretz, those two parties enjoyed significant wins, increasing their combined strength from 9 to 16 seats. The upshot of all this was that over a third of the members of the Fifteenth Knesset represented first and foremost the two poles of the religious–secular cleavage.

Other special-interest groups also did well in the elections. Yisrael ba-Aliyah and Yisrael Beitenu, both headed by immigrants from the former Soviet Union, together won ten seats. Three lists representing the Arab population, Ra'am, Balad, and Hadash, also won ten seats. In all, the religious, 'Russian', and Arab sectors of the population now controlled 47 seats.

Three new factions represented additional divisions. The National Unity Party, which controlled eight seats in the outgoing Knesset, had to content itself in 1999 with just four seats. The new Center Party, which before the elections had offered no fewer than four different candidates for Prime Minister, and which was united primarily by its hostility to the outgoing Prime Minister, won six seats. Even the new workers' party, One Nation, headed by Histadrut Secretary-General Amir Peretz, won two seats.

It is worth noting that, despite the strong element of proportionality in the Israeli electoral system, a few incongruities crept in. Thus, Yisrael Beitenu received one more seat than Hadash despite winning fewer popular votes. The reason for this was the better vote-surplus agreement it had with the One Nation Party. It is reasonable to assume that not a few supporters of the latter party had voted in the past for the Labor Party. Had a few hundred of these voters abstained from voting, Avigdor Lieberman's Yisrael Beitenu list would have received one seat fewer, and One Israel one seat more. Furthermore, the 'price' of a seat paid by the parties after the internal division of surplus votes was smaller than the price paid by parties without such agreements.

Examination of the 1999 elections reveals greater rifts in social and political life than Israel had ever seen. Security and foreign policy were once again perceived as major issues, by both political leaders and voters (see Table 22). However, this time around, issues surrounding the Arab–Israel conflict were judged to be less important than in the 1996 elections, while other issues assumed greater importance. Many Jewish voters gave as a reason for their party votes the feeling that 'the party represents people like themselves'. This consideration was widespread, and the effect is clearly discernible in the election results. The Arab populace too gave greater weight than in the past to the attractiveness of its political leadership. This leadership was different in the 1999 elections from what it had been in the past, articulating as it did the nationalistic urges of Israeli Arabs, whether traditional or modern.

Together with the fragmentation of the party map and the impressive showing of the sectarian parties, one particular factor more than any other underscored polarization between the two main camps. Even if the views of supporters of the different parties were not that different from one another,[116] the consistency of party identity and support for a given candidate for Prime Minister in itself expressed parallel streams of political commitments. Voters for One Israel, Meretz, the Center Party, Hadash, Balad, and Ra'am clearly preferred Barak over Netanyahu (see Table 23). A slightly weaker preference for Barak was discernible among Shinui and One Nation voters. Voters for the Likud, Shas, the National Religious Party, Yahadut ha-Torah, the National Unity Party, and Yisrael Beitenu clearly preferred Netanyahu. Only Yisrael ba-Aliyah voters split significantly.

The divisions in the Israeli political system are discernible on a number of other planes. Below we shall describe the political and social divisions as revealed by the vote in a number of communities and types of communities (see Table 24).

Ehud Barak won an overwhelming victory in Arab communities. However, Shimon Peres's showing among Arab in 1996 was no less impressive. In Jewish communities, Netanyahu won a decisive victory in 1996. This time Barak beat him by 3 percent. Electorally, this result has little meaning, but politically and symbolically it is significant. Despite Barak's victory in Jewish communities, it is doubtful which he won a majority of the total Jewish vote. This is because mixed towns with large Arab populations were also defined as Jewish and it is reasonable to assume that the Arabs there gave Barak massive support. Thus, while the voting body in Arab communities stood at 458,261 in the 1999 elections, or 10.7 percent of

Table 22: Reasons for Supporting Parties in the 1999 Elections

	Jews	Change since 1996	Non-Jews	Change since 1996
Foreign affairs and security issues	32%	–21	15%	–7
Parties' positions on other issues	9%	+3	15%	–4
Party leadership	14%	–	8%	–13
The party 'represents people like themselves'	26%	+8	39%	+6
Other reasons	19%	+10	23%	+19

Source: Public opinion survey, 1999.

Table 23: Preferences for Prime Minister among Party Supporters in the 1999 Elections (%)

Party	Netanyahu	Barak	Other Candidates
One Israel	0.8	98.8	0.4
Likud	93.9	5.3	0.8
Shas	82.2	10.0	7.8
Meretz	2.2	96.6	1.2
Yisrael ba'Aliyah	40.0	48.6	11.4
Shinui	26.8	61.0	12.2
Center Party	16.4	71.2	12.4
Mafdal	85.7	9.5	4.8
Yahadut ha'Torah	96.2	3.8	0.0
Ra'am	0.0	52.0	48.0
National Unity	97.6	0.0	2.4
Yisrael Beitenu	94.4	5.6	0.0
Hadash	4.3	87.0	8.7
Balad	5.6	72.2	22.2
One Nation	29.4	52.9	17.7

Source: Public opinion survey, 1999.

Table 24: Election results from votes for Prime Minister (17 May 1999) by Type of Community (%)

	Ehud Barak	Binyamin Netanyahu
Total	56	44
Jewish Communities	51.5	48.5
Arab Communities	94.5	5.5
Jerusalem	35.5	64.5
Tel Aviv	64	36
Haifa	68	32
Bnei Brak	11	89
Veteran Cities	56.5	43.5
New Cities	42.5	57.5
Kibbutzim	93	7
Moshavim	56	44
Judeah and Samaria	18.5	81.5
Golan Heights	58.5	41.5

Source: Based on data supplied by the Central Election Committee.

the total, the 'non-Jewish' vote reached 662,932, or 15.5 percent. If the non-Jews in 'Jewish' cities voted like the Arabs in the all-Arab areas, then Netanyahu also received a majority of the Jewish vote in 1999.

Among the big cities, Jerusalem is a special case. Barak lost by nearly 30 percent there while winning by a similar margin in Tel Aviv and by even more in Haifa. The difference stems among other things from the big ultra-Orthodox (and generally religious) population in

Jerusalem with its clear-cut preference for Netanyahu. This was even more marked in Bnei Brak, where Netanyahu won overwhelmingly, just as he had against Peres in 1996.

In this context it is customary to distinguish between 'veteran' communities, founded before the establishment of the state, and new urban settlements founded afterwards. Barak won a clear-cut victory in the old towns and lost by a similar margin in the new towns. Nonetheless it is precisely in this match-up that the shift of votes to Barak can be discerned. In the 1996 elections Peres had lost both in the old towns (by 48 percent to 52 percent) and in the new ones (36 percent to 64 percent). Despite losing there, Barak's showing was better in the new towns, too.

Israel's rural Jewish population has always voted left. This time the kibbutzim gave Barak 93 percent of their vote (as opposed to 90 percent for Peres in 1996). Barak did better in the moshavim as well, with 56 percent of the vote as opposed to 52 percent for Peres.

Unlike voters inside the Green Line, those beyond it, in the territories that were occupied in the Six-Day War, are far from conforming to the established patterns. Netanyahu won a majority of over 80 percent of the vote in Judeah and Samaria (the West Bank) but lost in settlements on the Golan Heights. In both these population groups, however, he suffered a big drop in strength, similar to his decline in nearly all other sectors of the population. After winning 49.7 percent of the vote in the Golan and 87.4 percent in Judeah and Samaria in 1996, his support fell to 41.5 percent and 81.5 percent, respectively, in 1999.

In Jerusalem there was a dramatic shift in party voting, reminiscent of what had occurred in the local elections to the Jerusalem municipal council in November 1998. While in 1999 Shas got the biggest vote in the city and Yahadut ha-Torah came in second, the Likud and One Israel were relegated to third and fourth place (see Table 25). In the 1996 elections Shas had been the fifth biggest party in Jerusalem, winning just 10 percent of the vote. The Likud, which had got over a quarter of the vote in 1996, dropped by over 10 percent. Many former Likud voters, in Jerusalem and elsewhere, went over to Shas. This can be seen by the breakdown of voting in different districts. Shas also increased its strength by 2 percent in Haifa and Tel Aviv, and by 7 percent in Bnei Brak. The rise in Shas's popularity in various localities bears witness to the deepening of religious/ethnic polarization among voters. This polarization also showed up when the Meretz–Shinui camp increased its strength from 5 to 7 percent in the three big cities, paralleling Shas's success.

Days of Storm and Stress 109

Table 25: 15th Knesset Election Results in Selected Cities (%)

Party	Jerusalem	Tel Aviv	Haifa	Bnei Brak
One Israel	14.1	27.4	28.3	4.3
Likud	15.2	15.4	12.7	6.5
Shas	17.3	10.8	5.5	22.5
Meretz	7.2	13.1	7.4	1.0
Yisrael ba'Aliyah	2.6	1.9	8.9	1.9
Shinui	4.6	5.9	5.2	1.3
Center Party	4.3	6.3	7.4	1.2
Mafdal	6.0	3.1	2.9	6.6
Yahadut ha'Torah	15.5	1.5	1.9	47.1
Ra'am	0.1	0.9	0.7	0.0
National Unity	5.5	1.9	2.4	3.6
Yisrael Beitenu	2.0	0.9	2.8	1.0
Hadash	0.5	1.1	2.7	0.0
Balad	0.2	0.2	2.7	0.0
One Nation	0.4	1.0	1.2	0.3

Source: Based on data supplied by the Central Election Committee.

The vote in Arab towns and villages runs counter to the established pattern among Jewish voters (see Table 26). The three Arab parties won about 70 percent of the vote there, reflecting almost perfectly their ultimate representation in the Knesset. Of all the 'Jewish' parties, One Israel scored the biggest success among Arabs, though its support there declined significantly in comparison with the elections to the Fourteenth Knesset.

Table 26: 15th Knesset Election Results in Jewish and Arab Settlements (%)

Party	Jewish Settlements	Arab Settlements
One Israel	21.6	7.7
Likud	15.4	1.3
Shas	14.1	4.1
Meretz	7.7	5.2
Yisrael ba'Aliyah	5.7	0.9
Shinui	5.3	1.8
Center Party	5.4	0.2
Mafdal	4.5	1.5
Yahadut ha'Torah	4.2	1.1
Ra'am	0.4	31.1
National Unity	3.2	0.1
Yisrael Beitenu	2.8	0.5
Hadash	0.5	21.3
Balad	0.3	16.7
One Nation	1.8	2.7

Source: Based on data supplied by the Central Election Committee.

Table 27: Fifteenth Knesset Election Results in Old and New Towns (%)

Party	Veteran Towns	New Towns
One Israel	24.8	13.8
Likud	16.9	15.7
Shas	11.4	21.9
Meretz	7.7	4.4
Yisrael ba'Aliyah	5.6	9.8
Shinui	6.5	4.1
Center Party	6.7	4.1
Mafdal	4.5	3.6
Yahadut ha'Torah	1.5	2.8
Ra'am	0.0	0.9
National Unity	2.6	2.4
Yisrael Beitenu	2.3	5.4
Hadash	0.1	0.6
Balad	0.0	0.6
One Nation	2.1	2.8

Source: Based on data supplied by the Central Election Committee.

The big parties maintained their strength in the 'veteran' towns, but in the new towns the most salient fact is that Shas took over first place (see Table 27). The ethnic roots of this turnaround are plain for all to see. It is also worth noting the impressive showing of the two 'Russian' parties in the new towns, the reason being that the immigrant populations are proportionately larger in the provincial towns than in the older and better-established localities. One Israel, the Center Party, Meretz, and Shinui had greater success in the old towns, this also being a reflection of the well-known demographic realities.

The 1999 election results in the kibbutzim were very similar to those in 1996 (see Table 28). One Israel won slightly more than half the kibbutz vote in the two elections though less in 1999. In both cases, Meretz came in second with a little over 30 percent of the vote.

Unlike the kibbutzim, the moshavim showed a big swing to Shas. Here too there was a big drop in the strength of One Israel in comparison with the 1996 elections, as was the case with the Likud. The Likud–Gesher–Tzomet list took 27 percent of the vote in 1996 and 16 percent in 1999.

The breakdown of voting in various localities beyond the Green Line yields a far from uniform picture (see Table 29). What is striking are the changes between 1996 and 1999. In the Gaza district (not included in Table 29), the National Unity Party took first place with 40 percent of the vote. Support for the Mafdal (National Religious Party) dropped from 62 percent to just 15 percent. Support

Table 28: Fifteenth Knesset Election Results in Kibbutzim and Moshavim (%)

Party	Kibbutzim	Moshavim
One Israel	50.5	30.8
Likud	1.8	16.3
Shas	0.5	14.6
Meretz	31.9	7.6
Yisrael ba'Aliyah	0.7	0.3
Shinui	2.4	6.1
Center Party	2.4	4.4
Mafdal	2.7	6.4
Yahadut ha'Torah	0.3	2.4
Ra'am	0.0	0.1
National Unity	1.4	3.1
Yisrael Beitenu	0.1	0.3
Hadash	0.5	0.1
Balad	0.0	0.0
One Nation	0.2	1.4

Source: Based on data supplied by the Central Election Committee.

Table 29: Fifteenth Knesset Election Results in Judeah and Samaria and in the Golan Heights (%)

Party	Judeah and Samaria	Golan Heights
One Israel	6.8	23.3
Likud	6.8	9.2
Shas	20.9	4.5
Meretz	11.6	6.8
Yisrael ba'Aliyah	2.0	4.9
Shinui	2.6	4.5
Center Party	3.6	4.6
Mafdal	4.1	8.6
Yahadut ha'Torah	10.9	0.6
Ra'am	9.7	0.0
National Unity	0.0	9.6
Yisrael Beitenu	4.1	2.9
Hadash	0.0	0.1
Balad	0.0	0.0
One Nation	0.6	0.5
Third Way	0.5	13.9

Source: Based on data supplied by the Central Election Committee.

for the Third Way, which this time around emphasized the issue of the Golan Heights much more than in 1996, dropped from 18 percent to 14 percent. Most of the settlers in the territories are concentrated in Judeah and Samaria. The number of qualified voters was 92,642. In 1996 the settlers gave the Likud–Gesher–Tzomet list the most votes, over 34 percent. This time the Likud got just 21 percent. Support for the National Religious Party also dropped significantly, from 27 percent to 11 percent. Shas became the second strongest party in Judeah and Samaria, with 19 percent of the vote as opposed to 6 percent in 1996. Moledet took 8 percent in 1996, but in 1999 the National Unity Party almost overtook the Likud, getting around 19 percent of the territories' vote.

The ethnic vote first made itself felt in the 1977 and 1981 elections. Surprisingly, North African and Oriental Jews were no better represented on the Likud list than on the Alignment list. It therefore appears that it was not sectoral representation in the big parties that produced the ethnic vote but, on the contrary, the ethnic vote that produced sectoral representation.

An additional aspect of strife and sectoral representation was revealed in the 1999 elections by the representation of 'discriminated-against' groups in the lists of candidates. In eight of the fifteen lists that won seats in the Knesset, a decisive majority of the MKs are Sephardim, religious, Arab, or Russian (see Table 30). As opposed to previous Knessets, the Sephardim were strongly represented in the two big parties as well, while women were present in force in only the Meretz and Hadash lists.

Table 30: Representation of Selected Population Groups in the 15th Knesset
(% of Knesset faction members)

Party	Women	Sephardim	Russians	Religious	Arabs
One Israel	11.5	32.7	3.8	7.7	7.7
Likud	15.8	28.9	–	–	5.3
Shas	–	100.0	–	100.0	–
Meretz	40.0	10.0	–	–	10.0
Yisrael ba'Aliyah	16.7	–	100.0	–	–
Shinui	16.7	–	16.7	–	–
Center Party	16.7	16.7	–	–	–
Mafdal	–	40.0	–	100.0	–
Yahadut ha'Torah	–	–	–	100.0	–
Ra'am	–	–	–	–	100.0
National Unity	–	–	–	25.0	–
Yisrael Beitenu	–	–	75.0	–	–
Hadash	33.3	–	–	–	66.7
Balad	–	–	–	–	100.0
One Nation	–	50.0	–	–	–
Percent of total	11.7	30.0	9.2	25.0	10.8

Source: Based on official data. All calculations are for 18 May 1999.

Table 31: Participation in Previous Knessets among Members of the 15th Knesset (% of Knesset faction members)

Party	0 Knessets	0–1 Knessets	0–2 Knessets	0–3 Knessets	0–4 Knessets
One Israel	11.5	34.6	61.5	76.9	84.6
Likud	21.1	31.6	42.1	63.2	84.3
Shas	52.9	88.2	94.1	100.0	100.0
Meretz	40.0	40.0	60.0	70.0	80.0
Yisrael ba'Aliyah	33.3	100.0	100.0	100.0	100.0
Shinui	66.7	66.7	83.3	100.0	100.0
Center Party	50.0	66.7	83.3	83.3	83.3
Mafdal	20.0	20.0	40.0	100.0	100.0
Yahadut ha'Torah	20.0	40.0	40.0	80.0	100.0
Ra'am	40.0	60.0	80.0	100.0	100.0
National Unity	0.0	25.0	25.0	75.0	100.0
Yisrael Beitenu	50.0	100.0	100.0	100.0	100.0
Hadash	66.7	66.7	66.7	100.0	100.0
Balad	50.0	100.0	100.0	100.0	100.0
One Nation	50.0	50.0	50.0	100.0	100.0
Percent of total	32.5	53.3	66.7	84.2	91.7

Source: Based on official data. All calculations are for 18 May 1999.

All the signs indicate that the Israeli political system has undergone far-reaching changes in recent years. In addition to an increase in the number of parties, the deepening of polarization among the different camps, the sectarian cleavages, and even new leadership patterns, are evolving. Thus the two Prime Ministers who preceded Sharon were relative outsiders until just before their election. Another sign of leadership change is the lack of seniority among Knesset members. About a third of the MKs elected to the Fifteenth Knesset had never served before,[117] while over half had only one term behind them.[118]

It therefore appears that the 1999 elections reflect even more than in previous elections the issues associated with Israel's 'basic social dilemma'. Conflict between 'the whole and its parts' has assumed more threatening proportions than in the past. One way to deal with this critical problem is related to how a governmental coalition is formed (and operates). We shall devote much space to this topic in the following section.

THE BARAK GOVERNMENT: FROM DILEMMA TO DILEMMA

Once elected, Barak confronted macropolitical parameters, which we have already noted. The central axis of the system divided right from left—as those terms are understood in Israel, that is to say, in accordance with views expressed on security and foreign-policy issues in general, and on the Arab–Israel and Israeli–Palestinian conflict in particular. Another axis separated voters and their elected representatives according to views on the issue of religion and the state. A third impulse was strong voter identification with defined population groups, such as the religious, Russians, and Arabs.

Assembling elements of these parameters into coalitions in the past had taken place according to two logical principles: (1) the overwhelming majority of coalitions in Israel and in other multiparty parliamentary regimes were 'closed', that is to say, all parties within the ideological range fixed by the partners at the opposite poles, on the right and the left, also participated in it. Therefore, no 'holes' existed within this range, owing to the absence of any party belonging there ideologically (unless by sectarian

Table 32: The Political Map after Elections to the 15th Knesset*

Opposition parties in the outgoing Knesset (60 seats)			Coalition parties in the outgoing Knesset (60 seats)			
			'Russian Parties'			'Nationalist Right'
Balad (2)		Shinui (6)	Yisrael ba'Aliyah (6)	Yisrael Beitenu (4)		
Hadash (3)	Meretz (10)	One Israel (26)	Center Party (6)	Likud (19)		National Unity (4)
Ra'am (5)		One Nation (2)	Shas (17)	Yahadut ha'Torah (5)		Mafdal (5)
'Arab Parties'	'Anticlerical Parties'		Religious Parties'			

*The parties along the central axis are shown in italicized boldface type in the middle of the diagram. These parties are from right to left: National Unity, Likud, Center Party, One Israel, Meretz, and Hadash. The parties on the central axis command 68 seats in the Knesset. Outside the central axis one finds the Russian parties (Yisrael ba-Aliyah and Yisrael Beitenu), the religious parties (National Religious—i.e. Mafdal, Yahadut ha-Torah and Shas), the Arab parties (Ra'am and Balad, to which Hadash may also be added) and Shinui, which ran on a platform attacking the Ultra-Orthodox parties (and to which Meretz may also be added as an anticlerical, and 'central axis', party). Another group of boxed-off parties is the Nationalist Right consisting of the Likud and National Unity Party.

Dark gray denotes 'third-circle' parties; light gray denotes 'second-circle' parties; white denotes 'central-circle' parties.

Days of Storm and Stress 115

parties); (2) since most coalitions were closed and backed by a real majority (or a blocking majority) in parliament, the participation of a pivotal party was always assured (this being the party, as previously defined, to the left and right of which no parliamentary majority is to be found).

In the Fifteenth Knesset there was no clear-cut pivotal party. In that Knesset, parties that were partners in the outgoing coalition are represented by exactly 60 Knesset members (see Table 32). It can be argued that the median line runs between the Center Party on the left and Yisrael ba-Aliyah on the right. But it can also be argued that Yisrael ba-Aliyah is closer to the pivotal position than the Center Party. This is because the latter insisted during the election campaign that it was unwilling to participate in a government headed by Netanyahu, while Yisrael ba-Aliyah expressed a willingness to participate in any coalition that might be formed.

Furthermore, under the system of elections in force in 1999, the Prime Minister elect was mandated to form the government. Consequently, and because of the way the elections turned out, the primacy of Ehud Barak and One Israel was assured. Yet one implication of these results was that another division in the above diagram, in terms of possible coalitions, is by proximity to One Israel.

Three parties aside from One Israel—Yisrael ba-Aliyah, the Center Party, and One Nation—seemed willing to join any reasonable coalition under Barak. These four parties are represented in the diagram as occupying the 'central circle'.

The camp comprising the 'second circle' includes parties whose participation in a coalition was possible but depended to a great extent on who the other partners would be. Yahadut ha-Torah and Shas were thus potential partners but it is doubtful whether they would join a coalition including the antireligious parties, Shinui and Meretz, which also belonged to the 'second circle'. Another party in this camp was the Likud, whose participation in the coalition was contingent on the exclusion of Meretz.

The parties of the 'third circle' are those whose inclusion in a Barak coalition was almost impossible. These are Yisrael Beitenu and National Unity on the right and Balad, Hadash and Ra'am on the left. The position of each is of course not identical to the position of the others and conceivably the National Religious Party had more of a chance of joining the coalition than the parties of the third circle.

The next diagram represents possible coalitions between One Israel and selected parties (see Table 33). Each of these coalitions would be difficult to form in its own way. However, each would also be difficult to run, i.e., would be limited in the policies which it would permit the government to implement.

One possibility was to create a minority coalition backed by a blocking majority of all parties on the left. If the parties of the central circle had joined it, it would have been able to function for some

Table 33: Possible Coalitions in the 15th Knesset

A. 'Left'

Left-wing Opposition (10 Seats)		Coalition (56 Seats)		Right-wing Opposition (56 Seats)	
Balad (2)		Shinui (6)	Yisrael ba'Aliyah (6)	Yisrael Beitenu (4)	
Hadash (3)	Meretz (10)	One Israel (26)	Center Party (6)	Likud (19)	National Unity (4)
Ra'am (5)		One Nation (2)	Shas (17)	Yahadut ha'Torah (5)	Mafdal (5)

B. 'Left-Right'

Left-wing Opposition (16 Seats)		Coalition (69 Seats)		Right-wing Opposition (35 Seats)	
Balad (2)		Shinui (6)	Yisrael ba'Aliyah (6)	Yisrael Beitenu (4)	
Hadash (3)	Meretz (10)	One Israel (26)	Center Party (6)	Likud (19)	National Unity (4)
Ra'am (5)		One Nation (2)	Shas (17)	Yahadut ha'Torah (5)	Mafdal (5)

C. 'National Reconciliation'

Left-wing Opposition (26 Seats)		Coalition (81 Seats)		Right-wing Opposition (13 Seats)	
Balad (2)		Shinui (6)	Yisrael ba'Aliyah (6)	Yisrael Beitenu (4)	
Hadash (3)	Meretz (10)	One Israel (26)	Center Party (6)	Likud (19)	National Unity (4)
Ra'am (5)		One Nation (2)	Shas (17)	Yahadut ha'Torah (5)	Mafdal (5)

time. The option of a leftist government ('A' in the diagram) envisages a broad minority coalition of this type. The parties of the central circle, controlling 40 seats, would be joined by Shinui and Meretz with 16. Such a coalition could rely on the blocking majority guaranteed by the ten MKs from the Arab parties. Rabin, and Peres after him, had led such coalitions from September 1993 on. These coalitions were reasonably stable and even implemented revolutionary and far-reaching policies. Such coalitions operated for dozens of years in other countries with multiparty parliamentary regimes, notably Denmark, Norway, and Sweden. However, in Israel, a minority coalition finds it hard to operate because of the deep ideological and social divisions cutting across the country on both the macro- and micropolitical levels. Therefore, past experience shows that there is little possibility of putting together such a coalition.

Tactically speaking, a coalition including only the parties of the central circle would be preferable, and even more stable. The latter could keep the rightist, leftist, religious, and antireligious parties in check by threatening to expand the coalition in one direction or another. In each case the support of the opposite camp could be expected at least on an ad hoc basis. However, such coalitions will be created only under duress. They contradict the declared intention to form a broad coalition or defy the will of the public, as mani-fested in the 1999 elections, to achieve a measure of national reconciliation.

Another possibility was to woo the right-wing and religious parties. This option may have seemed plausible once both Binyamin Netanyahu and Aryeh Deri left their positions of leadership after the elections. Plausible or not, the addition of the Likud to the parties in the central circle would have yielded a coalition of only 59 seats. Expansion of this coalition by inviting one of the leftist parties, Shinui or Meretz, to join is mapped out in the diagram under 'B'.

Two problems would plague such a team. First, there would be no chance of expanding the coalition by inviting the religious camp to come on board unless the leftist partner (or partners) made its exit. This brings to mind Rabin's dilemma after he formed his first government (Israel's 17th) in June 1974. At first none of the religious parties joined the coalition. Then the National Religious Party replaced Ratz. Secondly, the ideological range of this coalition's main axis, particularly with Meretz as a partner, could have turned out to be too broad and hindered the formulation and implementation of government policy.

A more likely possibility was the one represented in the diagram under 'C'. In this case a majority could have been obtained by adding the Likud and the religious parties to the central circle. It would also have been possible to have one of the ultra-Orthodox parties come in. The participation of only one ultra-Orthodox party would increase the dependence on the ultra-Orthodox partner but, given the narrowness of the coalition, reduce the price paid to the ultra Orthodox camp as such. In pursuit of peace, Yahadut ha-Torah would be a better partner than Shas. In terms of 'national reconciliation', Shas is preferable. Participation of both these parties would have considerably expanded the base of the coalition without broadening the ideological range of the central axis. However, in such a coalition One Israel would constitute a minority. Barak intended to give government portfolios to his partners in the One Israel bloc. But, if the Labor party itself with 23 seats were to become a minor coalition member, it would have to pay the price of reconciliation and unity. Nonetheless the possibility of putting together this third kind of coalition was 'the best', since election results and opinion polls showed that this was the coalition that most voters preferred.

The coalition that Barak actually put together diverged from all these options. Recent years had witnessed, for a variety of reasons, the increasing weight of personal considerations, narrow and shortsighted, in the choice of coalition partners. It might have been hoped that common and long-term interests would guide the task of forming the government. This does not seem to have been the case, because the man mainly responsible for putting together the coalition was Prof. David Libai, one of the doves of the Labor Party and a former Minister of Justice. Indeed, Libai had already demonstrated little understanding of the art of forming coalitions when he had gone all out in support of the Basic Law: the Government of 1992.

After the formation of Barak's coalition, Libai declared, on a number of occasions, that his priority was 'making it possible for Meretz to join the coalition'. Relying on a 'solid prop' in forming a coalition was a strategic mistake whose consequences had been witnessed time and again in the past. The best example of this error is the way Levi Eshkol formed the government on behalf of Ben-Gurion after the 1961 elections. Preferring the 'solid prop' of Ahdut ha-Avodah to the 'weak prop' of the Liberal Party was what led to the change in the party map in the 1965 elections and ultimately to the upheaval of 1977, despite Mapai's firm control of the pivotal position in the system.[119]

Under the circumstances created after the 1999 elections, leaning on the 'strong prop' was equally inadvisable. The third option in the above diagram, given the relatively narrow ideological range it embraced, would have made it possible to move ahead in the peace process or in any other reasonable political direction. Furthermore, this option was feasible because the events that marked the Netanyahu period (and the election campaign) along with the conviction of Aryeh Deri on criminal charges, had made it obvious that their participation in the government was impossible. Therefore, if Barak had formed a 'national reconciliation' government along the lines of option 'C', he could have perpetually threatened his partners with replacement by a leftist government. The split in Yisrael ba-Aliyah and the creation of the Democratic Choice faction by the two 'dovish' MKs of Yisrael ba-Aliyah made such a threat all the more real. There are good indications that the establishment of the Democratic Choice was encouraged by circles close to the Prime Minister. However, the lesson to be learned from the new party setup was neither absorbed nor put to use.

The government actually formed included the parties of the 'central circle' except for One Nation, all the religious parties, and Meretz. Meretz's leader, Yossi Sarid, had declared at the outset of negotiations that he would not sit in the same government as Shas, but these brave words proved to be empty. Even more surprising was the willingness of Meretz and the National Religious Party, more hawkish than ever before, to sit together. The supposed lack of choice according to conventional wisdom proved to lack any basis in fact in the light of later developments and the frequent changes in the composition of the coalition that they made necessary.

The Knesset cast its vote of confidence in the government on 6 July 1999. The Labor Party at first had eight ministers (44.4 percent of the 18). Gesher was represented by David Levi as Foreign Minister. This gave One Israel half the ministers in the government, though it only had 26 of the 75 MKs that supported the coalition. In other words, just as in the Netanyahu government, the Prime Minister's faction was overrepresented. Shas received four portfolios, Meretz three, the Center Party two, and Yisrael ba-Aliyah and the National Religious Party one each (see Table 34). The remaining partner in the coalition, Yahadut ha-Torah, declined ministerial representation as it had in all previous governments.

Five additional ministers were added to the government on 5 August 1999. To make this possible the Basic Law: the Government

Table 34: The 28th Government: Ministers, Ministries, and Period of Current Service

Name	Party	First Governmental Portfolio	Started service	Ended service
Ehud Barak	Labor	Prime Minister, Minister of Defence, Minister of Agriculture, Minister of Tourism, Minister of Science, and Minister of Immigrant Absorption	6.7.99	
Yossi Beilin	Labor	Minister of Justice	6.7.99	
Shlomo Ben-Ami	Labor	Minister of Internal Security	6.7.99	
Binyamin Ben-Eliezer	Labor	Minister of Communication	6.7.99	
Shlomo Benizri	Shas	Minister of Health	6.7.99	11.7.00
Ra'anan Cohen	Labor	Minister of Labor and Social Welfare	15.8.00	
Ran Cohen	Meretz	Minister of Industry and Trade	6.7.99	24.6.00
Yitzhak Cohen	Shas	Minister of Religious Affairs	6.7.99	11.7.00
Dalia Itzik	Labor	Minister of the Environment	6.7.99	
David Levi	Gesher	Minister of Foreign Affairs	6.7.99	4.8.00
Yitzhak Levi	Mafdal	Minister of Housing and Construction	6.7.99	11.7.00
Amnon Lipkin-Shahak	Center	Minister of Tourism	25.8.99	
Michael Malci'or	Meimad	Minister in charge of social and Diaspora affairs	5.8.99	
Roni Milo	Center	Minister of Health	15.8.00	
Yitzhak Mordechai	Center	Minister of Transport	6.7.99	30.5.00
Chaim Oron	Meretz	Minister of Agriculture and Rural Development	5.8.99	24.6.00
Shimon Peres	Labor	Minister of Regional Cooperation	6.7.99	
Chaim Ramon	Labour	Minister in charge of Jerusalem Affairs	6.7.99	
Yossi Sarid	Meretz	Minister of Education Culture and Sport	6.7.99	24.6.00
Natan Sharansky	Yisrael ba'Aliyah	Minister of the Interior	6.7.99	11.7.00
Avraham Shochat	Labor	Minister of Finance	6.7.99	
Eliyahu Suissa	Shas	Minister of National Infrastructure	6.7.99	11.7.00
Yael (Yuli) Tamir	Labor	Minister of Absorption	5.8.99	
Mathan Vilna'I	Labor	Minister of Science	5.8.99	
Eliyahu Yishai	Shas	Minister of Labor and Social Welfare	6.7.99	11.7.00

Source: Data supplied by the Secretary of the Government and the Knesset Archive.

had to be changed, since the original version limited the number of ministers to 18. Two of the new ministers represented Labor, one represented Meimad, one Meretz, and one the Center Party. The effect was to increase the relative representation of the Labor Party and One Israel even further.

It would be difficult to imagine a more bizarre coalition than this. Its broad ideological range on two key issues—security and foreign policy, and religion and the state—made movement in any direction almost impossible, since it was clear that any movement on either of the two issues would result in the resignation of part of the government. This was what happened soon enough.

The first coalition crisis occurred as early as the end of August. The government approved the transport of an electrical turbine on Friday night (27–28 August 1999) to avoid obstructing a major interurban traffic artery. The ultra-Orthodox factions strongly protested this Sabbath desecration while the other coalition partners supported the decision on the grounds that working then would keep traffic jams to a minimum. Two weeks later the debate was renewed over the movement of additional turbines, and as a consequence Yahadut ha-Torah left the coalition.

This initial crisis was a foretaste of what was to come. Many commentators point to Barak himself as a major factor in the repeated failures of the government. There can be no question that a politician's personality can have a decisive effect on events, and it is possible that in recent years Israel has lacked leaders of stature who place the good of the country (and even of their own party) ahead of personal advantage. Moreover, as we have seen, the flavor of coalitions is indeed influenced to a great extent by the character of their leaders. Nonetheless, it is the composition of the coalition as such that seems to have been the main reason for the failure of the 28th government. Every effort to make a meaningful move on the peace front produced a coalition crisis, and whenever such a crisis was produced the government changed direction, and sometimes radically. This was the main reason why Barak's government was soon called the 'zigzag government', and it is by this name that it will be remembered in Israel's political history.

The first minister to leave the government was Yitzhak Mordechai. This was the only departure not related to politics, coming as it did in the wake of Mordechai's indictment for sexual assault. The personal failings of Israeli leaders in this period were demonstrated on numerous occasions under both the Netanyahu and Barak administrations.

Aryeh Deri, the rising star of previous governments, began serving his prison sentence on 3 September 2000. On 28 May 2000, President Ezer Weizman announced his resignation despite the Attorney General's decision not to indict him for receiving hundreds of thousands of dollars' worth of gifts under questionable circumstances. In the meantime, the Attorney General instructed the police to continue investigating voluntary organizations linked to the political parties (27 January 2000). Prominent among the investigated organizations were those close to Prime Minister Barak. In December 2000, the police interrogated Government Secretary Yitzhak Herzog, an intimate of Barak, in the affair. According to news reports, Herzog invoked his right to remain silent. Former Prime Minister Netanyahu and his wife, also under investigation, were not indicted despite police recommendations. The Attorney General decided not to prosecute on 27 September 2000, although he strongly criticized Netanyahu for mixing personal and public finances as well as improperly disposing of gifts he had received as Prime Minister. The Attorney General's public report called to mind the Bar-On affair, which had also been concluded without Netanyahu's being indicted.

At the institutional level, clashes between Shas and Meretz produced pure comedy. Meretz's leader, Yossi Sarid, had declared before the elections that his party would not under any circumstances join a government in which Shas was a member. Afterwards, when both Meretz and Shas were installed in the government as senior partners, Shas MK Meshulam Nahari was named Deputy Minister of Education under Education Minister Sarid. Differences of opinion between the two, as between their respective parties, did not cease for a moment. Finally, on 24 June 2000, Meretz's three ministers, Yossi Sarid, Chaim Oron, and Ran Cohen, resigned from the government, for the odd purpose of allowing Shas to remain, a move that in any event did not work out.

Negotiations between Israel and the Palestinian Authority, which reached their high point in the Barak–Arafat talks at Camp David in 2000, were what ultimately brought the government down. The collapse of the government was a clear-cut result of ideological divisions as well as a reaction against Barak's penchant for concentrating power in his own hands. Mainly it reflected Barak's inability to direct policy in a coalition whose ideological bounds took in nearly the entire political map. Against the background of peace negotiations, Barak's partners abandoned him in rapid succession: Shas Ministers Eli Yishai, Shlomo Benizri, Yitzhak Cohen, and Eli

Suissa on 11 July 2000, Yisrael ba-Aliyah Minister Nathan Sharansky on the same day, National Religious Party Minister Yitzhak Levi on 12 July and Gesher and One Israel Foreign Minister David Levi on 4 August. In the wake of these resignations, the government was reduced to 12 members and no longer had a parliamentary majority. In its final phase, after bringing on board Raanan Cohen (One Israel) and Roni Milo (Center Party) in the middle of August, the government numbered 14 ministers.

As in the election of Weizman to the presidency during the Netanyahu period, the election of a new president, Moshe Katzav (31.7.2000), symbolized the loss of the government's majority in the Knesset. Katzav defeated Peres, Labor's candidate, by a 63–57 margin in a second-round Knesset vote.

The zigzagging policies of the government reached a peak on the issue of religion and state. Barak vacillated between his pledge to 'draft everyone' during his election campaign, and promotion of the Tal Law, which was intended to anchor the draft deferments of yeshiva students in legislation. Moreover, he was torn between efforts to impose the views of Shas on Meretz, which led to the latter's resignation from the government, and attempts to abolish the Ministry of Religious Affairs as a step in the direction of a 'secular revolution'. Ironically, the government decided to abolish the Ministry of Religious Affairs on the day that Aryeh Deri began serving his sentence.

In other areas as well, the government backed down on positions it had held at the beginning of its term. Thus, on 11 June 2000, the Finance Minister admitted the death of the tax reform that he had previously proclaimed. And, on 12 July 2000, Israel announced the cancellation of the Falcon plane sale to China in the face of American pressure, including a threat from the Appropriations Committee of Congress to cancel financial aid to Israel.

In one area the Barak government did display noteworthy consistency.[120] Right from the start it had given priority to the peace process, and it continued to pursue this policy right up to the end. Prior to the 1999 elections and in their aftermath, Barak had promised a comprehensive peace settlement within a year. In January 2000, he had held week-long talks with the Syrian Foreign Minister in Sheperdstown under the auspices of the American President. Many had praised him at first for extracting Israel from the Lebanese morass, though later the surrender of Israel in this other war of attrition was seen by some as what fanned the flames of the new Palestinian uprising. In every case Barak had been prepared to make greater concessions than his predecessors though the results were meager. Even so, there were those who argued that he had failed not because of Palestinian intransigence but because he had not gone far enough.

At the end of September 2000, a new wave of violence erupted, called by the Palestinians the Al-Aqsa Intifada. Overtly, this limited war began over the visit of the Likud leader Ariel Sharon and other party members to the Temple Mount. In actual fact, the events demonstrated the bankruptcy of prevailing views on the Arab–Israel conflict. The response of Israeli Arabs and the death of 13 Israeli Arab demonstrators during the first wave of riots revealed the depth of the crisis. On what was to be the eve of a permanent solution to the Israeli–Palestinian conflict, Israel found itself, in complete contradiction to the prediction of its leaders, in a violent confrontation in which arms given by Israel to the Palestinian Authority were being used against Israeli soldiers and civilians. While these events revealed the depth of Arab hostility, they also demonstrated the urgent need to change the situation and allow Arab aspirations fair and reasonable expression even if the immediate result was not the definitive end of the conflict.

At the end of 2000 it became apparent that early elections could not be avoided. Here, too, the Prime Minister responded inconsistently. At first opposed to elections and doing everything in his power to postpone them, he then surprised his rivals and intimates by announcing his agreement to early elections. The announcement was made from the podium of the Knesset in the midst of the first reading of the Early Elections Law, while members of his own party were preparing to vote against that law. A few days later, Barak handed in his resignation to the President to forestall general Knesset elections and ensure that his predecessor, Binyamin Netanyahu, would not be able to run against him for Prime Minister, since the latter was no longer an MK. This was followed almost immediately by still another reversal of direction: Barak voted on its preliminary reading in the Knesset for a 'Netanyahu Law', which would have enabled Netanyahu to run if he had wished to.

No doubt these moves were partly dictated by changing circumstances, and some might even be termed 'brilliant'. But when all is said and done they seemed destined to have the same results, for leaders and led alike, as similar exercises in sleight of hand in the past. Thus, in the elections of 2001, after seeing Barak waffle and zigzag again and again, the citizens of Israel had to settle for what seemed to many a choice between the lesser of two evils.

THE SHARON GOVERNMENT

On 6 February 2001, for the third time, Israel went to the polls to elect a Prime Minister by direct popular vote. Direct election of the Prime Minister, as will be remembered, had been introduced by the revised 1992 version of the Basic Law: the Government, and had been previously implemented in the 1996 and 1999 general elections.

In a reversal of his 12 percent 1999 victory, Barak now lost to Ariel Sharon by twice that margin. The election was a first in Israel in terms of both its form and its results. In form it was the first direct election for the Prime Minister alone. Unlike the 1996 and 1999 elections, the Knesset was not elected at the same time, since the Prime Minister had resigned and forced 'special' elections only for the Prime Minister, who would thus inherit a sitting parliament. In its results the election constituted not only an unprecedented rout but also reflected the lowest turnout of voters in the country's history.[121]

Though Barak had succeeded in his somewhat clumsy effort to maneuver the still fairly popular Netanyahu out of the race, he still had one more hurdle to surmount. Even with Netanyahu out of the way, Barak continued to slip in the polls while Likud leader Sharon's popularity continued to rise. A movement was therefore now afoot to replace Barak with Shimon Peres as the candidate of the left, or to run Peres as a third candidate who might finish ahead of Barak in the first round. While neither of these schemes bore fruit, they hardly contributed to Barak's popularity.

Barak was left to defend an almost indefensible record while his opponent could confine himself to pledging that he would restore the sense of personal security that many Israelis had lost, and lead the country down a safer, more conservative path toward peace. As the Palestinian violence escalated and the death toll mounted, the gap in polls results widened, only to be outdone by the elections themselves.

Barak not only lost the election but the vote of every sector that had supported him in 1999. However, even more noteworthy than Sharon's landslide victory was the across-the-board drop in voter turnout (see Table 35). The biggest decline was in the Arab sector, which dropped to 25 percent of what it had been in 1999. In the 15 elections held between 1949 and 1999, average Arab turnout had been 78 percent. Now, after giving Barak almost 95 percent of their vote in 1999, Arab citizens felt betrayed by the government. The reasons varied from the response of the Barak government to the Palestinian uprising in general and to Israeli Arab protests in particular, with their toll of 13 dead, to the feeling of social discrimination and of being taken for granted politically.

Paradoxically, with the gap between Sharon and Barak so great in the Jewish population alone, the drop in Arab turnout was not the factor that swung the election. Thus whether the expectation of a rout was what contributed to keeping Arabs away from the polls, or whether they would have done so even if their absence would have been the factor that assured Sharon's election, remains a moot point.

Ariel Sharon presented his government to the Knesset on 7 March 2001. It was a national-unity (grand-coalition) government in which the two biggest parties participated. Similar big governments had existed in 1952–55, 1967–70, and 1984–90. The main reasons for forming such a government were the apparent failure of the peace process, the Palestinian uprising, and the makeup of parliament. The mounting Palestinian violence was perceived as a crisis that demanded a stable government enjoying broad public support. Differences of opinion over concessions relating to the peace process seemed irrelevant. Indeed, after the elections, the creation of a national-unity government was supported by both sides of the political spectrum in Israel. Furthermore, Sharon had inherited the Knesset that had been elected with Barak in 1999 and therefore enjoyed only a bare majority among its representatives. A government based on the support of such a majority would have found it very difficult to function effectively or even survive. In many ways the coalition formed by Sharon was identical to the 'third option' described previously. This option was available to Barak, and rejected by him, following the 1999 elections. The major change, of course, was that this time it was the Likud leader who had decisively won the elections for Prime Minister. Sharon chose this latter path but included in his coalition, in addition to his 'natural/ ideal' partners, the merged National Unity–Yisrael Beitenu faction.

Table 35: Election results from votes for Prime Minister (7 February 2001)

	Votes	% of valid votes	% of all votes
Ariel Sharon	1,698,077	62.4	60.5
Ehud Barak	1,023,944	37.6	36.4

Electorate: 4,504,769
Turnout: 62.3% (2,805,938)
Valid votes: 97.0% (2,722,021)

Source: Based on data supplied by the Central Election Committee.

Days of Storm and Stress 127

The Sharon coalition included seven parties, controlling 72 of the 120 Knesset seats. The three biggest parties were all partners: One Israel (23 MKs), Likud (19), and Shas (17). Also represented were the National Unity–Yisrael Beitenu alliance (7), Yisrael ba-Aliyah (4), and One Nation (2). All 72 MKs voted their approval of the government, with 21 additional MKs opposed and 27 abstaining. Within a month the five Yahadut ha-Torah MKs and one from the Center Party joined the coalition. The Opposition consisted of the Arab parties and Meretz on the left, Shinui and the Center Party in the center, and the National Religious Party on the religious right. David Levi's Gesher faction, which at this point in time included three Knesset members, remained outside the coalition, as opposed to its position in the mooted 'third option' (see Table 36).

The new government included three women (within a total of 26 ministers), the largest number in Israeli history, and one Arab (Druze) for the first time. The government was slated to serve for a maximum of two and a half years, since the next parliamentary elections were scheduled for November 2003.[122]

Most of the more dovish Labor leaders, including Oslo architect Yossi Beilin, remained outside the government. Sharon wanted Barak in his government, but opposition within Labor made such a partnership impossible and Barak retired from active politic life 'for the time being'. From outside, he steadily criticized Arafat and the Palestinian Authority. On numerous occasions he pointed an accusing finger at Palestinian leaders, holding them responsible for the current wave of terrorism and calling into question the possibility of reaching any kind of real agreement with Arafat, let alone genuine peace. Even a dovish figure like outgoing Foreign Minister Shlomo Ben-Ami expressed unequivocal disappointment in Arafat. Shimon Peres, the new Foreign Minister, once again became Labor's leading political figure. Paradoxically, in the new configuration, his status was considerably enhanced in comparison with his problematic and even humiliating position under Barak.

The co-option of Peres made Sharon and his government far more palatable both to the dovish segments of the Israeli public and to foreign critics. Sharon was willing to risk the support of right-wingers in his government by declaring, on a number of occasions, that he was prepared to accept the establishment of a Palestinian state.[123] However, during the government's first year, Sharon and Peres clashed time and again on various issues related to the Israeli–Palestinian conflict. Notwithstanding, they always seemed

Table 36: The 29th Government (7.3.01)

Name	Party	First Governmental Portfolio
Ariel Sharon	Likud	Prime Minister, Minister of Immigrant Absorption
Shimon Peres	Labor	Deputy Prime Minister, Minister of Foreign Affairs
Eliyahu Yishai	Shas	Deputy Prime Minister, Minister of the Interior
Natan Sharansky	Yisrael ba'Aliyah	Deputy Prime Minister, Minister of Housing and Construction
Silvan Shalom	Likud	Deputy Prime Minister, Minister of Finance
Shmuel Avital	One Nation	Minister without Portfolio in Charge of Social Affairs Coordination
Binyamin Ben-Eliezer	Labor	Minister of Defence
Shlomo Benizri	Shas	Minister of Labor and Welfare
Ra'anan Cohen	Labor	Minister without Portfolio
Nisim Dahan	Shas	Minister of Health
Tzahi Hanegbi	Likud	Minister of the Environment
Dalia Itzik	Labor	Minister of Trade and Industry
Uzi Landau	Likud	Minister of Internal Security
Avigdor Lieberman	National Union–Yisrael Beitenu	Minister of National Infrastructure
Limor Livnat	Likud	Minister of Education
Tzipi Livni	Likud	Minister of Regional Cooperation
Danny Naveh	Likud	Minister without Portfolio in Charge of Government–Knesset Liaison
Asher Ohana	Shas	Minister of Religious Affairs
Reuven Rivlin	Likud	Minister of Communications
Meir Sheetrit	Likud	Minister of Justice
Shalom Simhon	Labor	Minister of Agriculture and Rural Development
Ephraim Sneh	Labor	Minister of Transport
Eli Suissa	Shas	Minister without Portfolio in Charge of Jerusalem Affairs
Salah Tarif	Labor	Minister without Portfolio
Matan Vilnai	Labor	Minister of Culture, Science, and Sport
Rehavam Ze'evi	National Union–Yisrael Beitenu	Minister of Tourism

Source: Data supplied by the Secretary of the Government and the Knesset Archive. As of February 2002, three additional ministers were nominated: Binyamin Elon (National Union–Yisrael Beitenu—substituting the assassinated Minister of Tourism, Rehavam Ze'evi), Dan Meridor (Center—Minister without portfolio), and Roni Milo (Center—Minister without portfolio). Salah Tarif resigned from the government as a result of a police investigation.

to find a way to patch up their partnership. In the eyes of most Israelis, the continued Palestinian violence and the reluctance of the Palestinian Authority to take decisive steps against terrorism seemed to justify the Likud–Labor alliance.

On 30 April 2001, the Sharm el-Sheikh Fact-Finding Committee headed by George J. Mitchell, former majority leader of the US Senate, published its report on the new Intifada. Other members of the Committee were distinguished statesmen from Turkey, Norway, the United States, and the European Union. The Committee called upon the government of Israel and the Palestinian Authority to 'act swiftly and decisively to halt the violence' and stated that the immediate objectives of the two parties 'should be to rebuild confidence and resume negotiations'. Given the continuation of terrorist activities, the implementation of these recommendations became almost impossible. On 14 June 2001, a Palestinian–Israeli Security Implementation Work Plan, better known as the Tenet Plan, proposed a six-stage timetable for the parties. Immediate implementation of this plan, too, seemed quite problematic. Later in 2001 and at the beginning of 2002, former General Anthony Zinni of the United States became the mediator between Israel and the Palestinians.

During 2001, more than 200 Israelis were killed in terrorist attacks. One of the most dramatic incidents occurred in October, when Cabinet Minister Rehava'am Ze'evi was shot dead in a Jerusalem hotel by terrorists belonging to the Popular Front for the Liberation of Palestine. Two days earlier, Ze'evi and Minister Avigdor Lieberman had handed in their resignations from the government because of their opposition to what they regarded as too moderate a government response to terrorism encouraged by the Palestinian Authority. The resignation would have come into effect later on the same day (17 October). Subsequently, Lieberman decided to withdraw his letter of resignation.

On 4 January 2002, Israeli Navy and Air Force units captured a 4,000-ton freighter in the Red Sea, the *Karine A*, carrying 50 tons of weaponry from Iran to the Palestinian Authority. The ship carried, among other weapons, long-range rockets, mines and 2.5 tons of sophisticated explosives—weapons regarded in Israel as earmarked for use in a variety of terrorist activities. Occuring during a visit by General Zinni in the area, the incident demonstrated to many not only the problematic nature of negotiations with the Palestinian Authority but also the global nature of modern-day terrorism.

During its first year the Sharon government found itself in embarrassing international situations more than once. On 2 July 2001, the Brussels public prosecutor's office announced that it had opened an investigation of Israeli Prime Minister Ariel Sharon for alleged crimes against humanity in the massacre of Palestinian civilians by Lebanese Christian militiamen in the Lebanese refugee camps of Sabra and Shatilla in September 1982. Early in September 2001, Israel and the United States decided to withdraw from the World Conference Against Racism (WCAR), Racial Discrimination, Xenophobia, and Related Intolerance, convened in Durban, South Africa, in protest against the virulent anti-Israel language of its draft resolution.

It seemed, however, that the atmosphere changed dramatically following the attack on America on 11 September 2001. The attack demonstrated to many that Israel was in the forefront of the war against a dangerous combination of terrorism, Islamic fundamentalism, and weapons of mass destruction.

A policy realm that confounded the Sharon government was the economy. While economic growth had reached an impressive figure of 6.4 percent in 2000, it fell to −0.5 percent in 2001 with per capita growth plummeting to −2.9 percent. Unemployment reached a rate of about 9 percent at the end of the year.[124] There is no question that the combination of terrorist violence in Israel and the depressed world market, especially in the hi-tech sector, contributed to Israel's economic woes. Nevertheless, despite the unfavorable climate, immigrants continued to pour into the country, to the extent of over 100,000 in the two Intifada years (60,000 in 2000 and 45,000 in 2001).

Public-opinion polls conducted at the beginning of 2002 indicated that Sharon and the Likud were very popular. One reason was that many Israelis continued to be disillusioned with the once popular Oslo process. Another was Sharon's continued partnership with the Ministers of Defence and Foreign Affairs (Ben-Eliezer and Peres of the Labor Party), an association that convinced many people that Sharon was not as extreme and dogmatic as his left-wing critics claimed. In fact, the Labor Party contributed to Sharon's popularity in more ways than one. The September 2001 elections for a new Labor Party chairman ended indecisively amid mutual recriminations that assumed the proportions of a political scandal. A return vote in a number of polling stations, where 'irregularities' were suspected, was held in December 2001. Binyamin Ben-Eliezer was declared the winner, defeating Knesset Speaker Avraham Burg. Neither, however, was seen by most Israelis as a charismatic or promising leader.

5
Conclusion: Solutions in the Absence of a Solution

The Israeli political situation we have analyzed in this book takes on a larger significance when viewed in game theory terms. On that score it is clear that decision making in any area of life involves countless dilemmas. Decisions are almost always made under conditions of uncertainty. In the social realm, much of this uncertainty springs from the mutual dependence of decision makers, that is to say, relationships that social scientists sometimes call 'games'[125]. Uncertainty deriving from the mutual dependence of various parties reaching decisions simultaneously often produces decision-making problems greater than the ones that existed in the first place. The reason for this is that it is impossible to overcome uncertainty by merely gathering information (since all the 'simultaneous' decisions will be wavering between alternatives). Thus application of relatively simple solutions deriving from a calculation of 'expected utilities', which are possible when dealing with 'state-of-nature' situations, is also liable to be far more complicated in situations of mutual dependence between various decision makers.

Although many professional publications on game theory point to a 'one and only solution' in games that resemble well-known social situations, the theory seems to demonstrate that in most actual social situations it is impossible to arrive at a solution that will meet at least the most minimal requirements of being 'correct', 'efficient', 'just', and 'rational'.[126] Actual circumstances become enormously complicated when one has to determine policy or make 'strategic decisions' (in the political and 'game' sense of these terms). And, in the Israeli political context, the problem of decision making may be even more complex than in other countries, both because Israel's very existence is on the line, and because of the many conflicts between 'binding' values and tangle of conditions that does not always allow conformity to these values.

There are of course a number of 'easy' solutions to the problem of making decisions on vital issues. Many try to convince themselves and others by 'rationalizing after the fact'. Some tend to ignore reality as long as they can stay in a state of 'cognitive dissonance'. Thus, for example, it is usual to deny failure (as well as the existence of problems).

It is also quite common to resort to slogans in order to simplify decision-making problems on both the personal and the social levels. In many instances the use of slogans (including bogus scales of value) seems to introduce a measure of order into a chaotic world, creating an illusion (pleasant on the personal level and convincing on the public level) of steadfastness, integrity, reason, and control of the situation. The first chapter of this book dealt with several such examples.

John Nash[127] showed half a century ago that there are social situations where there is an 'optimal equilibrium'. With just slight distortion it is possible to show that Nash's equilibrium enables everyone in the system to adopt an effective and undisguised strategy. In such situations each decision maker can adopt a strategy intended to serve his own interests, and expose the details of this strategy without violating his own interests. The only general situation in which Nash's equilibrium is always theoretically operative is, ironically, one in which there is a total conflict between the participants. This situation is sometimes described by the term 'zero-sum game' (as is any situation where it is possible to arrive at the zero-sum through a positive linear transformation of the utilities of the parties).

Even when there is a total conflict things are not so simple. Sometimes decision makers have to adopt a 'mixed strategy', that is a strategy in which a number of alternatives are used in accordance with probabilities that can be calculated in advance. In such cases as well, the decision makers need not hide their own strategies. They need not conceal the probability of each of the alternatives they will use but they cannot declare their specific 'moves' before each stage of the repetitive game.

Situations of total conflict are also relatively simple in another sense. Communication between the sides is entirely superfluous and there is nothing to be gained by it. It is sometimes possible to expose situations approaching total conflict by the lack of communication between the parties. International relations in the Middle East are replete with examples of this kind. Furthermore, communication can solve many problems, but it does not solve the basic social dilemma when it is in the form of the Prisoner's Dilemma. In this case, communication can bring about agreement, but then a 'second-degree dilemma' will be produced since the dominant alternative for the sides is violation of the agreement.

It seems reasonable that in the most critical policy dimension that Israel faces—the Arab–Israeli conflict—Israel is doomed to employ an open mixed strategy while decreasing its belief in communication solutions. This is not only because of the zero-sum aspects of the situation, but also because of its Prisoner's Dilemma features. In the latter case, 'tit for tat' seems the proper strategy that may lead the parties to a reasonably cooperative peace situation. One may claim that this line of behavior is rather more 'centrist' than extreme 'dovish' or extreme 'hawkish'.

Social and political life is generally more complex than the clear-cut situations depicted by both the zero-sum models and the Prisoner's Dilemma situation. Participants are usually not engaged in all-out conflicts and still share common interests. Under such circumstances there is still a glimmer of hope, though this generally complicates the decision-making process considerably. On the other hand, the apparent importance of social competition (and 'self-respect') diverts decision makers into seeking to increase their advantages over the other participants (rather than to increase their own utilities *per se*). When examining the loan of your neighbor becomes the supreme factor guiding the decisions of players, the danger of arriving at total conflict increases. Such tendencies do occur, from time to time, when the relations examined are between nations, communities, or individuals. Incidentally, it should be noted that treatment of the subject of 'relative advantage' in game theory (or of the 'sum of the payoffs', which, conversely, represents the 'common interest') is highly problematic, since interpersonal comparison of utilities is forbidden—and even impossible—in modern game theory.

John Nash, mentioned above, also published a 'single' solution for bargaining problems.[128] This solution meets four well-known requirements ('Pareto-optimality', 'symmetry', 'indifference to linear transformation', and 'indifference to irrelevant solutions').[129] However, the addition of a requirement or replacement of three of the requirements with another (such as 'perfect monotonicity') makes a solution impossible. Moreover, Nash's solution of the bargaining problem only works if the parties see the agreements as binding. As is known, agreements in general (and in the Middle East and internal Israeli politics in particular) are not always seen as binding by all actors.

From all the above it is clear that in many social situations it is very difficult to arrive at an efficient, correct, rational, and just solution. Aside from the problems discussed above, decision and policy makers must also solve many other universal problems, and first and foremost, as already seen, the prevalence of the 'basic social dilemma'. In the context of the democratic solution we must once again mention the Arrow Theorem,[130] already known in part from the analyses of Borda and Condorcet from before the French Revolution, that is to say, from before the advent of modern democracies.[131]

The nature of the Israeli political system and Israel's struggle for survival ever since it came into existence make the search for solutions to basic problems (as well as routine problems) a process necessarily involving alternatives fraught with danger and internal contradictions. The difficulties of decision makers are magnified by basic political problems that are more serious than is usual in Western countries. An inkling of these difficulties has been provided throughout the present work.

In Chapter 1 we dwelled on the difficulties and contradictions deriving from the central position of the concepts of democracy, Jewishness, peace, and security in the Israeli political experience.

In Chapter 2 we concluded that the development of the constitutional system in recent years has not only failed to provide a framework and solution for the country's basic problems and objectives, but has exacerbated the dilemmas of governance and greatly complicated the relations between the branches of government.

In Chapter 3 we described the evolution of the political-party map, which was characterized from the outset by rifts deeper and more complex than those found in most stable democratic regimes. With the passage of time, the situation has grown even more complicated. The loss of control of the pivotal position in the system by the dominant parties has produced instability and further fragmentation. This affected the makeup of coalitions (and consequently the constitutional framework as well). In recent years the party map has undergone more frequent changes than in the past, indicative of widening social and political gaps.

In Chapter 4 we surveyed political developments in recent years. In only a decade Israel has had six Prime Ministers. The Rabin assassination was a shocking reflection of the growing polarization on basic issues. Developments in relations with the Arabs were dramatic in the extreme. The shifts in power between the main camps produced a kind of a pendulum-like movement putting stable solutions out of reach.

From all the above it is clear that decision making and strategy formulation under the conditions of Israel is a challenge that few leaders in democratic countries have to face. In Israel, some of these challenges are of a permanent nature and it is hard to say whether Israel's new leadership has exhibited optimal talents and abilities under these conditions. It is clear that critical errors were made both in understanding the situation and in decisions and actions by leaders of all the political camps, not only in the last decade but in all the years of Israel's existence. Given the complexity of the problems it was indeed hard to avoid mistakes, but there is no doubt that they could have been minimized.

Most probably many of the 'solutions' to Israel's problems lie in, or near, the political center. Many political scientists, as well as the general public, politicians and the media, criticize 'centrist positions', 'centrist parties', and politicians who attempt to place themselves in the center of the political map. Often these critics zero in on the vagueness of the messages coming out of the center and the reluctance to make tough decisions when they are called for.

The truth, however, is that positions at the center need not always be vague. Thus, for example, a realistic centrist view of the Arab–Israel conflict might endorse the idea of separation and perhaps even propose generous territorial and political concessions while at the same time recognizing that stable peace lies beyond the horizon. Such an approach could emphasize efforts to deal meanwhile with a number of Israel's basic problems, such as the 'demographic problem' and the security problem. In other cases, the position of the center could prove to be more realistic just because of its vagueness, for we face political and social problems that may have no solution, in which case trying to deal with them decisively, whether from the 'left' or the 'right', is a delusion.

Paradoxically, in fact, recognition that perfect solutions are often unattainable in any social reality (and certainly not likely in Israel's) can produce better, albeit not ideal, solutions than those deriving from the illusion that we are living in a world amenable to equilibrium and optimal solutions.

Notes

1. For alternative possibilities of organizing a 'comparative' research, see, for example, Keman (1993) and, of course, Lijphart (1999).
2. The universal features of the dilemma were emphasized by Olson (1965) in his *The Logic of Collective Action*. But although the dilemma caused the collapse of many 'nations', he preferred to focus on other factors in his *The Rise and Decline of Nations* (Olson (1982).
3. The *coercion* and *solidarity* solutions are as old as history. One can suggest, for example, many biblical depictions of the dilemma and these solutions. One relevant quotation is used in Chapter 2 ('Make us a king to judge us'). A brilliant defense of the *coercion* solution is that of Hobbes in *Leviathan* (1651). Throughout history it seems that solidarity has been the more popular solution. Unfortunately, there are too many examples of its failure. Kant in his *Critique of Practical Reason* (1788) proposed a more realistic and yet an ethical type of *limited* solidarity.
4. Important works on the *repetition* solution are those of Robert Axelrod (e.g., 1984 and 1997). Rapoport and Chammah (1965) were probably the first to deal with it systematically, and also those to whom the *tit-for-tat* strategy should be attributed.
5. Cohen (1994) depicted democracy and its problems as a Prisoner's Dilemma situation. He focused, however, on only one level of the 'elements' versus the 'whole' conflict. I suggest that this conflict exists at every level, including the macro, the micro, and the institutional ones. Although Przeworski never mentioned the Prisoner's Dilemma overtly, in my opinion the findings included in Przeworski *et al.* (1999) and Przeworski *et al.* (2000) should be interpreted within the framework of the dilemma.
6. Like referendums on the future of the existing regime.
7. Arrow (1951).
8. For additional problems associated with voting procedures, see, for example, Felsenthal and Machover (1998) and Taylor (1995).
9. And those operating on their behalf.
10. And the Palestinian areas.
11. A critical yet more optimistic analysis is proposed, for example, by Dror (1997).
12. For a historical perspective, see, for example, Diskin (1980), Karsh (1999a).
13. See, for example, Sachar (1996).
14. After changes.
15. And the majority of the Jewish population.
16. While the lowest is among Christian Arabs.
17. Not including the children of immigrants who were born in Israel.
18. *Grundgesetz*.
19. *Sefer ha-Hukkim*, No. 1155 (7 Aug. 1985), p. 196.
20. *Sefer ha-Hukkim*, No. 1395 (9 April 1992).
21. Piskei Din, Vol. 19, Part 3, 1965.
22. Findings on the way Israel's Jews and Arabs perceive the enemy in recent years are presented in the following section.
23. See, for example, Sagie (1998). General Sagie served as the head of the military intelligence until the late 1990s.
24. See, for example, Karsh (1999b).
25. Differences of opinion between population groups and changes in positions in the late 1990s will be discussed below.
26. Peres with Naor (1993).

27. For the difficulty in belonging to the first camp, as faced by Egypt after 1978, see, for example, Diskin and Mishal (1981).
28. Compare, for example, with the data of the International Institute for Strategic Studies (2000).
29. Tal (1996).
30. For a historical survey of the developments since 1973, see, for example, Inbar (1998).
31. For internal party differences, see, for example, Diskin and Galnoor (1991).
32. The use of Spearman's correlation coefficient is more suitable than the Pearson coefficient when it comes to ordinal variables of the kind under discussion. As with the Pearson coefficients, results here vary between −1.00 'full negative correlation' and +1.00 'full positive correlation'.
33. Diskin (1991).
34. Abramson and Inglehart (1995) supply an important theoretical analysis and comparative data on similar issues.
35. The importance of political polarization was emphasized by many scholars. Most prominent is Sartori (1976; and also 1987 and 1994).
36. *Divrei ha'Knesset*, June 1950.
37. Basic Law: the Knesset.
38. Proclamation, Manifesto.
39. *Sefer ha'Hukkim*, No. 1155 (7 August 1985), p.195 (Original version 1958).
40. Most recently in a first reading in summer 2000.
41. See, for example, Gavison (1998).
42. See England (1991).
43. Which replaced the old Basic Law: the Government, of 1968.
44. *Sefer ha'Hukkim*, 1992.
45. *Sefer ha'Hukkim*, 1992, 1994. For the full text, see the appendix below.
46. Ibid.
47. Ibid.
48. The full text of the Declaration is quoted in the first appendix below.
49. It seems that the important background to the adoption of the 'direct elections' idea was the constant failure of those who actually preferred to change the Knesset electoral system. See, for example, Diskin and Diskin (1995) and Lijphart and Diskin (1989).
50. Bagehot (1857).
51. Bolivar (1819).
52. For additional historical and analytical perspectives, see, for example, Lijphart (1992).
53. Diskin (1995).
54. *Yedioth Ahronoth*, 8.11.1991, p. 21
55. Diskin and Diskin (1991), p. 11. See also Diskin and Diskin (1995).
56. *Yedioth Ahronoth*, 8.11.1991, p. 21.
57. *Sefer ha'Hukkim*, 1992.
58. This is the background to the requirement of an even greater majority to rescind the article, as set forth in the Attorney General's opinion mentioned above.
59. *Sefer ha'Hukkim*, 1992.
60. *Sefer ha'Hukkim*, 2001.
61. Ibid.
62. Ibid.
63. Ibid.
64. See, for example, Maor (1997). As far as the micro political level is concerned, it is interesting to compare the volatility of the Israeli voter with that of voters in other democracies. See, for example, Abramson and Inglehart (1995) and Miller and Shanks (1996).
65. For the impact of electoral systems under different conditions, see, for example, Lijphart (1994) and Smith (1990).
66. Laver and Schofield (1990) is one of the best modern surveys of both 'policy-distance' theories and practical behavior in multiparty systems. A modification of the 'closed (connected) coalition' theory, which improves predictive power considerably in most multiparty systems, was suggested by Diskin (2000).
67. For additional unique 'agenda' features, see, for example, Sachar (1996).

138   *The Last Days in Israel*

68. The Yemenite and Sephardi ethnic lists had three seats in 1951.
69. Over the issue of drafting women into the army.
70. Katz and Mair's (1995) general analysis is most relevant to the development of the Alignment, Gahal, and the Likud in Israel.
71. For the immediate impact of the war on domestic politics, see, for example, Pedatzur (1996).
72. But not Ben-Gurion, who had retired from political life.
73. Caspi *et al.* (1984).
74. Goldberg (1994).
75. For a comparative perspective, see, for example, Heidar and Koole (2000).
76. Better known as Lewis Carroll, author of *Alice's Adventure in Wonderland*.
77. Arrow (1951).
78. Abramson *et al.* (2001a, 2001b) focus on relevant questions in the Barak–Netanyahu–Mordechai race of the 1999 Prime Ministerial elections, and in strategic voting in these elections.
79. Downs (1957).
80. Hotelling (1929).
81. The theory of Downs is one of the most celebrated in modern political science. There are many impressive developments of his ideas. A good example for such elaboration is Gorfman (1993).
82. See, for example, Shamir and Shamir (1999) and Diskin (1991).
83. On the survival and durability of small governments, see, for example, Dodd (1976) and Warwick (1994).
84. Written by Yaakov Rotblit.
85. See, for example, Sachar (1996).
86. Pedatzur (1996).
87. The man charged with marking off unpopulated 'strips' in the occupied territories was Professor Yuval Ne'eman, who later became a leader of the extreme right-wing camp.
88. Bentsur (1997).
89. As in the matter of not seating Saib Erikat when he wore a Fatah-style *keffiyeh*.
90. It is interesting to compare the assessments of Arens (1995) and Shamir (1994) with those of Beilin (1997) and Savir (1998).
91. See, for example, Savir (1998) and Beilin (1997).
92. Beilin (1997).
93. With whom Beilin even met to keep things moving (Beilin, 1997).
94. On Rabin's latent ties with King Hussein, and on his national-security considerations, see, for example, Inbar (1999).
95. In the Land of Israel Movement.
96. See for this the letters appended to the Camp David Agreement of 1978.
97. Like the Third Way, which was founded mainly to oppose giving the Golan Heights back to Syria.
98. In a master's thesis in the framework of his academic studies.
99. Rabin (1979).
100. Usually Peres's assistant, Avi Gil, who currently serves in the 29th government as director general of the Ministry of Foreign Affairs.
101. Rabbi Toledano as Minister of Religious Affairs.
102. It should be pointed out that other ministers as well—Ehud Barak and Yaakov Tzur—were not MKs. The appointment of 'partisan' ministers who were not members of the Knesset had occurred a number of times in the past. The expedient of nonpartisan appointments was later adopted by Netanyahu when he—twice—appointed Professor Yaakov Ne'eman.
103. For the obvious intentions behind this nomination, see, for example, Kaspit and Kfir (1998).
104. Later it would be argued that the agreement greatly curtailed Israel's ability to operate in the security zone.
105. See the concluding part of Chapter 1 on 'Democracy, Jewishness, Security and Peace'.
106. See Taagapera and Shugart (1989).
107. Riker (1962).

108. The 'diagonal range' that fixed the upper and lower limits of the rate of exchange.
109. In the wake of a controversy about the costumes of dancers appearing in the country's 50th-anniversary celebrations.
110. This was unquestionably the most amusing saga of candidacy for the premiership in the country's history.
111. A thorough analysis of the sensitivities of the area is included in Shragai (1995).
112. See, for example, Karsh (1997).
113. For Netanyahu's stands on such issues prior to his election, see Netanyahu (1995, 1996).
114. Hazan and Diskin (2000).
115. Nonetheless, it should be emphasized that following the elections to the 14th Knesset the partners in the right-wing coalition and the Moledet list commanded 68 seats.
116. As we saw in a previous chapter.
117. And their number has in the meantime risen following changes since May 1999.
118. For comparison with previous Knessets, the *Who's Who in the Knesset* series (1993, 1996, 1999) is very useful.
119. My hypothesis is that the 'props proposition' is relevant to other multiparty parliamentary democracies. To the best of my knowledge, it has not been examined yet. (See, for example, Warwick, 1994.)
120. From a theoretical point of view, most relevant is the comparative research of Budge and Keman (1990).
121. Diskin and Hazan (2002).
122. Notwithstanding Barak's resignation and the election of Sharon.
123. For Sharon's previous stands, see, for instance, Sharon (1989).
124. Bank of Israel (2001).
125. Among the best introductions to game theory one should still count the pioneering von Neumann and Morgenstern (1944), and Luce and Raiffa (1957). One of the best introductions to the employment of the theory in the social sciences is Harsanyi (1977).
126. An opposite conclusion may derive from Rubinstein (1998).
127. Nash (1950).
128. Nash (1951).
129. There are a number of alternative 'solutions' to the bargaining problem. Felsenthal and Diskin (1982) proposed to modify the Pareto optimality demand, by substituting the 'conflict point' (the *status quo* point) by a 'minimum utility point'. Their solution tends to be by far more popular than the Nash solution in experimental environments.
130. Arrow (1951).
131. Many additional 'paradoxes' are mentioned in the literature. A useful introduction is that of Brams (1976).

Appendices

Appendix

Appendix i
The Declaration of the Establishment of the State of Israel

The Land of Israel (Eretz Yisrael) was the birthplace of the Jewish people. Here their spiritual, religious and political identity was shaped. Here they first attained to statehood, created cultural values of national and universal significance and gave to the world the eternal Book of Books.

After being forcibly exiled from their land, the people kept faith with it throughout their Dispersion and never ceased to pray and hope for their return to it and for the restoration in it of their political freedom.

Impelled by this historic and traditional attachment, Jews strove in every successive generation to re-establish themselves in their ancient homeland. In recent decades they returned in their masses. Pioneers, immigrants and defenders, they made deserts bloom, revived the Hebrew language, built villages and towns, and created a thriving community controlling its own economy and culture, loving peace but knowing how to defend itself, bringing the blessings of progress to all the country's inhabitants, and aspiring towards independent nationhood.

In the year 5657 (1897), at the summons of the spiritual father of the Jewish State, Theodore Herzl, the First Zionist Congress convened and proclaimed the right of the Jewish people to national rebirth in its own country.

This right was recognized in the *Balfour Declaration* of the 2nd November, 1917, and reaffirmed in the *Mandate of the League of Nations* which, in particular, gave international sanction to the historic connection between the Jewish people and the land of Israel and to the right of the Jewish people to rebuild its National Home.

The catastrophe which recently befell the Jewish people—the massacre of millions of Jews in Europe—was another clear demonstration of the urgency of solving the problem of its homelessness by re-establishing in the land of Israel the Jewish State, which would open the gates of the homeland wide to every Jew and confer upon the Jewish people the status of a fully privileged member of the comity of nations.

Survivors of the Nazi holocaust in Europe, as well as Jews from other parts of the world, continued to migrate to the land of Israel, undaunted by difficulties, restrictions and dangers, and never ceased to assert their right to a life of dignity, freedom and honest toil in their national homeland.

In the Second World War, the Jewish community of this country contributed its full share to the struggle of the freedom- and peace-loving nations against the forces of Nazi wickedness and, by the blood of its soldiers and its war effort, gained the right to be reckoned among the peoples who founded the United Nations.

On the 29th November, 1947, the United Nations General Assembly passed a resolution calling for the establishment of a Jewish State in the land of Israel; the General Assembly required the inhabitants of the land of Israel to take such steps as were necessary on their part for the implementation of that resolution. This recognition by the United Nations of the right of the Jewish people to establish their State is irrevocable.

This right is the natural right of the Jewish people to be masters of their own fate, like all other nations, in their own sovereign State.

Accordingly we, members of the People's Council, representatives of the Jewish community of the land of Israel and of the Zionist movement, are here assembled on the day of the termination of the British mandate over the land of Israel and, by virtue of our natural and historic right and on the strength of the resolution of the United Nations General Assembly, hereby declare the establishment of a Jewish state in the land of Israel, to be known as the State of Israel.

We declare that, with effect from the moment of the termination of the Mandate being tonight, the eve of Sabbath, the 6th Iyar, 5708 (15th May, 1948), until the establishment of the elected, regular authorities of the State in accordance with the Constitution which shall be adopted by the Elected Constituent Assembly not later than the 1st October 1948, the People's Council shall act as a Provisional Council of State, and its executive organ, the People's Administration, shall be the Provisional Government of the Jewish State, to be called 'Israel'.

The State of Israel will be open for Jewish immigration and for the Ingathering of the Exiles; it will foster the development of the country for the benefit of all its inhabitants; it will be based on freedom, justice and peace as envisaged by the prophets of Israel; it will ensure complete equality of social and political rights to all its inhabitants irrespective of religion, race or sex; it will guarantee freedom of religion, conscience, language, education and culture; it will safeguard the Holy Places of all religions; and it will be faithful to the principles of the Charter of the United Nations.

The State of Israel is prepared to cooperate with the agencies and representatives of the United Nations in implementing the resolution of the General Assembly of the 29th November, 1947, and will take steps to bring about the economic union of the whole of the land of Israel.

We appeal to the United Nations to assist the Jewish people in the building-up of its State and to receive the State of Israel into the comity of nations.

We appeal—in the very midst of the onslaught launched against us now for months—to the Arab inhabitants of the State of Israel to preserve peace and participate in the upbuilding of the State on the basis of full and equal citizenship and due representation in all its provisional and permanent institutions.

We extend our hand to all neighboring states and their peoples in an offer of peace and good neighborliness, and appeal to them to establish bonds of cooperation and mutual help with the sovereign Jewish people settled in its own land. The State of Israel is prepared to do its share in a common effort for the advancement of the entire Middle East.

We appeal to the Jewish people throughout the Diaspora to rally round the Jews of the land of Israel in the tasks of immigration and upbuilding and to stand by them in the great struggle for the realization of the age-old dream—the redemption of Israel.

Placing our trust in the rock of Israel, we affix our signatures to this proclamation at this session of the Provisional Council of State, on the soil of the homeland, in the city of Tel Aviv, on this Sabbath eve, the 5th day of Iyar, 5708 (14th May, 1948).

Appendix ii
Basic Law: Human Dignity and Freedom*

1a. Fundamental rights in Israel are founded on the recognition of the value of the human being, the sanctity of human life and the principle that all persons are free; these rights shall be upheld in the spirit of the principles set forth in the Declaration of the Establishment of the State of Israel.

1b. The purpose of the Basic Law is to protect human dignity and freedom, in order to establish in a basic law the values of the State of Israel as a Jewish and democratic state.

2. There shall be no violation of the life, body or dignity of any person as such.

3. There shall be no violation of the property of a person.

4. All persons are entitled to protection of their life, body and dignity.

5. There shall be no deprivation or restriction of the liberty of a person by imprisonment, arrest, extradition or otherwise.

6a. All persons are free to leave Israel.

6b. Every Israeli national has the right of entry into Israel from abroad.

7a. All persons have the right to privacy and to intimacy.

* The 1994 version.

7b. There shall be no entry into the private premises of a person who has not consented thereto.

7c. No search shall be conducted on the private premises of a person nor on his body or personal effects.

7d. There shall be no violation of the confidentiality of conversation or of the writings or records of a person.

8. There shall be no violation of rights under this Basic Law except by a law befitting the values of the State of Israel, enacted for a proper purpose, and to an extent no greater than is required or authorized.

9. There shall be no restriction of rights under this Basic Law held by persons serving in the Israel Defense Forces, the Israel Police, the Prisons Service and other security organizations of the State, nor shall such rights be subject to conditions except by virtue of a law, and to an extent no greater than is required by the nature and character of the service.

10. This Basic Law shall not affect the validity of any norm in force prior to the commencement of the Basic Law.

11. All government authorities are bound to respect the rights under this Basic Law.

12. This Basic Law cannot be varied, suspended or made subject to conditions by emergence regulations; notwithstanding, when a state of emergency exists, by virtue of a declaration under section 9 of the Law and Administration Ordinance, 5708 (1948), emergency regulations may be enacted by virtue of said section to deny or restrict rights under this Basic Law, provided the denial or restriction shall be for a proper purpose and for a period and extent no greater than is required.

Appendix iii
Basic Law: Freedom of Occupation*

1. Fundamental rights in Israel are founded on the recognition of the value of the human being, the sanctity of human life and the principle that all persons are free; these rights shall be upheld in the spirit of the principles set forth in the Declaration of the Establishment of the State of Israel.

2. The purpose of the Basic Law is to protect freedom of occupation, in order to establish in a Basic Law the values of the State of Israel as a Jewish and democratic state.

3. Every Israel national or resident has the right to engage in any occupation, profession or trade.

4. There shall be no violation of rights under this Basic Law except by a law befitting the values of the State of Israel, enacted for a proper purpose, and to an extent no greater than is required or authorized.

5. All governmental authorities are bound to respect the freedom of occupation of all Israeli nationals and residents.

6. This Basic Law cannot be varied, suspended or made subject to conditions by emergency regulations.

7. This Basic Law may not be amended except by a Basic Law passed by a majority of Knesset members.

* The 1994 version.

8. A provision of a law that violates freedom will be in effect though not in accordance with section 4 if it has been included in a law passed by a majority of the members of the Knesset which expressly states that it shall be in effect notwithstanding the provisions of this Basic Law; such a provision shall expire four years from its commencement unless a shorter duration has been stated therein.

9. Basic Law: Freedom of Occupation [1992] is hereby repealed.

10. The provisions of any enactment which, immediately prior to this Basic Law, would have been in effect but for this Basic Law or the Basic Law repealed in section 9, shall remain in effect two years from the commencement of this Basic Law, unless repealed earlier; however, such provisions shall be construed in the spirit of the provisions of this Basic Law.

Appendix iv
The Palestinian National Charter*

(AL-MITHAQ AL-WATANEE AL-PHILISTEENI)

Article 1: Palestine is the homeland of the Arab Palestinian people; it is an indivisible part of the greater Arab homeland, and the Palestinian people are an integral part of the Arab nation.

Article 2: Palestine, with the boundaries it had during the British Mandate, is an indivisible territorial unit.

Article 3: The Palestinian Arab people possess the legal right to their homeland and to self-determination after the completion of the liberation of their country in accordance with their wishes and entirely of their own accord and will.

Article 4: The Palestinian identity is a genuine, essential, and inherent characteristic; it is transmitted from fathers to children. The Zionist occupation and the dispersal of the Palestinian Arab people, through the disasters which befell them, do not make them lose their Palestinian identity and their membership in the Palestinian community, nor do they negate them.

Article 5: The Palestinians are those Arab nationals who, until 1947, normally resided in Palestine regardless of whether they were evicted from it or stayed there. Anyone born, after that date, of a Palestinian father—whether in Palestine or outside it—is also a Palestinian.

*The 1968 version.

Article 6: The Jews who had normally resided in Palestine until the beginning of the Zionist invasion are considered Palestinians.

Article 7: There is a Palestinian community and that it has material, spiritual, and historical connection with Palestine are indisputable facts. It is a national duty to bring up individual Palestinians in an Arab revolutionary manner. All means of information and education must be adopted in order to acquaint the Palestinian with his country in the most profound manner, both spiritual and material, that is possible. He must be prepared for the armed struggle and ready to sacrifice his wealth and his life in order to win back his homeland and bring about its liberation.

Article 8: The phase in their history, through which the Palestinian people are now living, is that of national (*watani*) struggle for the liberation of Palestine. Thus the conflicts among the Palestinian national forces are secondary, and should be ended for the sake of the basic conflict that exists between the forces of Zionism and of colonialism on the one hand, and the Palestinian Arab people on the other. On this basis the Palestinian masses, regardless of whether they are residing in the national homeland or in Diaspora (*mahajir*) constitute—both their organizations and the individuals—one national front working for the retrieval of Palestine and its liberation through armed struggle.

Article 9: Armed struggle is the only way to liberate Palestine. This is the overall strategy, not merely a tactical phase. The Palestinian Arab people assert their absolute determination and firm resolution to continue their armed struggle and to work for an armed popular revolution for the liberation of their country and their return to it. They also assert their right to normal life in Palestine and to exercise their right to self-determination and sovereignty over it.

Article 10: Commando (*Feday'ee*) action constitutes the nucleus of the Palestinian popular liberation war. This requires its escalation, comprehensiveness, and the mobilization of all the Palestinian popular and educational efforts and their organization and involvement in the armed Palestinian revolution. It also requires the achieving of unity for the national (*watani*) struggle among the different groupings of the Palestinian people, and between the Palestinian people and the Arab masses, so as to secure the continuation of the revolution, its escalation, and victory.

Article 11: Palestinians have three mottoes: national unity, national (*al-qawmiyya*) mobilization, and liberation.

Article 12: The Palestinian Arab people believe in Arab unity. In order to contribute their share toward the attainment of that objective, however, they must, at the present stage of their struggle, safeguard their Palestinian identity and develop their consciousness of that identity, oppose any plan that may dissolve or impair it.

Article 13: Arab unity and the liberation of Palestine are two complementary goals, the attainment of either of which facilitates the attainment of the other. Thus, Arab unity leads to the liberation of Palestine, the liberation of Palestine leads to Arab unity; and the work toward the realization of one objective proceeds side by side with work toward the realization of the other.

Article 14: The destiny of the Arab Nation, and indeed Arab existence itself, depend upon the destiny of the Palestinian cause. From this interdependence springs the Arab nation's pursuit of, and striving for, the liberation of Palestine. The people of Palestine play the role of the vanguard in the realization of this sacred (*qawmi*) goal.

Article 15: The liberation of Palestine, from an Arab viewpoint, is a national (*qawmi*) duty and it attempts to repel the Zionist and imperialist aggression against the Arab homeland, and aims at the elimination of Zionism in Palestine. Absolute responsibility for this falls upon the Arab nation—peoples and governments—with the Arab people of Palestine in the vanguard. Accordingly, the Arab nation must mobilize all its military, human, moral, and spiritual capabilities to participate actively with the Palestinian people in the liberation of Palestine. It must, particularly, in the phase of the armed Palestinian revolution, offer and furnish the Palestinian people with all possible help, and material and human support, and make available to them the means and opportunities that will enable them to continue to carry out their leading role in the armed revolution, until they liberate their homeland.

Article 16: The liberation of Palestine, from a spiritual viewpoint, will provide the Holy Land with an atmosphere of safety and tranquillity, which in turn will safeguard the country's religious sanctuaries and guarantee freedom of worship and of visit to all, without discrimination of race, color, language, or religion. Accordingly, the Palestinian people look to all spiritual forces in the world for support.

Article 17: The liberation of Palestine, from a human point of view, will restore to the Palestinian individual his dignity, pride, and freedom. Accordingly, the Palestinian Arab people look forward to the support of all those who believe in the dignity of man and his freedom in the world.

Article 18: The liberation of Palestine, from an international point of view, is a defensive action necessitated by the demands of self-defense. Accordingly, the Palestinian people, desirous as they are of the friendship of all people, look to freedom-loving and peace-loving states for support in order to restore their legitimate rights in Palestine, to re-establish peace and security in the country, and to enable its people to exercise national sovereignty and freedom.

Article 19: The partition of Palestine in 1947, and the establishment of the State of Israel are entirely illegal, regardless of the passage of time, because they were contrary to the will of the Palestinian people and their natural right in their homeland, and were inconsistent with the principles embodied in the Charter of the United Nations, particularly the right to self-determination.

Article 20: The Balfour Declaration, the Palestine Mandate, and everything that has been based on them, are deemed null and void. Claims of historical or religious ties of Jews with Palestine are incompatible with the facts of history and the conception of what constitutes statehood. Judaism, being a religion, is not an independent nationality. Nor do Jews constitute a single nation with an identity of their own; they are citizens of the states to which they belong.

Article 21: The Arab Palestinian people, expressing themselves by armed Palestinian revolution, reject all solutions which are substitutes for the total liberation of Palestine and reject all proposals aimed at the liquidation of the Palestinian cause, or at its internationalization.

Article 22: Zionism is a political movement organically associated with international imperialism and antagonistic to all action for liberation and to progressive movements in the world. It is racist and fanatic in its nature, aggressive, expansionist and colonial in its aims, and fascist in its methods. Israel is the instrument of the Zionist movement, and the geographical base for world imperialism placed strategically in the midst of the Arab homeland to combat the hopes of the Arab nation for liberation, unity, and progress. Israel is a constant source of threat *vis-à-vis* peace in the Middle East and the whole world. The liberation of Palestine will destroy the Zionist and imperialist presence and will contribute to the establishment of peace in the Middle East. That is why the Palestinian people look to the progressive and peaceful forces and urge them all, irrespective of their affiliations and beliefs, to offer the Palestinian people all aid and support in their just struggle for the liberation of their homeland.

Article 23: The demand of security and peace, as well as the demand of right and justice, require all states to consider Zionism an illegitimate movement, to outlaw its existence, and to ban its operations, in order that friendly relations among peoples may be preserved, and the loyalty of citizens to their respective homelands safeguarded.

Article 24: The Palestinian people believe in the principles of justice, freedom, sovereignty, self-determination, human dignity, and the right of peoples to exercise them.

Article 25: For the realization of the goals of this Charter and its principles, the Palestine Liberation Organization will perform its role in the liberation of Palestine.

Article 26: The Palestine Liberation Organization, the representative of the Palestinian revolutionary forces, is responsible for the Palestinian Arab peoples movement in its struggle—to retrieve its homeland, liberate and return to it and exercise the right to self-determination in it—in all military, political, and financial fields and also for whatever may be required by the Palestinian cause on the inter-Arab and international levels.

Article 27: The Palestine Liberation Organization shall cooperate with all Arab states, each according to its potentialities; and will adopt a neutral policy among them in light of the requirements of the battle of liberation; and on this basis does not interfere in the internal affairs of any Arab state.

Article 28: The Palestinian Arab people assert the genuineness and independence of their national revolution and reject all forms of intervention, trusteeship, and subordination.

Article 29: The Palestinian people possess the fundamental and genuine legal right to liberate and retrieve their homeland. The

Palestinian people determine their attitude toward all states and forces on the basis of the stands they adopt *vis-à-vis* the Palestinian revolution to fulfill the aims of the Palestinian people.

Article 30: Fighters and carriers of arms in the war of liberation are the nucleus of the popular army, which will be the protective force for the gains of the Palestinian Arab people.

Article 31: This Organization shall have a flag, an oath of allegiance, and an anthem. All this shall be decided upon in accordance with a special law.

Article 32: A law, known as the Basic Statute of the Palestine Liberation Organization, shall be annexed to this Covenant. It will lay down the manner in which the Organization, and its organs and institutions, shall be constituted; the respective competence of each; and the requirements of its obligation under the Charter.

Article 33: This Charter shall not be amended save by [vote of] a majority of two-thirds of the total membership of the National Council of the Palestine Liberation Organization [taken] at a special session convened for that purpose.

Appendix v
Declaration of Principles on Interim Self-Government Arrangements*

The Government of the State of Israel and the PLO team (in the Jordanian–Palestinian delegation to the Middle East Peace Conference) (the 'Palestinian Delegation'), representing the Palestinian people, agree that it is time to put an end to decades of confrontation and conflict, recognize their mutual legitimate and political rights, and strive to live in peaceful coexistence and mutual dignity and security and achieve a just, lasting and comprehensive peace settlement and historic reconciliation through the agreed political process. Accordingly, the, two sides agree to the following principles:

ARTICLE I: AIM OF THE NEGOTIATIONS

The aim of the Israeli–Palestinian negotiations within the current Middle East peace process is, among other things, to establish a Palestinian Interim Self-Government Authority, the elected Council (the 'Council'), for the Palestinian people in the West Bank and the Gaza Strip, for a transitional period not exceeding five years, leading to a permanent settlement based on Security Council Resolutions 242 and 338.

It is understood that the interim arrangements are an integral part of the whole peace process and that the negotiations on the permanent

* The 'Oslo I' agreement. Signed in Washington, DC, 13 September 1993.

status will lead to the implementation of Security Council Resolutions 242 and 338.

ARTICLE II: FRAMEWORK FOR THE INTERIM PERIOD

The agreed framework for the interim period is set forth in this Declaration of Principles.

ARTICLE III: ELECTIONS

1. In order that the Palestinian people in the West Bank and Gaza Strip may govern themselves according to democratic principles, direct, free and general political elections will be held for the Council under agreed supervision and international observation, while the Palestinian police will ensure public order.

2. An agreement will be concluded on the exact mode and conditions of the elections in accordance with the protocol attached as Annex I, with the goal of holding the elections not later than nine months after the entry into force of this Declaration of Principles.

3. These elections will constitute a significant interim preparatory step toward the realization of the legitimate rights of the Palestinian people and their just requirements.

ARTICLE IV: JURISDICTION

Jurisdiction of the Council will cover West Bank and Gaza Strip territory, except for issues that will be negotiated in the permanent status negotiations. The two sides view the West Bank and the Gaza Strip as a single territorial unit, whose integrity will be preserved during the interim period.

ARTICLE V: TRANSITIONAL PERIOD AND PERMANENT STATUS NEGOTIATIONS

1. The five-year transitional period will begin upon the withdrawal from the Gaza Strip and Jericho area.

2. Permanent status negotiations will commence as soon as possible, but not later than the beginning of the third year of the interim period, between the Government of Israel and the Palestinian people representatives.

3. It is understood that these negotiations shall cover remaining issues, including: Jerusalem, refugees, settlements, security arrangements, borders, relations and cooperation with other neighbors, and other issues of common interest.

4. The two parties agree that the outcome of the permanent status negotiations should not be prejudiced or preempted by agreements reached for the interim period.

ARTICLE VI: PREPARATORY TRANSFER OF POWERS AND RESPONSIBILITIES

1. Upon the entry into force of this Declaration of Principles and the withdrawal from the Gaza Strip and the Jericho area, a transfer of authority from the Israeli military government and its Civil Administration to the authorised Palestinians for this task, as detailed herein, will commence. This transfer of authority will be of a preparatory nature until the inauguration of the Council.

2. Immediately after the entry into force of this Declaration of Principles and the withdrawal from the Gaza Strip and Jericho area, with the view to promoting economic development in the West Bank and Gaza Strip, authority will be transferred to the Palestinians in the following spheres: education and culture, health, social welfare, direct taxation, and tourism. The Palestinian side will commence in building the Palestinian police force, as agreed upon. Pending the inauguration of the Council, the two parties may negotiate the transfer of additional powers and responsibilities, as agreed upon.

ARTICLE VII: INTERIM AGREEMENT

1. The Israeli and Palestinian delegations will negotiate an agreement on the interim period (the 'Interim Agreement').

2. The Interim Agreement shall specify, among other things, the

structure of the Council, the number of its members, and the transfer of powers and responsibilities from the Israeli military government and its Civil Administration to the Council. The Interim Agreement shall also specify the Council's executive authority, legislative authority in accordance with Article IX below, and the independent Palestinian judicial organs.

3. The Interim Agreement shall include arrangements, to be implemented upon the inauguration of the Council, for the assumption by the Council of all of the powers and responsibilities transferred previously in accordance with Article VI above.

4. In order to enable the Council to promote economic growth, upon its inauguration, the Council will establish, among other things, a Palestinian Electricity Authority, a Gaza Sea Port Authority, a Palestinian Development Bank, a Palestinian Export Promotion Board, a Palestinian Environmental Authority, a Palestinian Land Authority and a Palestinian Water Administration Authority, and any other Authorities agreed upon, in accordance with the Interim Agreement that will specify their powers and responsibilities.

5. After the inauguration of the Council, the Civil Administration will be dissolved, and the Israeli military government will be withdrawn.

ARTICLE VIII: PUBLIC ORDER AND SECURITY

In order to guarantee public order and internal security for the Palestinians of the West Bank and the Gaza Strip, the Council will establish a strong police force, while Israel will continue to carry the responsibility for defending against external threats, as well as the responsibility for overall security of Israelis for the purpose of safeguarding their internal security and public order.

ARTICLE IX: LAWS AND MILITARY ORDERS

1. The Council will be empowered to legislate, in accordance with the Interim Agreement, within all authorities transferred to it.

2. Both parties will review jointly laws and military orders presently in force in remaining spheres.

ARTICLE X: JOINT ISRAELI-PALESTINIAN LIAISON COMMITTEE

In order to provide for a smooth implementation of this Declaration of Principles and any subsequent agreements pertaining to the interim period, upon the entry into force of this Declaration of Principles, a Joint Israeli–Palestinian Liaison Committee will be established in order to deal with issues requiring coordination, other issues of common interest, and disputes.

ARTICLE XI: ISRAELI-PALESTINIAN COOPERATION IN ECONOMIC FIELDS

Recognizing the mutual benefit of cooperation in promoting the development of the West Bank, the Gaza Strip and Israel, upon the entry into force of this Declaration of Principles, an Israeli–Palestinian Economic Cooperation Committee will be established in order to develop and implement in a cooperative manner the programs identified in the protocols attached as Annex III and Annex IV.

ARTICLE XII: LIAISON AND COOPERATION WITH JORDAN AND EGYPT

The two parties will invite the Governments of Jordan and Egypt to participate in establishing further liaison and cooperation arrangements between the Government of Israel and the Palestinian representatives, on the one hand, and the Governments of Jordan and Egypt, on the other hand, to promote cooperation between them. These arrangements will include the constitution of a Continuing Committee that will decide by agreement on the modalities of admission of persons displaced from the West Bank and Gaza Strip in 1967, together with necessary measures to prevent disruption and disorder. Other matters of common concern will be dealt with by this Committee.

ARTICLE XIII: REDEPLOYMENT OF ISRAELI FORCES

1. After the entry into force of this Declaration of Principles, and not later than the eve of elections for the Council, a redeployment of

Israeli military forces in the West Bank and the Gaza Strip will take place, in addition to withdrawal of Israeli forces carried out in accordance with Article XIV.

2. In redeploying its military forces, Israel will be guided by the principle that its military forces should be redeployed outside populated areas.

3. Further redeployments to specified locations will be gradually implemented commensurate with the assumption of responsibility for public order and internal security by the Palestinian police force pursuant to Article VIII above.

ARTICLE XIV: ISRAELI WITHDRAWAL FROM THE GAZA STRIP AND JERICHO AREA

Israel will withdraw from the Gaza Strip and Jericho area, as detailed in the protocol attached as Annex II.

ARTICLE XV: RESOLUTION OF DISPUTES

1. Disputes arising out of the application or interpretation of this Declaration of Principles, or any subsequent agreements pertaining to the interim period, shall be resolved by negotiations through the Joint Liaison Committee to be established pursuant to Article X above.

2. Disputes which cannot be settled by negotiations may be resolved by a mechanism of conciliation to be agreed upon by the parties.

3. The parties may agree to submit to arbitration disputes relating to the interim period, which cannot be settled through conciliation. To this end, upon the agreement of both parties, the parties will establish an Arbitration Committee.

ARTICLE XVI: ISRAELI-PALESTINIAN COOPERATION CONCERNING REGIONAL PROGRAMS

Both parties view the multilateral working groups as an appropriate instrument for promoting a 'Marshall Plan', the regional programs and other programs, including special programs for the West Bank and Gaza Strip, as indicated in the protocol attached as Annex IV.

ARTICLE XVII: MISCELLANEOUS PROVISIONS

1. This Declaration of Principles will enter into force one month after its signing.

2. All protocols annexed to this Declaration of Principles and Agreed Minutes pertaining thereto shall be regarded as an integral part hereof.

Appendix vi
Report of the Sharm el-Sheikh Fact-Finding Committee*

SUMMARY OF RECOMMENDATIONS

The Government of Israel (GOI) and the Palestinian Authority (PA) must act swiftly and decisively to halt the violence. Their immediate objectives then should be to rebuild confidence and resume negotiations.

During this mission our aim has been to fulfill the mandate agreed at Sharm el-Sheikh. We value the support given our work by the participants at the summit, and we commend the parties for their cooperation. Our principal recommendation is that they recommit themselves to the Sharm el-Sheikh spirit and that they implement the decisions made there in 1999 and 2000. We believe that the summit participants will support bold action by the parties to achieve these objectives.

The restoration of trust is essential, and the parties should take affirmative steps to this end. Given the high level of hostility and mistrust, the timing and sequence of these steps is obviously crucial. This can be decided only by the parties. We urge them to begin the process of decision-making immediately.

Accordingly, we recommend that steps be taken to:

---

* The 'Mitchell Report' of 30 April 2001.

End the Violence

The GOI and the PA should reaffirm their commitment to existing agreements and undertakings and should immediately implement an unconditional cessation of violence. The GOI and PA should immediately resume security cooperation.

Rebuild Confidence

The PA and GOI should work together to establish a meaningful 'cooling off period' and implement additional confidence building measures, some of which were detailed in the October 2000 Sharm el-Sheikh Statement and some of which were offered by the US on January 7, 2001 in Cairo.

The PA and GOI should resume their efforts to identify, condemn and discourage incitement in all its forms.

The PA should make clear through concrete action to Palestinians and Israelis alike that terrorism is reprehensible and unacceptable, and that the PA will make a 100 percent effort to prevent terrorist operations and to punish perpetrators. This effort should include immediate steps to apprehend and incarcerate terrorists operating within the PA's jurisdiction.

The GOI should freeze all settlement activity, including the 'natural growth' of existing settlements.

The GOI should ensure that the IDF adopt and enforce policies and procedures encouraging non-lethal responses to unarmed demonstrators, with a view to minimizing casualties and friction between the two communities.

The PA should prevent gunmen from using Palestinian populated areas to fire upon Israeli populated areas and IDF positions. This tactic places civilians on both sides at unnecessary risk.

The GOI should lift closures, transfer to the PA all tax revenues owed, and permit Palestinians who had been employed in Israel to return to their jobs; and should ensure that security forces and settlers refrain from the destruction of homes and roads, as well as trees and other agricultural property in Palestinian areas. We acknowledge the GOI's position that actions of this nature have been taken for security reasons. Nevertheless, the economic effects will persist for years.

The PA should renew cooperation with Israeli security agencies to ensure, to the maximum extent possible, that Palestinians workers employed within Israel are fully vetted and free of connections to organizations and individuals engaged in terrorism.

The PA and GOI should consider a joint undertaking to preserve and protect holy places sacred to the traditions of Jews, Muslims, and Christians.

The GOI and PA should jointly endorse and support the work of Palestinian and Israeli non-governmental organizations involved in cross-community initiatives linking the two peoples.

Resume Negotiations

In the spirit of the Sharm el-Sheikh agreements and understandings of 1999 and 2000, we recommend that the parties meet to reaffirm their commitment to signed agreements and mutual understandings, and take corresponding action. This should be the basis for resuming full and meaningful negotiations.

Appendix vii
Palestinian-Israeli Security Implementation Work Plan*

The security organizations of the Government of Israel (GOI) and of the Palestinian Authority (PA) reaffirm their commitment to the security agreements forged at Sharm el-Sheikh in October 2000, embedded in the Mitchell Report of April 2001.

The operational premise of the work plan is that the two sides are committed to a mutual, comprehensive cease-fire, applying to all violent activities, in accordance with the public declaration of both leaders. In addition, the joint security committee referenced in this work plan will resolve issues that may arise during the implementation of this work plan.

The security organizations of the GOI and PA agree to initiate the following specific, concrete, and realistic security steps immediately to reestablish security cooperation and the situation on the ground that existed prior to 28 September.

1. **The GOI and the PA will immediately resume security cooperation.**

A senior-level meeting of Israeli, Palestinian, and US security officials will be held immediately and will reconvene at least once a week, with mandatory participation by designated senior officials.

Israeli–Palestinian District Coordination Offices (DCOs) will be reinvigorated. They will carry out their daily activities, to the

---

* The 'Tenet Plan' of 14 June 2001.

maximum extent possible, according to the standards established prior to September 28, 2000. As soon as the security situation permits, barriers to effective cooperation—which include the erection of walls between the Israeli and Palestinian sides—will be eliminated and joint Israeli–Palestinian patrols will be reinitiated.

US-supplied video conferencing systems will be provided to senior-level Israeli and Palestinian officials to facilitate frequent dialogue and security cooperation.

2. **Both sides will take immediate measures to enforce strict adherence to the declared cease-fire and to stabilize the security environment.**

Specific procedures will be developed by the senior-level security committee to ensure the secure movement of GOI and PA security personnel travelling in areas outside their respective control, in accordance with existing agreements.

Israel will not conduct attacks of any kind against the Palestinian Authority Ra'is facilities: the headquarters of Palestinian security, intelligence, and police organization; or prisons in the West Bank and Gaza.

The PA will move immediately to apprehend, question, and incarcerate terrorists in the West Bank and Gaza and will provide the security committee the names of those arrested as soon as they are apprehended, as well as a readout of actions taken.

Israel will release all Palestinians arrested in security sweeps who have no association with terrorist activities.

In keeping with its unilateral cease-fire declaration, the PA will stop any Palestinian security officials from inciting, aiding, abetting, or conducting attacks against Israeli targets, including settlers.

In keeping with Israel's unilateral cease-fire declaration, Israeli forces will not conduct 'proactive' security operations in areas under the control of the PA or attack innocent civilian targets.

The GOI will re-institute military police investigations into Palestinian deaths resulting from Israel Defense Forces actions in the West Bank and Gaza in incidents not involving terrorism.

3. **Palestinian and Israeli security officials will use the security committee to provide each other, as well as designated U.S. officials, information on terrorist threats, including information on known or suspected terrorist operation in—or moving to—areas under the other's control.**

Legitimate terrorist and terror threat information will be acted upon immediately, with follow-up actions and results reported to the security committee.

The PA will undertake preemptive operations against terrorists, terrorist safe houses, arms depots, and mortar factories. The PA will provide regular progress reports of these actions to the security committee.

Israeli authorities will take action against Israeli citizens inciting, carrying out, or planning to carry out violence against Palestinians, with progress reports on these activities provided to the security committee.

4. **The PA and GOI will move aggressively to prevent individuals and groups from using areas under their respective control to carry out acts of violence. In addition, both sides will take steps to ensure that areas under their control will not be used to launch attacks against the other side nor be used as refuge after attacks are staged.**

The security committee will identify key flash points, and each side will inform the other of the names of senior security personnel responsible for each flash point.

Joint Standard Operating Procedures (SOPs) will be developed for each flash point. These SOPs will address how the two sides handle and respond to security incidents; the mechanisms for emergency contact; and the procedures to deescalate security crises.

Palestinian and Israeli security officials will identify and agree to the practical measures needed to enforce 'no demonstration zones' and 'buffer zones' around flash points to reduce opportunities for confrontation. Both sides will adopt all necessary measures to prevent riots and to control demonstrations, particularly in flash-point areas.

Palestinian and Israeli security officials will make a concerted effort to locate and confiscate illegal weapons, including mortars, rockets, and explosives, in areas under their respective control. In addition, intensive efforts will be made to prevent smuggling and illegal production of weapons. Each side will inform the security committee of the status and success of these efforts.

The Israeli Defense Forces (IDF) will adopt additional non-lethal measures to deal with Palestinian crowds and demonstrators, and more generally, seek to minimize the danger to lives and property of Palestinian civilians in responding to violence.

5. **The GOI and the PA, through the auspices of the senior-level security committee, will forge—within one week of the commencement of security committee meetings and resumption of security cooperation—an agreed-upon schedule to implement the complete redeployment of IDF forces to positions held before September 28, 2000.**

Demonstrable on-the-ground redeployment will be initiated within the first 48 hours of this one-week period and will continue while the schedule is being forged.

6. **Within one week of the commencement of security committee meetings and resumption of security cooperation, a specific timeline will be developed for the lifting of internal closures as well as for the reopening of internal roads, the Allenby Bridge, Gaza Airport, the Port of Gaza, and border crossings. Security checkpoints will be minimized according to legitimate security requirements and following consultation between the two sides.**

Demonstrable on-the-ground actions on the lifting of the closures will be initiated within the first 48 hours of this one-week period and will continue while the timeline is being developed.

The parties pledge that even if untoward events occur, security cooperation will continue through the joint security committee.

The parties pledge that even if untoward events occur, security cooperation will continue through the joint security committee.

Appendix viii
Basic Profiles of Israel, Gaza Strip, West Bank, and Selected Middle Eastern Countries*

	Area (sq. km.)	Population (millions)	Density (population per sq. km.)	GDP (purchasing power parity—billion $)	GDP per capita (purchasing power parity—$)	Literacy (% of population over 15)	Life Expectancy (at birth—years)
Israel	20,770	5.9	286	110	18,900	95	79
West Bank	5,860	2.1	358	3	1,500	(90)	73
Gaza Strip	360	1.2	3,300	1	1,000	(90)	71
Egypt	1,001,450	69.5	69	247	3,600	51	64
Iran	1,648,000	66.1	40	413	6,300	72	70
Iraq	437,032	23.3	53	57	2,500	58	67
Jordan	92,300	5.1	56	17	3,500	87	78
Libya	1,759,540	5.2	3	45	8,900	76	76
Saudi Arabia	1,960,582	22.8	12	232	10,500	63	68
Syria	185,180	16.7	88	51	3,100	71	68

*2000 and 2001 estimates based on the CIA World Fact Book web site (January 2002).

Appendix ix
Knesset Elections: 1949–99

Constituent										
Assembly 25.1.1949 (First Knesset)	Maki 4	Mapam 19		Mapai 46	Minorities 2	Progressive Party 5	General Zionists 7	Herut 14	Religious Front 16	Sephardies-4 Yemenites-1 Fighters-1 WIZO-1
Second Knesset 30.7.1951	Maki 5	Mapam 15		Mapai 45	Minorities 5	Progressive Party 4	General Zionists 20	Herut 8	Ha-Poel ha-Mizrachi 8 Hamizrachi 2	Poalei Aguda 2 Agudat Israel 3 Sephardies-2 Yemenites-1
Third Knesset 26.7.1955	Maki 6	Mapam 9	Ahdut ha-Avodah 10	Mapai 40	Minorities 5	Progressive Party 5	General Zionists 13	Herut 15	National Religious Front 11	Torah Front 6
Fourth Knesset 3.11.59	Maki 3	Mapam 9	Ahdut ha-Avodah 7	Mapai 47	Minorities 5	Progressive Party 6	General Zionists 8	Herut 17	Mafdal 12	Torah Front 6
Fifth Knesset 15.8.1961	Maki 5	Mapam 9	Ahdut ha-Avodah 8	Mapai 42	Minorities 4	Liberal Party 17		Herut 17	Mafdal 12	Poalei Aguda 2 Agudat Israel 4
Sixth Knesset 2.11.1965	Rakah 3	Maki 1	Ha-Olam ha-Zeh 1	Mapam Alignment 8 45	Minorities 4		Rafi 10	Independent Liberals 5	Gahal 26	Mafdal 11	Poalei Aguda 2 Agudat Israel 4

172 The Last Days in Israel

Appendix ix continued

Seventh Knesset 28.10.1969	Rakah 3	Maki 1	Ha-Olam ha-Zeh 2	Alignment 56	Minorities 4	State List 4	Independent Liberals 4	Gahal 26	Free Center 2		Mafdal 12	Poalei Aguda 2	Agudat Israel 4		
Eighth Knesset 31.12.1973	Rakah 4	Moked 1	Ratz 3	Alignment 51	Minorities 3	Independent Liberals 4	Likud 39	Mafdal 10		Torah Front 5					
Ninth Knesset 17.5.1977	Hadash 5	Sheli 2	Ratz 1	Alignment 32	Minorities 1	Dash 15	Independent Liberals 1	Likud 43	Shlomzion 2		Mafdal 12	Poalei Aguda 1	Agudat Israel 4	Flato Sharon 1	
Tenth Knesset 30.6.1981	Hadash 4	Ratz 1	Alignment 47	Shinui 2	Telem 2	Likud 48	Tehiyyah 3	Tami 3	Mafdal 6				Agudat Israel 4		
Eleventh Knesset 23.7.1984	Hadash 4	Progressive List 2	Ratz 3	Alignment 44	Shinui 3	Yahad 3	Ometz 1	Likud 41	Tehiyyah Tzomet 5		Tami 1	Mafdal 4	Morasha 2	Agudat Israel 2	Shas 4	Kach 1
Twelfth Knesset 1.11.1988	Hadash 4	Mada 1	Progressive 1	Ratz 5	Mapam 3	Alignment 39	Shinui 2	Likud 40	Tehiyyah 3		Tzomet 2	Moledet 2	Mafdal 5	Degel ha-Torah 2	Agudat Israel 5	Shas 6
Thirteenth Knesset 23.6.1992	Hadash 3	Mada 2	Meretz 12	Labor 44				Likud 32	Tzomet 8		Moledet 3	Mafdal 6	Yahadut ha-Torah 4	Shas 6	
Fourteenth Knesset 29.5.1996	Hadash Balad 5	Mada Ra'am 4	Meretz 9	Labor 34	Third Way 4	Yisrael ba-Aliyah 7		Likud Gesher-Tzomet 32	Moledet 2		Mafdal 9	Yahadut ha-Torah 4	Shas 10		
Fifteenth Knesset 17.5.1999	Hadash 3	Balad 2	Ra'am 5	Meretz 10	One Israel 26	Shinui 6	One Nation 2	Center 6	Yisrael ba-Aliyah 6		Yisrael Beitenu 4	Likud 19	National Unity 4	Mafdal 5	Yahadut ha-Torah 5	Shas 17

Appendix x
The Governments of Israel: 1949–2002

Knesset	Government Number	Date of Investiture	Prime Minister	Political Parties at Formation	Reason for End of Term
First	1	9.3.1949	Ben-Gurion	Mapai, Religious Front, Progressive Party, Sephardi List, Minorities	Resignation of the Prime Minister
	2	30.10.1950	Ben-Gurion	Mapai, Religious Front, Progressive Party, Sephardi List, Minorities	Resignation of the Government and Elections
	3	7.10.1951	Ben-Gurion	Mapai, Ha-Poel ha-Mizrachi, Mizrachi, Agudat Israel, Poalei, Agudat Israel, Minorities	Resignation of the Prime Minister
	4	23.12.1952	Ben-Gurion	Mapai, General Zionists, Ha-Poel ha-Mizrachi, Mizrachi, Progressive Party, Minorities	Resignation of the Prime Minister
	5	26.1.1954	Sharet	Mapai, General Zionists, Ha-Poel ha-Mizrachi, Mizrachi, Progressive Party, Minorities	Resignation of the Prime Minister
Second	6	29.6.1955	Sharet	Mapai, Ha-Poel ha-Mizrachi, Mizrachi, Progressive Party, Minorities	Elections

Appendix x continued

Knesset	Government Number	Date of Investiture	Prime Minister	Political Parties at Formation	Reason for End of Term
Third	7	3.11.1955	Ben-Gurion	Mapai, Mafdal, Ahdut ha-Avodah, Mapam, Progressive Party, Minorities	Resignation of the Prime Minister
	8	7.1.1958	Ben-Gurion	Mapai, Mafdal, Ahdut ha-Avodah, Mapam, Progressive Party, Minorities	Elections
Fourth	9	16.12.1959	Ben-Gurion	Mapai, Mafdal, Ahdut ha-Avodah, Mapam, Progressive Party, Minorities	Resignation of the Prime Minister and Elections
Fifth	10	2.11.1961	Ben-Gurion	Mapai, Mafdal, Ahdut ha-Avodah, Poalei Agudat Israel, Minorities	Resignation of the Prime Minister
	11	24.6.1963	Eshkol	Mapai, Mafdal, Ahdut ha-Avodah, Poalei Agudat Israel, Minorities	Resignation of the Prime Minister
	12	22.12.1964	Eshkol	Mapai, Mafdal, Ahdut ha-Avodah, Poalei Agudat Israel, Minorities	Elections
Sixth	13	12.1.1966	Eshkol	Alignment, Mafdal, Mapam, Independent Liberals, Poalei Agudat Israel, Minorities	Death of the Prime Minister
	14	17.3.1969	Meir	Labor, Mapam, Gahal, Mafdal, Independent Liberals, Poalei Agudat Israel, Minorities	Elections
Seventh	15	15.12.1969	Meir	Alignment, Gahal, Mafdal, Independent Liberals, Minorities	Elections
Eighth	16	10.3.1974	Meir	Alignment, Mafdal, Independent Liberals, Minorities	Resignation of the Prime Minister
	17	3.6.1974	Rabin	Alignment, Independent Liberals, Ratz, Minorities	Resignation of the Prime Minister and Elections
Ninth	18	20.6.1977	Begin	Likud, Madal, Agudat Israel	Elections

Appendix x continued

Knesset	Government Number	Date of Investiture	Prime Minister	Political Parties at Formation	Reason for End of Term
Tenth	19	5.8.1981	Begin	Likud, Madal, Agudat Israel, Tami	Resignation of the Prime Minister
	20	10.10.1983	Shamir	Likud, Madal, Agudat Israel, Tami, Tehiyya	Resignation of the Prime Minister and Elections
Eleventh	21	13.9.1984	Peres	Labor, Likud, Mafdal, Yahad, Shas, Morasha, Agudat Israel, Shinui, Ometz	Resignation of the Prime Minister ('Rotation')
	22	21.10.1986	Shamir	Labor, Likud, Mafdal, Yahad, Shas, Morasha, Agudat Israel, Shinui, Ometz	Elections
Twelfth	23	22.12.1988	Shamir	Likud, Labor, Shas, Mafdal, Agudat Israel	Vote of No Confidence
	24	11.6.1990	Shamir	Likud, Mafdal, Shas, Tehiyya, Tzomet, Moledet, The Zionist Idea, Degel ha-Torah, Agudat Israel	Resignation of the Prime Minister and Elections
Thirteenth	25	12.7.1992	Rabin	Labor, Meretz, Shas	Assassination of the Prime Minister
Fourteenth	26	22.11.1995	Peres	Labor, Meretz, Yi'ud	Elections
	27	17.6.1996	Netanyahu	Likud, Gesher, Tzomet, Shas, Mafdal, Yisrael ba-Aliyah, Third Way	Resignation of the Prime Minister and Elections
Fifteenth	28	6.7.1999	Barak	One Israel, Meretz, Yisrael ba-Aliyah, Center Party, Shas, Mafdal, Yahadut ha-Torah	Resignation of the Prime Minister
	29	7.3.2001	Sharon	One Israel, Likud, Shas, National Unity-Yisrael Beitenu, Yisrael ba-Aliyah, One Nation	Resignation of the Prime Minister and 'Special' Elections

Bibliography

Abramson, P., Aldrich, J.H., Diamond, M. *et al.* 'Prime Minister and Parliament: Strategic Split Ticket Voting', paper presented at the 2001 Annual Meeting of the American Political Science Association (2001).

Abramson, P., Aldrich, J.H., Diamond, M. *et al.* 'Strategic Abandonment or Sincerely Second Best? Strategic Voting in the 1999 Israeli Election', paper presented at the 2001 annual meeting of the Midwest Political Science Association (2001).

Abramson, P. R. and Inglehart, R., *Value Change in Global Perspective* (Ann Arbor, MI: Michigan University Press, 1995).

Arens, M., *Broken Covenant*, (Tel Aviv: Yedioth Ahronoth, 1995) [Hebrew].

Arrow, K.J., (1951), *Social Choice and Individual Values* (New York, NY: Wiley, 1951).

Axelrod, R., 'An Evolutionary Approach to Norms', *American Political Science Review*, 80, 4, (1987) pp. 1095–112.

Axelrod, R., *The Complexity of Cooperation: Agent-Based Models of Competition and Collaboration* (Princeton, NJ: Princeton University Press, 1997).

Axelrod, R., *The Evolution of Cooperation* (New York, NY: Basic Books, 1984).

Bagehot, W., *The English Constitution* (London: Chapman and Hall (in Lijphart, 1992), 1857).

Bank of Israel, *Annual Reports 1990–2001* (Jerusalem) [Hebrew].

Beilin, Y., *Touching Peace*, (Tel Aviv: Miskal-Yedioth Ahronoth Books/Chemed Books, 1997) [Hebrew].

Bentsur, E., *The Road to Peace Crosses Madrid* (Tel Aviv: Miskal-Yedioth Ahronoth Books/Chemed Books, 1997) [Hebrew].

Bolivar, S., 'Address Delivered at the Inauguration of the Second National Congress of Venezuela in Angostura' (1819) (in Lijphart, 1992).

Brams, S., *Paradoxes in Politics: An Introduction to the Nonobvious in Political Science* (New York, NY: The Free Press, 1976).

Budge, I., and Keman, H., *Parties and Democracy: Coalition Formation and Government Functioning in Twenty States* (Oxford: Oxford University Press, 1990).

Caspi, D., Diskin, A., and Gutmann, E. (eds), *The Roots of Begin's Success* (London: Croom Helm/New York: St Martin's Press, 1984).

Central Bureau of Statistics, *Statistical Abstract of Israel, 1990–2001*, (Jerusalem: Central Bureau of Statistics, 1990–2001).

Central Bureau of Statistics, *Statistical Abstract of Israel 1995–2000*, (Jerusalem: Central Bureau of Statistics, 1995–2000).

Cohen, Y., *Radicals, Reformers, and Reactionaries: The Prisoner's Dilemma and the Collapse of Democracy in Latin America* (Chicago, IL: Chicago University Press, 1994).

Cox, G.W., 'Centripetal and Centrifugal Incentives in Electoral Systems', *American Journal of Political Science*, 34, 4, (1990) pp. 903–35.

Data supplied by the Knesset Archive, the Central Election Committee, the Register of Parties and the Secretary of the Government.

Diskin, A., *Das Politische System Israels: Eine Raumlich-Zeitliche Untersuchung 1949–1973* (Koln/Wien: Bohlau, 1980).

Diskin, A., *Elections and Voters in Israel* (New York, NY: Praeger, 1991).

Diskin, A., *The Courage to Repent before the Fall* (Jerusalem: Movement for Better Government, 1995).

Diskin, A., 'Rethinking De Swaan (1973): A Note on Closed Coalitions, Uni-dimentionality and the Role of Sectarian Political Parties', in Hazan, R.Y. and Maor, M., *Parties, Elections and Cleavages: Israel in Comparative Perspective* (London: Frank Cass, 2000), pp. 141–7; also published in *Israel Affairs*, 6, 2 (1999), pp. 141–7.

Diskin, A., 'Israel', *European Journal of Political Research (Political Data Yearbook 1992–2001)* (Dordrecht: Kluwer, 1992–2001).

Diskin, A., 'The New Political System of Israel', *Government and Opposition*, 34, 4, (Autumn 1999), pp. 498–515

Diskin, A. and Diskin H., 'The Coming Power of the Small Parties', in *First Analysis of the New Version of Basic Law: the Government* (Jerusalem: Jerusalem Institute for Israel Studies, 1991).

Diskin, A. and Galnoor, I., 'Political Distances between Individual Parliament Members and Coalition Behaviour', *Political Studies*, 27, 4, (1991), pp. 710–17.

Diskin, A. and Hazan, R., 'The 2001 Prime Ministerial Elections in Israel', *Electoral Studies*, 21, 4 (December 2002).

Diskin, A., and Mishal, S., 'Spatial Models and Centrality of International Communities: Meetings between Arab Leaders 1966–1978', *Journal of Conflict Resolution*, 25, 4 (1981), pp. 655–75.

Diskin, H., and Diskin, A., 'The Politics of Electoral Reform in Israel', *International Political Science Review*, 16, 1 (1995), pp. 31–45. [Also published in: Mahler, G.S., *Israel*, Aldershot: Ashgate, 1999].

Divrei ha'Knesset, 1990–2002 [Hebrew].

Dodd, L.C., *Coalitions in Parliamentary Government* (Princeton, NJ: Princeton University Press, 1976).

Downs, A., *An Economic Theory of Democracy* (New York, NY: Harper & Row, 1957).

Dror, Y., *Refounding Zionism* (Jerusalem: Publishing House of the World Zionist Organization, 1997) [Hebrew].

Englard, I., *Introduction to the Theory of Law* (Jerusalem: Yahalom, 1991) [Hebrew].

Felsenthal, D. and Diskin, A., 'The Bargaining Problem Revisited: The Minimum Utility Point, The Restricted Monotonicity Axiom and the Employment of the Mean as an Estimate of Expected Utility', *The Journal of Conflict Resolution*, 26, 4 (1982), pp. 664–91.

Felsenthal, D.S. and Machover, M., *The Measurement of Voting Power: Theory and Practice, Problems and Paradoxes* (Cheltenham, UK/Northampton, MA: Edward Elgar, 1998).

Gavison, R., *The Constitutional Revolution: Reality of Self-Fulfilling Prophecy* (Jerusalem: IDI, 1998) [Hebrew].

Goldberg, G., *The Israeli Voter 1992* (Jerusalem: Magnes, 1994) [Hebrew].

Grofman, B. (ed.), *Information, Participation, and Choice: An Economic Theory of Democracy in Perspective* (Ann Arbor, MI: University of Michigan Press, 1993).

Ha'Aretz, daily newspaper, 1990–2002 [Hebrew].

Harsanyi, J.C., *Rational Behavior and Bargaining Equilibrium in Games and Social Situations* (Cambridge, UK: Cambridge University Press, 1997).

Hazan, R. Y. and Diskin, A., 'The 1999 Knesset and Prime Ministerial Elections in Israel', *Electoral Studies*, 19, 4 (December 2000), pp. 628–37.

Hazan, R.Y. and Maor, M., (eds), *Parties, Elections and Cleavages: Israel in Comparative and Theoretical Perspective* (London: Frank Cass, 2000).

Heidar, K. and Koole, R.A., *Parliamentary Party Groups in European Democracies: Political Parties Behind Closed Doors* (London: Routledge, 2000).

Heller, M. (ed.), *The Middle East Military Balance 1984* (Tel Aviv: Tel Aviv University, Jaffe Center for Strategic Studies, 1984).

Hobbes, T., *Leviathan* (1651) (Harmondsworth: Penguin Classics, 1999).

Hotelling, H., 'Stability and Competition', *The Economic Journal*, 39, 1 (1929), pp. 41–57.

Inbar, E., *Israeli National Security, 1973–96* (Ramat Gan: Begin-Sadat Center for Strategic Studies, Bar-Ilan University, 1998).

Inbar, E., *Rabin and Israel's National Security*, Washington, DC: Woodrow Wilson Press, 1999).

International Institute for Strategic Studies, *The Military Balance 1999–2000* (London: Oxford University Press, 2000).

Interviews with members of the government, the Knesset and the Supreme Court, 1990–2002.

Jerusalem Post, daily newspaper, 1990–2002.

Jerusalem Report, weekly magazine, 1996-2001.

Kam, E., (ed.), *The Middle East Military Balance 1994–5*, (Tel Aviv: Tel Aviv University, Jaffe Center for Strategic Studies, 1996).

Kant, I., *Critique of Pure Reason* (Cambridge: Cambridge University Press, 1998).

Kant, I., *Critique of Practical Reason* (Cambridge: Cambridge University Press, 1997).

Karsh, E. (ed.), *From Rabin to Netanyahu: Israel's Troubled Agenda* (London: Frank Cass, 1997).

Karsh, E. (ed.), *Israel: The First Hundred Years—Israel's Transition from Community to State* (London: Frank Cass, 1999a).

Karsh E., *Fabricating Israeli History: The 'New Historians'* (London: Frank Cass, 1999b).

Kaspit, B. and Kfir, I., *Ehud Barak: Israel's Number 1 Soldier* (Tel Aviv: Alpha Tikshoret, 1998) [Hebrew].

Katz, R.S. and Mair, P., 'Changing Models of Party Organization and Party Democracy: The Emergence of The Cartel Party', *Party Politics*, 1, 1 (1995), pp. 5–28.

Keesing's Record of World Events, 1990–2002 (Washington, DC: Keesing's World Wide).

Keman, H., (ed.), *Comparative Politics: New Directions in Theory and Method* (Paul and Company Publishers Consortium, 1993).

Knesset.gov.il (website).

Laver, M. and Schofield, N., *Multiparty Government: The Politics of Coalition in Europe* (Oxford: Oxford University Press, 1990).

Lijphart, A. (ed.), *Parliamentary versus Presidential Government* (Oxford: Oxford University Press, 1992).

Liphart, A., *Electoral Systems and Party Systems: A Study of Twenty-Seven Democracies 1945–1990* (Oxford: Oxford University Press, 1994).

Lijphart, A., *Patterns of Democracy: Government Forms and Performance in Thirty-Six Countries* (New Haven, CT: Yale University Press, 1999).

Lijphart, A. and Diskin, A., 'Electoral Reform in Israel: The Basic Options', unpublished working paper presented at the IDI conference, Israel (March 1989).

Luce, R.L. and Raiffa, H., (1957), *Games and Decisions: Introduction and Critical Survey* (New York, NY: Wiley, 1957).

Maor, M., *Political Parties and Party Systems: Comparative Approaches and the British Experience* (London: Routledge, 1997).

Miller, W. E., and Shanks, J. M., *The New American Voter* (Cambridge, MA: Harvard University Press, 1996).

Mishal, S. and Diskin, A., 'Palestinian Voting in the West Bank: Traditional Community without Sovereignty', *Journal of Politics*, 44 (1982), pp. 538–58.

Nash, J., The Bargaining Problem', *Econometrica*, 18 (1951), pp. 155–62.

Nash, J., 'Equilibrium Points in N-Person Games', *Proceedings of the National Academy of Sciences, USA*, 36 (1950), pp. 48–9.

Netanyahu, B., *A Place Among the Nations* (Tel Aviv: Yedioth Ahronoth, 1995) [Hebrew].

Netanyahu, B., *Fighting Terrorism* (Tel Aviv: Miskal-Yedioth Ahronoth Books/Chemed Books, 1996) [Hebrew].

Palestine-Net.com (website).

Olson, M., *The Logic of Collective Action: Public Goods and the Theory of Groups* (Cambridge, MA: Harvard University Press, 1965).

Olson, M., *The Rise and Decline of Nations: Economic Growth, Stagflation, and Social Rigidities* (New Haven, CT: Yale University Press, 1982).

Pedatzur, R., *The Triumph of Embarrassment: Israel and the Territories after the Six-Day War* (Tel Aviv: Yad Tabenkin/Bitan Publishers, 1996) [Hebrew].
Peres, S., with Naor, A., *The New Middle East*, 2nd edn (Bnei Brak: Steimatzki, 1993) [Hebrew].
Piskei Din, 1965–2000 [Hebrew].
pmo.gov.il (Prime Minister's office, website).
Przeworski, A., Stokes, S.C. and Manin, B., (eds), *Democracy, Accountability, and Representation* (Cambridge: Cambridge University Press, 1999).
Przeworski, A., Limongi, F., Alvarez, M.E. *et al.*, *Democracy and Development: Political Institutions and Well-Being in the World, 1950–1990* (Cambridge: Cambridge University Press, 2000).
Public Opinion Surveys (1996).
Public Opinion Survey (1999).
Rabin, Y., *The Rabin Memoirs* (Boston, MA: Little, Brown and Co., 1979).
Rapoport, A. and Chammah, A.M., *Prisoner's Dilemma: A Study in Conflict and Cooperation* (Ann Arbor, MI: University of Michigan Press, 1965).
Riker, W.H., *The Theory of Political Coalition*, (New Haven, CT: Yale University Press, 1962).
Rubinstein, A., *Modeling Bounded Rationality* (Cambridge, MA: MIT Press, 1998).
Sachar, H.M., *The History of Israel from the Rise of Zionism to Our Time* (London: Random House, 1996).
Sagie, U., *Lights Within the Fog* (Tel Aviv: Miskal-Yedioth Ahronoth Books/Chemed Books, 1998) [Hebrew].
Sartori, G., *Parties and Party Systems: A Framework for Analysis* (Cambridge: Cambridge University Press, 1976).
Sartori, G., *The Theory of Democracy Revisited* (Chatham: Chatham House, 1987).
Sartori, G., *Comparative Constitutional Engineering: An Inquiry into Structures, Incentives, and Outcomes* (New York, NY: New York University Press, 1994).
Savir, U., *The Process* (Tel Aviv: Miskal-Yedioth Ahronoth Books/Chemed Books, 1998) [Hebrew].
Sefer Ha'Hukkim (1992–2000) [Hebrew].
Shamir, I., *Summing Up: An Autobiography* (Boston, MA: Little, Brown and Co., 1994).
Shamir, J. and Shamir, M., *The Anatomy of Public Opinion* (Ann Arbor, MI: University of Michigan Press, 1999).

Sharon, A., with Chanoff, D., *Warrior: The Autobiography of Ariel Sharon* (New York, NY: Simon and Schuster, 1989).

Shragai, N., *The Temple Mount Conflict* (Jerusalem: Keter, 1995) [Hebrew].

Smith, G., 'Stages of European Development: Electoral Change and System Adaptation', in Urwin, D.W. and Paterson, W. E. (eds), *Politics in Western Europe Today* (London: Longman), pp. 251–69.

Taagapera, R. and Shugart, M.S., *Seats and Votes: The Effects and Determinants of Electoral Systems* (New Haven, CT: Yale University Press, 1989).

Tal, I., *National Security: The Few Against the Many* (Tel Aviv: Dvir Publishing House, 1996) [Hebrew].

Taylor, A.D., *Mathematics and Politics: Strategy, Voting, Power and Proof* (New York, NY: Springer-Verlag, 1995).

Von Neumann, J. and Morgenstern, O., *Theory of Games and Economic Behavior* (Princeton, NJ: Princeton University Press, 1994).

Warwick, P.V., *Government Survival in Parliamentary Democracies* (Cambridge: Cambridge University Press, 1994).

Who's Who in the Thirteenth Knesset (Jerusalem: The Knesset, 1993) [Hebrew].

Who's Who in the Fourteenth Knesset (Jerusalem: The Knesset, 1996) [Hebrew].

Who's Who in the Fifteenth Knesset (Jerusalem: The Knesset, 1999) [Hebrew].

Index

Abramson, P., 3, 137, 138, 177
Abu Ala, 83
Abu-Hazeirah, A., 65
Adiv, U., 87
ADL, see Arab Democratic List/Party
Agranat, Sh., 14, 63
Agudat Israel, 23, 24, 57, 58, 59, 61, 65, 68, 171, 172, 173, 174, 175
Ahdut ha-Avoda, 58, 60, 61, 62, 63, 118, 171, 174
Aldrich, J.H., 177
Alignment, 62, 63, 64, 65, 66, 77, 88, 112, 137, 172, 174
Allon, Y. (Allon Plan), 81, 86
Aloni, Sh., 63, 64
Alvarez, M.E., 182
Amir, Y., 79, 80, 86
Arab Democratic List/Party, 23, 66
Arens, M., 138,177
Arrow, K.J., 6, 64, 70, 134, 136, 138, 139, 177
Artzi, Y., 77
Attrition, War of, 16, 21, 81, 123
Avital, S., 83, 128
Axelrod, R., 136, 177

Bagehot, W., 43, 137, 177
Balad, 24, 67, 68, 69, 104, 105, 106, 107, 109, 110, 111, 112, 113, 114, 115, 116, 172
Balfour, Lord, 143, 153
Barak, A., 33, 37, 38,
Barak, E., 3, 26, 27, 30, 47, 51, 71, 88, 92, 101, 102, 106, 107, 108, 113, 115, 118, 119, 120, 121, 122, 123, 124, 125, 126, 127, 138, 139, 175, 180

Bar-On, R., 97, 99, 122
Basic Law(s), 6, 12, 13, 22, 35, 36, 37, 38, 39, 40, 41, 44, 45, 46, 47, 50, 52, 53, 56, 58, 65, 66, 96, 118, 119, 125, 137, 146, 147, 148, 149, 178, 184
Begin, B.Z., 68, 72, 96, 97, 100
Begin, M., 51, 62, 64, 65, 77, 81, 82, 86, 174, 178, 180
Beilin, Y., 41, 83, 120, 127, 138, 177
Ben-Ami, S., 120, 127
Ben-Eliezer, B., 120, 128, 130
Ben-Gurion, D., 35, 61, 62, 63, 76, 77, 118, 137, 173, 174
Benizri, S., 120, 122, 128
Bentsur, E., 138, 177
Bergman, A., 36,37
Bernadotte, Count, 59
Bishara, A., 68,72
Bnei Brak, 107,108,109,182
Bolivar, S., 43,137,178
Borda, 70,71,134
Brams, S., 137,138,139,177, 178
Budge, I., 139,178
Burg, A., 130
Bush, G. W., 15

Carroll, Lewis, see Dodgson, Ch.
Caspi, D., 137,178
Center Party, 23,24, 69,70,71, 98,104, 105, 106, 107, 109, 110, 111, 112, 113, 114, 115, 116, 119, 121, 123, 127, 175
Chammah, A.M., 136, 182
Chanoff, D., 183
Cheibub, A., 182
Chirac, M., 43
Christopher, W., 84

Civil Rights Movement, see Ratz
Clinton, W. (B.), 44, 84, 101
Cohen, Chaim, 14
Cohen, Geula, 65
Cohen, Ra'anan, 120, 123, 128
Cohen, Ran, 120, 122
Cohen, Yitzhak, 120, 122
Cohen, Youssef, 136, 178
Condorcet, 70, 71, 134
Confidence Vote, see no-confidence vote
Constituent Assembly, 35, 56, 58, 59, 76, 103, 145,175
Constractive Vote of no-confidence, see no-confidence vote
Common Goods Dilemma, see Prisoner's Dilemma
Cox, G.W., 178

Dahan, N., 128
Darawshe, A., 66
Dash, 64, 65, 67, 69, 72, 77, 172
Dayan, Ch., 68
Dayan, M., 62, 64, 65, 77, 78, 81
Declaration of Independence, 35, 39, 40, 57, 143, 144, 146, 148
Degel ha-Torah, 23, 24, 65, 68, 172, 175
Democratic Choice, 119
Democratic Movement for Change, see Dash
Deri, A., 96, 99, 117, 119, 122, 123
Diamond, M., 177
Diskin, H., 3, 41, 48, 137, 139, 178, 179
DMC, see Dash
Dodd, L.C., 138, 179
Dodgson, Ch., 70, 138
Dror, Y., 136, 179

Egypt, 20, 21, 81, 82, 136, 160, 170
Eitan, R., 65, 67, 68, 92, 93
El-Ard decision, see Yardor Election Appeal
England, I., 38, 137, 179
Eshkol, L., 62, 81, 118, 174

Flato-Sharon, S., 172
Felsenthal, D.S., 136, 139, 179,
Fighters' List, 39, 171
Foursome Club, the, 61, 62
Free Center, 63
Friedman Yellin-Mor, N., 59

Gahal, 62, 63, 64, 76, 102, 136, 172
Gavison, R., 34, 137, 179
General Zionists, 57, 59, 60, 61, 62, 76, 102, 171, 173
Gesher, 23, 24, 67, 68, 92, 93, 95, 96, 97, 98, 102, 110, 111, 119, 120, 123, 127, 172, 175
Gil, A., 138, 189
Goldberg, G., 137, 179
Goldstein, B., 86
Greater Israel Movement, 64
Grofman, B., 179
Gulf War, 15, 16, 22, 85
Gutmann, E., 178

Hadash, 23, 24, 59, 62, 66, 67, 68, 69, 75, 83, 95, 104, 105, 106, 107, 109, 110, 111, 112, 113, 114, 115, 116, 172
Haj, R., 69
Hamas, 90
Hanegbi, Tz., 99, 128
Ha-Olam ha-Zeh, 62, 172
Ha-Poel ha-Mizrahi, 58, 61, 171, 173
Harari, Y., ('Harari Decision', 13 June 1950), 35
Harel, Y., 84, 95
Harsanyi, J.C., 139, 180
Hazan, R.Y., 139, 178, 179, 180
Hebron, 86, 97, 99, 101
Heidar, K., 138, 180
Heller, M., 20, 180
Hendel, Z., 68
Herut, 23, 24, 59, 61, 62, 63, 64, 68, 102, 171
Herzl T., 18, 143
Histadrut, 84, 88, 105,
Hizbullah, 90
Hobbes, T., 136, 180
Holst, J. J., 82
Hotelling, H., 72, 138, 180
Hurwitz, Y., 65, 77
Hussein, King, 83, 84, 85, 101, 138

Inbar, E., 136, 138, 180
Independent Liberals, 62, 64, 72, 76, 77, 174
Inglehart, R., 137, 177
Intifada, 16, 17, 30, 81, 82, 100, 124, 129, 130
Iran, 20, 21, 129, 170

Iraq, 20, 85, 170
Islamic Arab Party, 23
Islamic Jihad, 90
Itzik, D., 120, 128

Jerusalem, 8, 18, 28, 29, 30, 76, 84, 86, 89, 90, 91, 99, 100, 107, 108, 109, 120, 128, 129, 158, 177, 178, 179, 180, 183
Judeah and Samaria, *see* West Bank and Gaza Strip
Jordan, 8, 14, 20, 28, 79, 82, 83, 84, 85, 100, 156, 160, 170
Jordan valley, 28, 29, 30, 81

Kach, 12, 65, 172
Kahalani, A., 84, 95
Kahane, M., 12
Kam, E., 20, 180
Kant, I., 136, 180
Karsh, E., 3, 136, 138, 180
Kaspit, B., 138, 180
Katz, R.S., 137, 180
Katzav, M., 123
Keman, H., 136, 139, 178, 181
Kfir, I., 138, 180
Koole, R.A., 138, 180
Kozirev, A., 84

Labor Party, 23, 24, 46, 49, 63, 64, 66, 67, 68, 69, 75, 79, 80, 81, 82, 83, 84, 88, 89, 91, 92, 94, 95, 96, 98, 105, 118, 119, 120, 121, 123, 127, 128, 129, 130, 172, 174, 175, 177
Landau, M., 34
Landau, U., 128
Lankri, Y., 68
LAOR movement, 37
Laver, M., 137, 181
Lavon, P. (Lavon Affair), 57, 61, 62
Law and Administration Ordinance, 1948, 36, 58, 147
Law of Parties, 1992, 56
Law of Transition, 1949, 35, 36, 46, 52, 58
Lebanon, 14, 16, 81, 82, 90, 100
Levi, D., 67, 68, 92, 93, 96, 97, 119, 120, 123, 127
Levi, M., 68,
Levi, Y., 120, 123
Levine, R. 177
Libai, D., 44, 45, 118

Liberal Party (Liberals), 61, 62, 63, 64, 72, 102, 118, 171, 174
Libya, 20, 170
Lieberman, A., 68, 97, 98, 105, 128, 129
Lijphart, A., 136, 137, 177, 175, 181
Likud, 23, 24, 46, 49, 63, 64, 65, 67, 68, 69, 75, 76, 77, 80, 91, 92, 93, 94, 95, 96, 97, 98, 102, 104, 106, 107, 108, 109, 110, 111, 112, 113, 114, 115, 116, 117, 118, 124, 125, 126, 127, 128, 129, 130, 137, 172, 174, 175
Limongi, F., 182
Lin, U., 44
Lincoln, A., 44
Lipkin-Shahak, A., 71, 72, 120
Livnat, L., 128
Livni, Tz., 128
Luce, R.L., 139, 181

Machover, M., 136, 179
MAD (Mutual Assured Distruction), 21
Mada, *see* Arab Democratic List/Party
Madison, 42
Mafdal, *see* National Religious Party
Magen, D., 68
Mahmid, H., 68
Mair, P., 137, 180
Maki, 24, 58, 60, 61, 63, 171, 172
Malci'or, M., 120
Manin, B., 182
Maor, M., 137, 178, 180, 181
Mapai, 35, 57, 58, 59, 60, 61, 62, 63, 64, 75, 76, 77, 88, 102, 118, 171, 173, 174
Mapam, 58, 60, 61, 63,
Masala, A., 68
Median Party/Position, *see* Pivotal Party/Position
Meimad, 23, 24, 88, 102, 120, 121
Meir, G., 64, 79, 81, 174
Meretz, 66, 67, 68, 69, 83, 84, 94, 95, 104, 106–23, 127, 172, 175
Meridor, D., 68, 71, 72, 96, 97, 128
Merom, H., 68
Miller, W.E., 137, 181
Milo, R., 71, 98, 120, 123, 128
Minority/Minorities (Parties), 64, 66, 171–4
Minshar, 36, 58
Mishal, K., 100
Mishal, S., 136, 179, 181
Mitchell Report, the, 129, 163–5

Mitterand, F., 43
Mixed Strategies/Solutions, 70, 132, 133
Mizrachi, 35, 57, 58, 59, 61, 171, 173
Moked, 63, 172
Moledet, 23, 24, 65, 67, 68, 84, 94, 95, 96, 112, 139, 172, 175
Montesquieu, 42
Morasha, 65, 172, 175
Mordechai, Y., 68, 71, 72, 98, 120, 121, 138
Morgenstern, O., 139, 183
Movement for Better Government, the, 41, 178

Nahari, M., 122
Naor, A., 136, 182
Nash, J., 132, 133, 134, 139, 181
National Council, 57
National Religious Party, 23, 24, 51, 61, 64, 65, 68, 69, 88, 95, 96, 101, 103, 104, 106, 107, 109, 110, 111, 112, 113, 114, 115, 116, 117, 119, 120, 123, 127, 171, 172, 174, 175
National Unity (Party), 68, 69, 104, 105, 106, 107, 109, 110, 111, 112, 113, 114, 115, 116, 127, 175
National Unity Government, 62, 64, 65, 66, 95, 96, 126
Naveh, D., 128
Ne'eman, Ya'akov, 98
Ne'eman, Yuval, 138
Netanyahu, B., 26, 27, 30, 47, 49, 51, 71, 80, 87, 90–102, 106, 107. 108, 112, 115, 117, 119, 121–5, 138, 175, 180, 181
no-confidence vote, 42, 43, 45, 46, 50–5, 60, 75, 119, 129, 175
NRP, *see* National Religious Party
Nudelman, M., 68

Ohana, A., 128
Olson, M., 136, 181
Ometz, 65, 77, 172, 175
One Israel, 23, 24, 69, 102, 104–16, 118, 119, 121, 123, 127, 175
One Nation, 23, 24, 69, 104, 105, 106, 107, 109–16, 119, 127, 128, 175
Oron, Ch., 120, 122
Oslo Agreement(s), 18, 82, 83, 84, 85, 86, 100, 127, 130, 156–62

Palestinian Authority (PA), 6, 14, 19, 83, 84, 85, 89, 97, 100, 122, 124, 127, 129, 156, 158, 159, 163–9
Palestinian Charter/Covenant, 19, 22, 82, 85, 89, 101, 150–5
Palestinian Liberation Organization, *see* PLO
Palestinian National Council (PNC), 89, 101, 155
Pedatzur, R., 137, 138, 182
Peel Commission, 8
Peled, M., 68
Peres, S., 30, 47, 75, 77, 79, 80, 83–94, 97, 106, 108, 117, 120, 123, 125, 127, 128, 130, 136, 138, 175, 182
Peretz, A., 68, 83, 88, 105
Pivotal Party/Position, 55, 58, 61, 62, 64, 66, 69, 74, 75, 76, 77, 92, 96, 115, 118, 134
PLO, 14, 19, 22, 79, 80, 82, 83, 85, 89, 100, 156
Poalei Agudat Israel, 59, 171, 172, 173, 174
Porat, H., 68
Poraz, A., 67, 69
Prisoner's Dilemma, 2, 5, 33, 133, 136, 178, 182
Progressive Party (Progressives), 35, 59, 60, 61, 62, 72, 76, 171, 173, 174
Progressive List, 66, 172
Provisional State Council, 36, 57, 145
Przeworski, A., 136, 182

Ra'am, 24, 67, 69, 104, 105, 106, 107, 109–16, 172
Rabin, Y., 40, 46, 47, 64, 66, 75, 79–89, 91, 92, 117, 135, 138, 174, 175, 180, 182
Rafi, 62, 63, 65, 69, 72, 77, 172
Raiffa, H., 139, 181
Rakah, 63, 66, 172
Ramon, Ch., 83, 88, 120
Rapoport, A., 136, 182
Ratz, 23, 24, 63, 64, 66, 67, 117, 172, 174
Ravitz, A., 68
Re'em, D., 68
Refugees, 14, 17, 130, 158
Religious Front, 35, 59, 60, 61, 171, 173
Revisionist Movement, 57, 59
Riker, W.H., 96, 138, 182
Rivlin, R., 128

Rotblit, Y., 138
Rubinstein, Amnon, 44, 67, 77
Rubinstein, Ariel, 139, 182
Rubinstein E., 38, 99

Sachar, H.M., 136, 137, 138, 182
Sadat, A., 82, 180
Sagie, U., 136, 182
Sapir, Y., 62
Sarid, Y., 119, 120, 122
Sartori, G., 137, 182
Saudi Arabia, 20, 170
Savir, U., 83, 138, 182
Schofield, N., 137, 181
Scotto, T.J., 177
Sephardi Party/List, 59, 60, 137, 171, 173
September 11 (2001), 15, 130
Shalom, S., 128
Shamgar, M., 79, 86, 87
Shamir, Yitzhak, 66, 75, 77, 82, 85, 89, 92, 138, 175, 182
Shamir, Jacob, 138, 182
Shamir, Michal, 138, 182
Shamir, Moshe, 65
Shanks, J.M., 137, 181
Sharansky, N., 67, 94, 120, 123, 128
Sharet, M., 76, 173,
Sharon, A., 3, 51, 63, 64, 96, 113, 124, 125–30, 139, 172, 175, 183
Shas, 23, 24, 65, 66, 69, 75, 83, 84, 95, 96, 99, 103, 104, 106–16, 118, 119, 120, 122, 123, 127, 128, 172, 175
Sheetrit, M., 128
Sheli, 66, 172
Shem-Tov–Yariv formula, 82
Shinui, 23, 24, 65, 66, 67, 69, 70, 77, 104, 106–17, 127, 172, 175
Shlomzion, 64, 172
Shochat, A., 120
Shragai, N., 138, 183
Shugart, M.S., 138, 183
Six-Days (1967) War, 6, 8, 18, 21, 62, 74, 79, 80, 86, 96, 108, 182
Simhon, S., 128
Smith, G., 137, 183
Sneh, E., 128
Sneh, M., 60
State List, 63, 77
Stern, Y., 68
Stokes, S.C., 182

Suissa, E., 120, 122, 128
Sussman, E., 69, 84, 95
Sussman, Y., 14
Syria, 14, 20, 21, 28, 29, 30, 81, 123, 138, 170

Taagapera, R., 138, 183
Tal, I., 136, 183
'Tal Law', 123
Tami, 63, 65, 103, 172, 174, 175
Tamir, Sh., 63
Tamir, Y., 120
Tarif, S., 128
Taylor, A.D., 136, 183
Tehiyya, 65, 172, 175
Telem, 65, 77, 88, 172
Temple Mount, 100, 124, 183
Tenet Plan, the, 129, 166-169
Terrorism, 21, 45, 50, 59, 80, 82, 85, 86, 87, 90, 96, 127, 129, 130, 164, 165, 167, 168, 181
Third Way, 67, 69, 70, 72, 78, 84, 95, 96, 100, 104, 110, 111, 138, 175
Toledano, Rabbi Y., 138
Torah Front, 61,
Tzomet, 65, 67, 68, 69, 83, 92, 93, 95, 96, 97, 98, 110, 111, 172, 175
Tzur, Y., 138

United Nations, 8, 40, 144, 145, 153
UNRWA, 14
UNSCOP, 8

Vietnam War, 15
Vilnai, M., 128
von Neumann, J., 139, 183

Warhaftig, Z., 35
War of Independence (1948), 9, 10, 11, 14, 17, 19, 58
Warwick, P.V., 138, 139, 183
WCAR, 130
Weizman, E., 65, 77, 98, 122, 123
West Bank and Gaza Strip, 9, 14, 28, 81, 83, 84, 85, 89, 90, 100, 101, 107, 108, 110, 111, 112, 156–62, 167, 169, 170, 171
Wilson, W., 44, 180
WIZO, 59, 171
World Wars, 10, 15, 18, 43, 144
Wye Plantation Agreement, 101

Yahadut ha-Torah, 65, 68, 69, 75, 94, 95, 96, 104, 106–16, 118, 119, 121, 127, 171, 172, 175
Yardor Election Appeal, 13
Yishai, E., 120, 122, 128
Yisrael ba-Aliyah, 24, 67, 68, 69, 70, 78, 94, 95, 96, 103–16, 119, 120, 123, 127, 128, 175
Yisrael ba-Merkaz, 68
Yisrael Beitenu, 24, 69, 94–116, 126, 127, 128, 175
Yahad, 65, 77
Yemenite Party/List, 59, 137, 171
Yi'ud, 83, 175

Yom Kippur (1973) War, 16, 18, 21, 63, 64, 81

Zandberg, E., 68, 69
Ze'evi, R., 84, 128, 129
Zeidel, H., 77
Zidon, Y., 44
Zionist Idea (Party), 175
Zionism, 8, 10, 12, 17, 18, 19, 21, 22, 58, 61, 76, 81, 86, 87, 143, 144, 150, 151, 152, 153, 154, 179, 182
Zinni, A., 129
Zucker, D., 68
Zvili, N., 68